KV-191-101

SPIRAL GUIDE

ANDALUCÍA

AA
Publishing

Contents

the magazine 5
- ✦ Moorish Andalucía
- ✦ Romantic Andalucía
- ✦ The Bullfight
- ✦ Flamenco: Fire in the Blood
- ✦ Festival Diary ✦ Movers and Shakers
- ✦ 5 of the Best
- ✦ Liquid Gold: The Sherry Experience
- ✦ Time for Tapas

Finding Your Feet 33
- ✦ First Two Hours
- ✦ Getting Around
- ✦ Accommodation
- ✦ Food and Drink
- ✦ Shopping
- ✦ Entertainment

Málaga and Cádiz 45
Getting Your Bearings
In Four Days
Don't Miss
- ✦ Málaga ✦ Ronda ✦ Jerez de la Frontera
- ✦ Cádiz ✦ Costa del Sol

At Your Leisure✦ 8 more places to explore
Where to...
- ✦ Stay ✦ Eat and Drink ✦ Shop ✦ Be Entertained

Granada and Almería 77
Getting Your Bearings
In Four Days
Don't Miss✦ Granada ✦ Las Alpujarras
- ✦ Almería

At Your Leisure✦ 6 more places to explore
Where to...
- ✦ Stay ✦ Eat and Drink ✦ Shop ✦ Be Entertained

Córdoba and Jaén 109

Getting Your Bearings
In Five Days
Don't Miss
✦ Córdoba ✦ Priego de Córdoba ✦ Baeza
✦ Parque Natural de Cazorla y Segura ✦ Úbeda
At Your Leisure ✦ 5 more places to explore
Where to...
✦ Stay ✦ Eat and Drink ✦ Shop ✦ Be Entertained

Seville and Huelva 137

Getting Your Bearings
In Four Days
Don't Miss
✦ Seville ✦ Carmona ✦ Aracena and Gruta de las
Maravillas ✦ Parque Nacional de Doñana
At Your Leisure ✦ 5 more places to explore
Where to...
✦ Stay ✦ Eat and Drink ✦ Shop ✦ Be Entertained

Walks and Tours 169

✦ **1** Granada's Albaicín
✦ **2** Hidden Corners of Córdoba
✦ **3** Sierra de Grazalema
✦ **4** Pottery Villages and Cowboy Country
✦ **5** Sierra de Aracena

Practicalities 185

✦ Before You Go ✦ When to Go ✦ When You are There
✦ Useful Words and Phrases

Atlas 193

Index 203

Written by Des Hannigan
Where to... sections by Josephine Quintero
Copy edited by Audrey Horne
Page layout by Nautilus Design (UK) Limited
Verified by Mona King
Indexed by Marie Lorimer

Published by AA Publishing, a trading name of Automobile
Association Developments Limited, whose registered office is
Millstream, Maidenhead Road, Windsor, Berkshire SL4 5GD
Registered number 1878835.

ISBN 0 7495 3210 6

A CIP catalogue record for this book is available from the
British Library.

Cover design and binding style by permission of AA Publishing
Colour separation by Leo Reprographics
Printed and bound in China by Leo Paper Products

Find out more about AA Publishing and the wide range of travel
publications and services the AA provides by visiting our website at
www.theAA.com.

Reprinted Jul 2003.
© Automobile Association Developments Limited 2002
Maps © Automobile Association Developments Limited 2002

A01914

the magazine

Moorish
Andalucía

Andalucía will always be defined by its Moorish legacy. In the 8th century AD, a mixed force of Arabs, Syrians, Berbers and Egyptians, the "Moors" of North Africa, gained a foothold on Spain's Mediterranean coast, from where they began their advance into Western Europe. The Moors maintained a significant presence in Andalucía until the late 15th century.

The name Moor derives from the word "Maurus", used by the Greeks and Romans to describe the inhabitants of Mauritania in northwestern Africa, and subsequently by Europeans as a blanket term covering Muslims in general.

Like many invaders, the Moors probably came out of curiosity, or out of hunger for new land. They stayed for over 700 years. The legacy of their subtle and beautiful craftsmanship and their social and political skills is seen everywhere in Andalucía today, but especially in the starry fretwork and swirling arabesques of great buildings such as the Alhambra in Granada, the Mezquita in Córdoba and Seville's Giralda tower. It is seen too in scores of clifftop castles, in the labyrinthine Moorish quarters in many Andalucian towns and villages, and in the ceramic tiles that grace the patios of Andalucian houses.

> "Like many invaders, the Moors probably came out of curiosity, or out of hunger for new land"

Guitar Man

The 9th-century Muslim poet and musician Ziryab is said to have introduced hairstyling, advanced culinary skills, table manners, and even an early form of toothpaste to Moorish Spain. For music lovers, though, his most important innovation was to add a fifth string to the Arab lute, a development that would lead to the evolution of the Spanish guitar.

Earthly Paradise

The Moors who came to Andalucía found the kind of earthly paradise that they had only dreamt of in the desert wastes of their Moroccan home, the Maghrib. The key ingredient was plentiful water; it transformed arid lands into green oases and furnished Moorish palaces and modest homes alike with lush gardens enriched by the music of fountains and the glitter of pools.

The Moors had long called the land across the Straits of Gibraltar al-Andalus. One suggested origin of the name relates to the Vandals who occupied Spain and parts of North Africa during the 5th century. Other sources believe that it may

have derived from a phrase used by the Muslims of the east to describe "Western Islam", and was first applied to all of Spain as the Moors advanced northwards until checked on the banks of the River Loire near Poitiers by Charles Martel. As soon as the Moors retreated south across the Pyrenees, the Christian Reconquest of al-Andalus began. It took seven centuries to achieve, chiefly because the forces of Christian Spain were sparse, fragmented and often at odds with each other.

Above: The Moors found plentiful water in their new lands

Below: Detail from a painting of the Battle of Poitiers by Charles Steuben (1838). The battle, fought in 732, marked a turning point in the advance of Moorish forces

A Golden Age

After their initial sweep through Spain and into France in the 8th century, the Moors dug in their heels in the region now known as Andalucía and made it their own. In this contracted al-Andalus they tolerated other religions, and made wise agreements and concessions with Christian neighbours. But Islamic rule was occasionally tumultuous as well as enlightened. Fierce rivalries existed between competing Muslim dynasties, and throughout the centuries, successive confederations of fellow Muslims invaded from North Africa, usurping established rulers. In spite of these upheavals and the sporadic, but relentless, capturing of towns and small estates by the Christian Spanish, the Moors created a Golden Age within their Spanish lands. Córdoba became the Moorish capital of al-Andalus, and its rulers, or caliphs, rivalled those of Baghdad and Damascus for

Los Reyes Católicos, Fernando (above) and Isabel (above right), the final conquerors of Islamic al-Andalus

Left: The conquest of Málaga by Fernando V in 1487

their wealth and accomplishments. In 756 the building of Córdoba's Great Mosque, the Mezquita, began, and over the next 200 years the city became enriched by trade in gold and silver, leather, silk, perfumes and spices, becoming a beacon of scientific and artistic achievement.

Muslim Kingdoms

By the beginning of the 11th century, factionalism and internal rivalries brought an end to the Golden Age of the Córdoban caliphate, and al-Andalus fragmented into a number of small independent Muslim kingdoms called *taifas*. During the following centuries, fresh waves of Muslim incomers from North Africa ensured that the Moorish character of al-Andalus survived, even as the Christian Reconquest of the region continued. The Christian king, Fernando III, took Córdoba from the Moors in 1236 and then Seville in 1248. There was a lull in the Christian advance during the 14th century, but by the late 15th century, the kingdom of Granada, under the rule of the Nasrid sultans, was the last substantial Moorish stronghold in al-Andalus.

In 1485 the *taifa* of Ronda surrendered to the Christians, and Moorish Málaga followed. By 1492 the formidable monarchs Fernando V and Isabel I, known as Los Reyes Católicos (the Catholic Monarchs), had taken

Granada; al-Andalus, as a Moorish "state", was no more.

The Moorishness of the region, however, has proved to be indestructible. The skills and artistry of the Moors were absorbed into the Christian culture of European Spain. This, in its turn, gave Andalucía a legacy of magnificent Renaissance buildings and baroque churches. Yet always, as you travel through Andalucía, it is the persuasive magic of Moorish al-Andalus that grips and captivates.

The magnificent ceiling of the Salón de los Embajadores (Hall of the Ambassadors) in Granada's Alhambra Palace

"The skills and artistry of the Moors were absorbed into the Christian culture"

Who brought down the cool waters from rocky prisons, turning whole wastes into sunny vineyards and gardens? The Moors...Who planted the orange tree and the palm, the fig and the olive? The Moors...
Matilda Betham-Edwards
Through Spain to the Sahara (1866)

Romantic

The romantic image that still clings to Andalucía was born in large part out of the writings of 19th-century travellers from northern Europe and from popular literature. Persuasive, enticing and enduring though their portrayal of life in the region was, the reality was often very different.

Nineteenth-century visitors to Andalucía conjured up an image of the region as a seductive other world, a world of heat and passion, of scented orange groves, of raffish characters and mountain brigands, of licentious Don Juans and alluring Carmens. It was an image that was self-perpetuating because many of these visitors exaggerated their experiences to make them sound more romantic in what was easily portrayed – at least in cooler northern climes – as an exotic and even dangerous land. This had been the al-Andalus of the Moors after all, a land where Europe gave way to

> "...raffish characters and mountain brigands..."

Andalucía

Africa, an exciting alternative to what seemed the staid predictability of northern Europe. The English writer Richard Ford, who first visited Andalucía in 1830, described Spain as an escape to "racy freshness" from the "dull uniformity" of Europe.

Ford wrote superbly of the Andalucía of his day. He first came to Spain in 1830 and over the next few years produced his epic *Handbook for Travellers in Spain and Readers at Home*, published in 1845 and still revered as one of the finest evocations of Spain ever written – exhaustive, witty and opinionated. Washington Irving came to Spain to work for the American Legation in Madrid in 1826, and in 1928 set off on a tour of Andalucía. He lived for some time in the semi-derelict Alhambra and there wrote *The Conquest of Granada* before beginning his famous work *The Alhambra: A Series of Tales*, now known universally as *Tales of the Alhambra*. The book mixes romantic stories of the Alhambra's Moorish past with vivid portrayals of the palace's decaying grandeur. It triggered

Below: The Alhambra, an enduring symbol of Moorish Andalucía

Begging for Bandits

Andalucian bandits were all the rage among 19th-century travellers, who arrived in the region with their heads filled with the imaginative tales of previous visitors. There were certainly lawless *bandoleros* in the Sierra Morena, the Alpujarras and the Serranía de Ronda during the 19th century, but records show that only one foreign visitor was known to have been kidnapped by them. And that happened in Andalucía's neighbouring province of La Mancha. Hope sprang eternal in the romantic breast, however. The French novelist Alexandre Dumas is said to have sent money to an Andalucian bandit chief in return for a promise that he and his party would be held up as they crossed wild country – with the proviso that no harm would be done to them. And the Danish writer Hans Christian Andersen expressed great disappointment that he passed unchallenged through the hills of the Sierra Morena.

movements in Spain and in northern Europe that led to the Alhambra's preservation, and fuelled interest in the palace. Irving and Ford were thoughtful and accomplished writers who had spent much time in Andalucía, but they set the tone for an exaggerated and sentimental romanticising of the region by the flood of travellers and commentators who followed in their wake.

Fictional writings about Andalucía set the seal on the region's romantic image. The popular opera *Carmen* was based on a novel of 1845 by the Frenchman Prosper Mérimée. *Carmen* had it all: a gypsy heroine of sultry good looks who worked in Seville's tobacco factory, a notorious bandit from the Ronda mountains, and a dashing bull-fighter, all three locked into a passionate story of love, betrayal and death. Georges Bizet's musical adaptation of the novel immortalised the heroine of *Carmen*; yet Bizet never visited Spain. Carmen's male counterpart was the fictional Don Juan, who first made his appearance in a 17th-century drama, *The Seducer of Seville*. Again the crucial ingredients of seduction, betrayal and murder stirred the romantic pot, and this time with a splendid ghost and eternal damnation thrown in. In turn, the Don Juan legend was immortalised by subsequent adaptations, not least by Mozart's opera *Don Giovanni*. But Mozart never made it to Andalucía either.

For modern visitors, the romance of Andalucía is as essential as its sun – even if it should be tempered by a gentle touch of scepticism.

THE BULLFIGHT

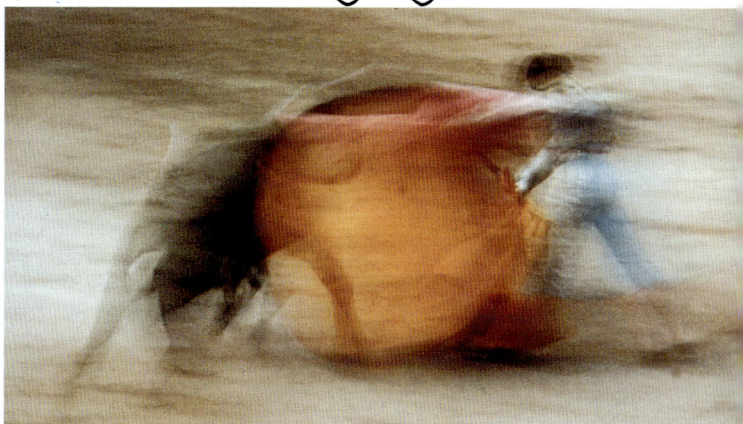

ART, SPORT OR OUTRAGE?

Bullfighting may be abhorrent to many visitors to Spain – and there is growing opposition to it within Spain itself – but the *corrida*, the bullfight, still commands great devotion in Andalucía. Its potent mix of skill, spectacle and cruel finality still draws the crowds, makes for prime-time viewing on television, and fills the bars and cafés with fiercely argued opinion.

To the *aficionado*, bullfighting is art rather than sport. Bullfight reviews come under the arts pages in Spanish newspapers, with the *corrida* receiving the same superlatives as stage and ballet productions. Theatrical performance is certainly present in bullfighting, in the costumes the bullfighters wear and in the athleticism and balletic movements of the *matador* and his supporting team: the cape-wielding *toreros*, the *banderilleros*, who implant barbed darts in the bull's neck, and the mounted *picadors*, who weaken the bull further with lance thrusts. In spite of the patent cruelty, the pageantry and ritual of the *corrida* can be spellbinding. The ultimate confrontation is sometimes a riveting performance of courage and of grace by the *matadores*, and of heart-stopping bravery by the bull.

Outside Spain, bullfighting receives mixed reactions, though still finds passionate supporters. Writer Ernest Hemingway and actor Orson Welles were both *aficionados*.

> "The pageantry and ritual of the *corrida* can be spellbinding"

Corrida art: matador, cape and bull

Hemingway wrote two exhaustive books on bullfighting, *Death in the Afternoon* and *The Dangerous Summer*. Welles was a devotee of the Ronda bullring and his ashes rest at the estate of the famous Ronda bullfighter, Antonio Ordóñez. Hemingway acquired encyclopaedic knowledge of bullfighting – one of the few non-Spaniards to do so – but he was not the only American to be closely associated with it. Sidney Franklin, a highly successful

Maestranza (▶ 168), are the places to experience the atmosphere of the bullfight at its most intense; and it is in the main rings that you are likely to see the best *matadores* confronting the biggest and fiercest Andalucian fighting bulls.

Even the smallest villages try to stage a *corrida* at least once a year. This is usually during a local fiesta and in a bullring located within a semi-ruinous Moorish castle or in the village plaza boarded

The celebrated Córdoban matador Manuel Benítez, known as El Cordobés, leads his *cuadrilla*, or "team", into the bullring

matador in Mexico and in Spain during the 1930s, was greatly celebrated in Spanish bullfighting circles and filled the Madrid ring to capacity on several occasions.

There are plenty of opportunities to see bullfighting in Andalucía. The season runs from Easter to October, although *novilladas*, novice fights, take place in Costa del Sol bullrings as late as November. The major bullrings, such as Seville's

Dirty Tricks

Opponents of bullfighting condemn the spectacle outright, but even enthusiasts argue that the modern *corrida* has become debased, not least by such practices as shaving the tips of a bull's horns to reduce its accuracy and sensitivity to movement. There are hints of worse practices being inflicted on "dangerous" bulls, before they are released into the ring, in order to reduce their potential lethality. *Aficionados* complain that the *arte*, the indefinable style of good bullfighting, is being lost.

Attending a Bullfight

- For city *corridas*, buy tickets at the bullring box office. Avoid buying tickets from touts, who usually hang about on the approaches to bullrings and charge hugely inflated prices, especially for major events.
- Seats on the shaded side of the bullring are the most expensive because, as well as being out of direct sunlight, they are where the box of the "President", the bullfight's "judge", is located. The *matador* tends to concentrate the action on this side of the ring.
- Most bullfights in Costa del Sol resorts are *novilladas*, events that feature novice *matadores* and young, untried bulls, or bulls that are not considered fit for senior bullfights.

Bullfight posters are an art form in themselves

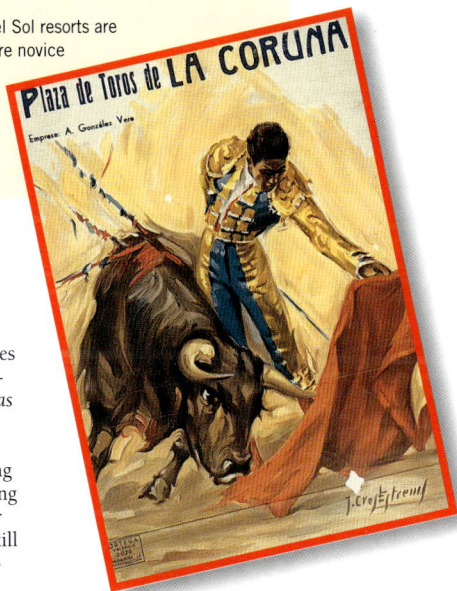

Plaza de Toros de LA CORUÑA

Empresa: A. González Vera

round for the event. Big-name *matadores*, such as Enrico Ponce, will often perform at tiny bullrings in remote villages, being well aware that rural communities are the bedrock of bullfighting's support. Village *corridas* are also something of a training ground for local talent, with novices as young as 16 taking part – and taking the ultimate risk. Death, for *matador* as well as bull, is still the price to pay in any bullring, great or small.

Lady in Lights

There were several accomplished female bullfighters (right) prior to 1908, when a ban was placed on them becoming *toreras*. One such was Martina García, who took part in her last bullfight in 1880 at the age of 76. When the ban was lifted in 1975, one woman who donned the *traje de luces*, the bullfighter's glittering, sequinned costume, was Cristina Sánchez. She outshone many of her male peers and at one memorable *corrida* killed all six bulls. Sánchez retired early in 1997, on the grounds that she was finding difficulty in securing top-level fights because so many big-name male bullfighters refused to share the bill with her.

FLAMENCO

FIRE IN THE BLOOD

Flamenco is the soul music of Andalucía, a fusion of voice, guitar and dance that rarely fails to set the blood tingling. There is nothing quite like the raw, passionate singing, the hand-clapping and the rippling guitar that accompany the staccato footwork and sinuous movements of the flamenco dancer.

There are claims that flamenco harks back to the music of the Arabs or the Jews, to India or Byzantium, or to Christian sacred song. But the flamenco of today seems to have emerged as a distinctive folk art during the late 18th century among the gypsy communities of the lower Guadalquivir Basin in the Cádiz and Jerez de la Frontera area, and Triana, the gypsy district of Seville (▶ 152).

Flamenco Secret

The finest flamenco singers are said to possess *duende* – the soul, the "ghost", the inspirational gift that transforms an ordinary performance into something sublime. Before achieving *duende*, singers may wait for hours, during which they massage their vocal chords with endless smoking and glassfuls of the fiery liqueur *aguardiente*, a combination that would render most people speechless, if not songless.

Even today the best flamenco singers are invariably from gypsy families, and Andalucía is acknowledged as the home of this thrilling art.

In its purest form flamenco is *el cante* (the song), of which *cante jondo* (deep song) is the ultimate expression, especially when performed by the best *cantaores* (singers), whose scorched voices express real grief, yet with a triumphant reaffirmation of the human spirit. For most visitors to Andalucía, however, it is the magical combination of *el cante* with *el toque*, the guitar, and *el baile*, the dance, that gives flamenco its appeal.

Opportunities to see some form of flamenco in Andalucía are legion, but it may not always be authentic. You may have to settle for a set-piece flamenco evening booked through hotels and tour operators.

The next best thing to an impromptu flamenco event, and a better alternative to phoney "gypsy" shows, are *tablaos*, performances of "classical" flamenco by trained artistes. Flamenco clubs and associations called *peñas* are also open to visits (see panel above). The best *tablaos* and *peñas* do succeed in capturing the passion and art of flamenco.

Experts will tell you that the real thing emerges spontaneously, and usually in the early hours of the morning, in hidden-away bars and in semi-private all-night parties called *juergas*, but for the visitor such events are usually untraceable and out of bounds. There are numerous official flamenco festivals staged throughout Andalucía,

Finding Flamenco

Ask for details of flamenco *tablaos* and *peñas* at tourist offices in cities and towns. Hotels often have information about local flamenco shows, but these may often be expensive all-in-one "variety" performances or stylised cabaret, with a meal as part of the bill. Steer clear of anyone touting in the street for "flamenco", especially in areas such as Sacromonte in Granada (► 108). You may end up paying a great deal for very little. There is accessible flamenco at the following venues:

Tablao Cardenal and **La Bulería** in Córdoba (► 136)
El Corral del Príncipe in Granada (► 108)
Teatro Miguel de Cervantes in Málaga (► 76)
Casa Santa Pola in Ronda (► 76)
El Laga in Jerez de la Frontera (► 76)
La Cava in Cádiz (► 76)
Los Gallos and **El Tamboril** in Seville (► 168)

A dancer's hands: pure expression, pure passion

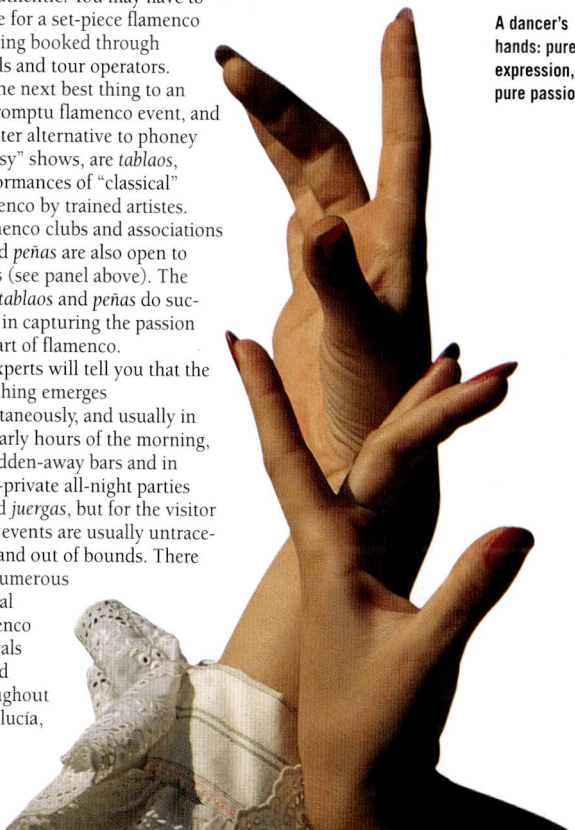

but these often concentrate on song alone, and for the non-devotee the relentless intensity of *cante jondo*, the wailings, sobbings and ululations performed by a succession of transfixed singers for hours on end, may quickly pall. Perhaps the best experience for a visitor to Andalucía is to come across spontaneous flamenco at a village fiesta. You'll hear it before you see it, and you'll never forget it.

Left: Flamenco glamour owes much to the dancers' colourful dresses, known as *batas de cola*

Below: Paco de Lucía, Algeciras-born maestro of the flamenco guitar

Famous Flamenco Names

The best-known flamenco singers are usually known by nicknames. Among the greatest was the late **Manolo Caracol** (Manolo the Snail), a gypsy from Seville province. He began his career in 1922, aged just 11, at a flamenco event staged by the Spanish composer Manuel de Falla, the poet Federico García Lorca and the guitarist Andrés Segovia. The most acclaimed singer of modern times was **Camarón de la Isla** (the Shrimp of the Island), whose harsh, impassioned singing expressed perfectly the fatalism and pain of the flamenco spirit. Camarón's heroin addiction contributed to his death in 1992. Two of the finest contemporary female singers are the sisters **Fernanda and Bernarda de Utrera**. Among flamenco's greatest guitarists are **Paco Peña** and **Paco de Lucía**, both non-gypsies and both great innovators. In the realm of flamenco dance, **Carmen Amaya** (1913–63), a gypsy dancer from Barcelona, became an international star and is still widely considered to have been the greatest flamenco dancer of all time. One of the best contemporary dancers is **Cristina Hoyos**, who has taken flamenco into the world of theatrical companies and ballet. If you want to capture the essence of great flamenco song and music, there are numerous discs and cassettes that feature the best flamenco singers and guitarists.

Festival Diary

The terms *festival*, *fiesta* and *feria* describe the whole range of celebratory events in Andalucía. The *fiesta* originated as a rural holiday and the *feria* as a country fair, and even in big cities their outdoor nature survives, with horses and bulls still figuring largely in the proceedings. Then there are religious festivals, notably Easter, centred on revered images carried in procession to the beating of drums and the sonorous ringing of bells, and accompanied by hooded penitents.

A hooded penitent during Seville's Semana Santa celebrations

FEBRUARY
Carnaval Spectacular carnivals in Cádiz and Málaga and, to a lesser extent, Córdoba, Carmona, Nerja and many other towns and villages, are held in the days preceding the beginning of Lent.

MARCH/APRIL
Semana Santa Religious processions are staged in all the main cities and in many country towns and villages throughout Holy Week, which precedes Easter.

APRIL
Feria de Abril Seville's April festival, held about two weeks after Easter, is a week-long celebration. It is the biggest and most colourful festival in Spain.

Nothing Less Than Excess

There is an enduring claim that more sherry is drunk during Seville's week-long Feria de Abril (above) than in the whole of Spain in one year. Yet, in spite of almost constant drinking, there are very few instances of outrageous behaviour or violence to disturb the Sevillian sense of style.

Left: Hooded *cofradía* during Semana Santa

Feria de la Manzanilla
Sanlúcar de Barrameda wine festival (last week in May).
Corpus Christi
Processions and celebrations in main towns and many villages (late May/early June).

MAY

Feria del Caballo Colourful horse fair, with marvellous displays of equestrianism (Jerez de la Frontera, early May).

"Moors and Christians" Carnival Mock battles and other events (Pampaneira, Las Alpujarras, 3 May).

Fiesta de los Patios Many of Córdoba's beautiful private patios open to the public (early May).

Romería del Rocío The biggest religious pilgrimage and festival in Spain (El Rocío, seventh week after Easter, ➤ 162).

Feria de Primavera Puerta de Santa María wine festival (last week in May).

JUNE

Feria de San Bernabé
Marbella's very lavish festival (second week in June).
Fiestas Patronales de

Above: Flamenco is an integral part of many Andalucian festivals

Left: The Feria del Caballo

Fun and Sun

Andalucians have long been noted for their love of festival and fun. "Every day seems to be a holiday," commented the 19th-century writer Richard Ford, in a rather sniffily English way, on his first visit. The English politician and writer Benjamin Disraeli was more enthusiastic.
"It is all the Sun," he exclaimed when he visited Andalucía in 1830 after an illness and felt rejuvenated.

San Antonio Festival where mock battles between "Moors" and "Christians" are played out (Trevélez, Las Alpujarras, 13/14 June).
Moors and Christians Fiesta Mojácar (10 June).
International Guitar Festival Córdoba (two weeks June/July).

JULY
International Festival of Music and Dance A programme of dance and chamber music is performed in various venues throughout the Alhambra (Granada, late June/early July).
Virgen de la Mar Almería's lively summer festival (last week in July).

AUGUST
Feria de Málaga Málaga's summer festival, noted for its good humour and exuberance (mid-Aug).
Sanlúcar de Barrameda Horse Races A series of exciting horse races along the beach at Sanlúcar de Barrameda (last two weeks in Aug).
Feria de Grazalema Grazalema's village festival includes bull-running through the streets (last week in Aug).
Fiestas Patronales San Augustín Mojácar festival (last week in Aug).

SEPTEMBER
Fiesta de la Vendimia Major wine festival at Jerez de la Frontera (first/second week in Sep).
Romería del Cristo de la Yedra Baeza's main festival (7 Sep).
Feria y Fiesta de Pedro Romero Fiesta featuring flamenco and traditional bull-fighting (Ronda, first two weeks in Sep).

OCTOBER
Fiesta de San Miguel Festival at Úbeda and in many other towns and villages (1 Oct).
Feria de San Lucas Jaén's main festival (mid-Oct).

Above: Jerez de la Frontera's Feria del Caballo, an equestrian extravaganza

Festival Tips

• Ask at tourist offices for a copy of the official Andalucian annual guide to festivals, the *Ferias y Fiestas de Andalucía*.
• For big city festivals like Seville's Semana Santa and Feria, or Cádiz's Carnaval, you have to book accommodation in advance. Be prepared to pay more for a bed during the festival period.
• If you are in any of Andalucía's larger cities during Semana Santa (Holy Week), try to get hold of a programme of the week's events. Local papers publish daily programmes and your hotel may well have its own guide. Be prepared for enormous crowds, especially in Seville.
• During Carnaval in cities like Cádiz and Málaga, it pays to dress up to some extent or you may find yourself the target of good-natured teasing.

The Man Who Gave It All Away

Roderick, king of Visigothic Spain, was probably more unfortunate than culpable in being the ruler whose unprepared army was trounced by the invading Moors in 711 near the present-day town of Jerez de la Frontera. The Moors probably came to Spain looking for new land, but legend blackens Roderick's name, claiming that a prominent fellow Visigoth, whose daughter had been violated by Roderick, persuaded the Moors to invade Spain in revenge by proxy.

MOVERS &

SHAKERS

> **"The army of Roderick, king of Visigothic Spain, was trounced by the invading Moors"**

The First and Last of the Moors

Tariq Ibn Ziyad, the Governor of Tangier in Morocco, was the man who first gained a military foothold in southern Spain by landing at Gibraltar in 711. The famous Rock was named after him: Jabal Tariq, the "mountain of Tariq".

Abur Abd Allah, known in Spanish as **Boabdil**, was the last of the Nasrid dynasty of sultans of Granada, and the last Moorish ruler of any substance in Spain. The story goes that, as he made his sad withdrawal from Granada, he kept looking back, much to his proud and severe mother's despair. The place where he caught his final regretful glimpse of the city is still known as Puerta del Suspiro – the Pass of the Sigh.

Two faces to fear: Fernando V of Aragón (left) and his wife Isabel I of Castile (below left)

Los Reyes Católicos

It was the marriage of **Isabel I of Castile** and **Fernando V of Aragón** in 1479 that heralded the end of Islamic authority (though not of Islamic influence) in Spain. Prior to the uniting of these most powerful of the Catholic kingdoms, the Christian Spanish had been far too divided to mount a complete Reconquest of Islamic al-Andalus. Isabel and Fernando, still revered in Spain as Los Reyes Católicos, the Catholic Monarchs,

> ## "Los Reyes Católicos – one of the most terrifying double acts in history"

brought renewed vigour to the ideal of a wholly Christian Spain. To their non-Christian subjects they represented one of the most terrifying double acts in history. Muslims were

Hard Headed

The Catholic Monarchs, Isabel and Fernando, are buried in the crypt of the Capilla Real (Royal Chapel), adjoining Granada cathedral (▶ 88–9). The royal pair are represented by recumbent effigies in marble, the centrepiece of the chapel. Isabel's head is more deeply sunk into her marble cushion than is Fernando's, a subtle conceit that is said to represent the well-attested fact that Isabel had a much "heavier" brain, and a much harder head, than did her husband.

at first granted religious tolerance, but within a few years they, like the Jewish community before them, were forced to accept either conversion to Christianity or expulsion from Spain. Following the Reconquest, the notorious Spanish Inquisition was established. Using threats of torture and the confiscation of property, the Inquisition was able to ensure the loyalty those who had converted to Christianity.

The surrender of Granada to Los Reyes Católicos in 1492

Artistic Andalucía

Two great classical Spanish painters associated with Andalucía are Francisco de **Zurbarán** (1598–1664), born in Andalucía's neighbouring province of Extremadura but

based for most of his life in Seville, and his contemporary, the Seville-born Bartolomé Esteban **Murillo** (1617–82). Zurbarán's haunting paintings of robed monks and saints reflect an austere nature rarely associated with Andalucía, yet even 17th-century Seville was a harsh enough place: Zurbarán lost the children of his second marriage to the Seville plague of 1649. Murillo was a genuinely popular artist who interpreted life with a typical Andalucian enthusiasm that, even in the religious sculptures that grace so many churches today, seems to mix sensuality and gaiety with piety. In his early years Murillo produced richly colourful and often sentimental Madonnas by the dozen as

well as numerous picturesque urchins, although his later work reflected a darker side. Works by Zurbarán and Murillo can be seen in a number of churches and galleries in Andalucía's main cities.

Most famous of all the region's artistic sons is Pablo Ruiz y **Picasso** (1881–1973), who was born in Málaga (although he moved with his family at the age of nine to Galicia and then to Barcelona, and lived for most of his life in France). You can see examples of his work in Málaga (▶ 52).

Left: Writer Miguel de Cervantes, whose colourful life provided him with much material

Literary Andalucía

Miguel de **Cervantes** Saavedra (1547–1616) was born near Madrid, but worked as a tax collector in Andalucía during the 1590s. He was jailed for a time because of alleged financial "inaccuracies" and, ever resourceful, is said to have written much of his great novel *Don Quixote* while in prison.

Federico García **Lorca** (1898–1936), a poet and

Above: Artist Pablo Picasso was born in Málaga

playwright of immense lyrical gifts, was one of Andalucía's greatest writers. Lorca was born in Granada, but his relationship with his native city was uneasy; he was a poet, and a homosexual, in Andalucía's least liberal-minded city. His work was what he saw as the spirit of the real Andalucía as exemplified by Málaga and Cádiz, cities that he felt were more open-minded and creative than Granada.

Lorca's most famous works include the plays *Bodas de Sangre* (Blood Wedding) and

Tragic Fall

The lives of 17th-century painters could be hazardous. Murillo fell from scaffolding while painting an altarpiece in a church in Cádiz and later died from the injuries he sustained. He was 64 years old when the accident happened (in an era when lifespans were far shorter): testimony to his remarkable energy.

closely bound up with Andalucía's Moorish past, with its gypsy culture, especially flamenco, and with *La Casa de Bernarda Alba* (The House of Bernarda Alba). Lorca was killed by Nationalist forces in 1936.

Flamenco diva in action

...buzzes

- **Halfway into a good flamenco performance** when singer, musicians and dancers really start to fly.
- **The first sip of great sherry**, a top *fino* from Jerez de la Frontera or a chilled *manzanilla* from Sanlúcar de Barrameda, followed by the first bite of *jamón serrano* (cured mountain ham) or *boquerones fritos* (deep-fried anchovies).
- **Being at Seville's Feria de Abril** (➤ 19) or at *Carnaval* in Cádiz or Málaga…or at almost any local fiesta for that matter.
- **A floodlit visit to the Palacio Nazaries** in the Alhambra (➤ 84).
- **Slipping into the sea from a lonely beach** on the Costa de la Luz (➤ 68–9) or Cabo de Gata (➤ 99).

The fun of the festival

...for kids

- **Mini Hollywood** near Tabernas, a Wild West theme park (➤ 102).
- **Isla Mágica**, a theme park in Seville with plenty of rides and attractions to keep the kids entertained (➤ 152).
- **Dolphin-watching** boat trips off the Tarifa coast or at Gibraltar (➤ 76).

- **Tivoli World** at Benalmádena Costa, a huge theme park with plenty of family attractions (➤ 62).
- **Parque de las Ciencias** (Science Park), Granada – fun as well as educational (➤ 90).

...beaches

- **Estepona**, the most relaxed of the Costa del Sol resorts and with a superbly maintained beach (➤ 61).
- **Nerja**: everything you could want in a beach resort, but with much more individual character than any of the Costa del Sol resorts (➤ 65).
- **Cabo de Gata**'s small isolated beaches north of the lighthouse, reached on foot, or by road to the small beach resort of San José (➤ 99).
- **Los Caños de Meca**, on Cádiz's Costa de la Luz, a delightful beach without too much development (➤ 68).
- **Playa Cuesta de Maneli**, on the western section of the Costa de la Luz. A 2-km walk takes you to a huge beach with room to breathe (➤ 162).

...wilderness areas

• **Sierra de Grazalema**, probably the most dramatic and most beautiful of Andalucian mountain areas: rocky peaks, deep pine forests, and all sorts of adventure experiences, from walking to rock climbing, birdwatching to hang-gliding (► 66–7).

• **Parque Natural del Torcal**, a dramatic lunar landscape of limestone pinnacles, with waymarked and longer guided walks through a superb nature reserve (► 66).

• **Las Alpujarras**, the beautiful, wooded foothills of the Sierra Nevada, giving opportunities for walking and horse riding (► 92–5).

• **Sierra Morena**, away-from-it-all, wooded hills in Seville province's Aracena region; good for walking and cycling (► 168).

• **Sierra de Cazorla**, a remote area of rugged, pine-clad mountains tucked away on Andalucia's northeastern border; walking, horse riding, jeep safaris (► 124–5).

...restaurants

• **Moochers Jazz Café and Restaurant**, Fuengirola (► 73), for the best live music (jazz and blues) around. The food's pretty good too!

• **Habanita**, Seville (► 165), for the best vegetarian food, with an emphasis on Cuban cui-

sine and not a slice of quiche in sight!

• **Restaurante Chinitas**, Málaga (► 71), for the best traditional Andaluz décor: beams, bricks and an evocative historic atmosphere.

• **Restaurante El Lido**, Estepona, best for elegance and top-quality cuisine, with views to match (► 73).

...if you go to only one...

• **Islamic monument**: the Alhambra, Granada (► 83–6).

• **art gallery**: Museo de Bellas Artes, Seville, for one of the finest collections of paintings in Spain, displayed in delightful surroundings (► 148–50).

• **baroque church**: Granada's Monasterio de la Cartuja, (Carthusian Monastery). Spectacularly over-the-top decorativeness in the main church (► 90).

• **mountain village**: Zahara de la Sierra, in Cádiz province (► 66–7, 178), for its dramatic castle and wide views.

• **Costa del Sol resort**: Marbella and its "port" of Puerto Banús, for glitz and glamour (► 61–2).

Above: The village of Zahara de la Sierra, crowning glory of the Sierra de Grazalema

Left: Setting off for a day's walking in the Alpujarras

Flamenco – an unmissable experience

Liquid Gold
The Sherry Experience

THIS CASK WAS DEDICATED
MATUSALEM
TO THE RT HON SIR
WINSTON CHURCHILL
K.G. O.M. C.H. M.P.
IN HONOUR OF HIS
80 TH BIRTHDAY

Below: An expert examining the sherry for taste and clarity

I n Andalucía, you don't simply drink sherry, you experience the entire sherry culture that goes with it – as befits one of the world's most exquisite wines.

By international law the wine can only be labelled as "sherry" if it is produced within the "Sherry Triangle", the corner of land that lies in the northwestern part of Cádiz province between the towns of Jerez de la Frontera, Sanlúcar de Barrameda and El Puerto de Santa María.

The Jerez area was producing wine from the time of the Phoenicians, but the specialised production of sherry began in the 16th century when British adventurers, exiled from Protestant England because of their Catholicism, became involved in wine production in the south of Spain, intermarried with local families and founded sherry dynasties. Sherry had been known as "sack" to the medieval English, and it became a favourite tipple after Sir Francis Drake and the Earl of Essex attacked Cádiz in the 1580s and 1590s and carried off thousands of barrels of sherry. The British are still the biggest consumers of the sweetened "cream" sherry.

Sherry is produced from three types of white grape: palomino, the basis of all sherry production, and muscat and Pedro Ximénez, both used in the blending of different types of sherry. The secret of sherry-making lies in the time-honoured

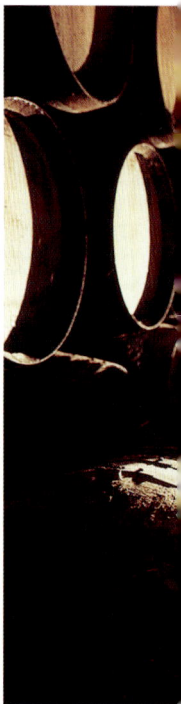

Harvesting palomino grapes

system of fortifying the palomino grape with alcohol, then storing it in huge casks of American oak, in warehouses known as *bodegas*. The yeast retained in the wine creates a surface film called *velo de flor* (veil of flowers) which prevents oxidation. It is this "locking in" of the wine that preserves the pale colour of *fino*, the most popular sherry in Spain, and creates its dryness and distinctive bouquet. In the absence of *flor*,

On hilltops overlooking main roads all over Spain, you'll see huge metal silhouettes of fighting bulls (below). They were erected by the Osborne sherry company of El Puerto de Santa María from the 1950s onwards. When roadside advertising was banned in the late 1980s, Osborne removed its name from the bulls, but left the silhouettes in place. There was a national outcry when the authorities threatened to dismantle them, and about 100 of the original 500 "sherry" bulls remain defiantly in place.

Domecq, González Byass, Sandeman and Osborne (▶ 56–7), you'll see thousands of casks, in rows called *criaderas* up to five casks high, where the sherry remains for between three and seven years. Sherry for bottling is drawn off at intervals from the ground-level row of casks, the *solera*. The amount taken is made up from the casks above, and the eventual shortfall in the top casks is then replenished with new wine. The results of this blending are the delicious sherries of the officially denominated *Jerez-Xérès-Sherry y Manzanilla-Sanlúcar de Barrameda*. And if you can get your tongue around that, you fully deserve another glass of liquid gold…

oxidation takes place, producing darker and fuller *amontillado* and *oloroso* sherries, which are often blended with the sweet wines made from muscat and Pedro Ximénez grapes to create pale, medium and cream sherries.

If you take a tour of one of the *bodegas* of famous-name sherry empires such as

Time for Tapas

Eat Andalucian and you eat *tapas*. These little dishes of food are a delicious accompaniment to a glass of dry sherry. Andalucía has more *tapas* bars than anywhere else in Spain and is the best place on earth to enjoy the real *tapa* experience.

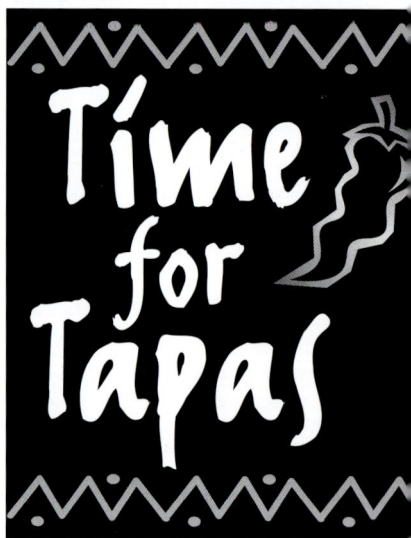

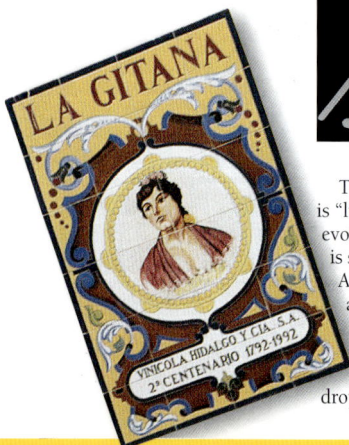

The literal meaning of *tapa* is "lid" or "cover", and its evolution as a culinary term is said to come from the old Andalucian habit of placing a small dish on a glass of sherry to protect it from flies and dust. Bar staff got into the habit of dropping morsels of bread

A local *tapas* bar in Seville, a city famous for its *tapas*

Café poster advertising La Gitana *manzanilla*

• Expect to pay around €2 for a *tapa*, but always check prices, especially when ordering expensive *jamón* (cured ham) dishes. A good idea for a group of friends is to order a few *raciones*, larger portions of your choice, which can then be shared.

• Some of the most satisfying *tapas* are served in modest bars in Andalucian provincial towns and villages. Look for a busy place with obvious locals and a crew of fast-moving, alert and friendly young bar staff. Don't be surprised to see them mark your "bill" on the counter in front of you with chalk.

and cheese and a couple of olives onto the dish and the custom grew. Today a good *tapas* bar will often have honey-coloured cured hams hanging from the ceiling, a row of stainless steel dishes filled with a selection of cold and hot *tapas*, a great choice of sherries and other drinks, and an atmosphere of enjoyment and good cheer.

Tapas are a civilised solution to the problem of what to eat during the hottest part of the day and in the early

Tapas temptation

"a delicious accompaniment to a glass of sherry"

There are many different *tapas* to choose from, be it a simple dish of olives or a tempting plate of squid

Some Tasty Tapas

The varieties of *tapas* are legion. Seville even has a Feria de la Tapa, an annual *tapas* fair. Here are some tasty and popular *tapas* to start you off (although different bars may serve them under slightly different names).

Fish and meat

Gambas a la plancha grilled prawns
Puntillitas fritas deep-fried baby squid
Boquerones fritos deep-fried anchovies
Boquerones en vinagre anchovies marinated in vinegar
Cazón en adobo fish marinated in vinegar, lemon, spices, and then deep fried
Croquetas croquettes filled with anything from ham to spinach
Jamón Serrano fabled cured ham of the mountains. Usually expensive
Habas con jamón broad beans and ham
Flamenquin casero sliced pork, boiled egg and vegetables, rolled tightly in breadcrumb batter
Lomo al Jerez fresh loin of pork cooked with sherry

Cinta de lomo pork in a cream and onion sauce
Pollo al ajillo chicken in garlic
Pincho muruño small meat kebabs

Vegetarian

Acietunas olives
Ensalada mixta mixed salad
Revueltos scrambled eggs with delicious additions, such as asparagus
Pimientos rellenos stuffed peppers
Champiñones a la plancha grilled mushrooms
Tortilla de patatas potato omelette
Patatas bravas fried potato chunks in a spicy sauce
Arroz rice

---

evening, when a full-scale meal seems inappropriate. They can be a precursor to dinner, but can also be a relaxed alternative to a more formal sit-down meal.

There are fashionable bars in Andalucian towns and cities that base their entire reputation on the variety of *tapas* on offer, but there is still a special pleasure, after ordering a glass of *fino* or beer in a quiet bar, to find a little dish of bread, olives and a sliver of *jamón* or cheese being slid across the counter, unsolicited. This can still happen in rural *tabernas* and in the neighbourhood bars of Granada and Almería.

Some *tapas* bars have menus in several languages, but where the menu is in Spanish only, be careful; if you don't speak the language, you may end up playing *tapas* roulette. Choosing "blind" can bring enjoyable surprises, but it can also lead to the cruel reality of finding that the *criadillas* or *sesos* that you ordered, and that sounded so delicious, are actually fried testicles of pig and scrambled brains. When in doubt, ask…

Facing page:
Pilgrims and their decorated wagon on the way to El Rocío

Five Best Tapas Bars

- **Bar Logüeno**, Málaga (► 71): best in town (possibly even in Andalucía) for sheer variety, with more than 75 *tapas* to choose from.
- **El Faro** (► 72): best seafood *tapas* in Cádiz, more innovative than some, with an upmarket yet traditional atmosphere.
- **La Chacha** (► 73): best old-world *tapas* bar in Torremolinos, with a fabulous selection of seafood and fish.
- **La Gran Taberna**, Granada (► 105): best for its traditional atmosphere, with hams curing above the bar and seating around giant barrels.
- **El Patio**, Seville (► 165): famous *tapas* bar, serving a wide range of *tapas*.

Finding Your Feet

First Two Hours

Arriving in Málaga

Málaga International Airport

Málaga International Airport (tel: 952 04 88 44), about 6km west of Málaga city and 4km east of Torremolinos, is the main point of entry for most visitors.

■ An **electric train service** (Línea C-1) between Málaga city and Fuengirola connects with the airport, Torremolinos and Benalmádena. This is the best option for getting to and from the airport by public transport. For the airport station (Aeropuerto), turn right outside the airport building upper-level exit and follow signs that direct you over a footbridge to the station. Tickets are obtained from a machine by the end of the footbridge, or on the train. Trains to Málaga city run from 7 am, then at 45 and 15 minutes past the hour until 11.45 pm; journey time: 12 minutes. First train for Torremolinos and Fuengirola: at 5.58 am, then at 13 and 43 minutes past the hour until 10.43 pm; journey time: Torremolinos 10 minutes, Fuengirola 29 minutes.
■ **Bus service** No 19 runs between the airport and Málaga city every 30 minutes, 6.30 am–11.30 pm. Journey time is about 30 minutes, fare around €1. Ask for the Alameda Principal 9 (Málaga's central thoroughfare).
■ A **taxi** to Málaga city should cost between €7 and €9; to Marbella about €34. Licenced taxis (which are usually white) line up outside the airport exit. Make sure the meter is operating before setting out, especially late at night. For more information on taxis ➤ 37.
■ Leaving the airport **by car**, follow the exit road. Approaching the N340, the left-hand lane will take you across a flyover and on to Málaga and the Málaga Ring Road (Ronda de Málaga) for Granada, Almería and destinations north and east of Málaga city; the right-hand lane will take you on to the N340 heading west for the Costa del Sol and onwards to Cádiz and Seville.

Málaga Railway Station (Málaga RENFE)

Málaga's main railway station (tel: 952 36 02 02) lies about 0.75km from Málaga city centre. **Electric train** (Línea C-1) connects to Alameda Centro in the city centre. Buses 1, 4, 5, 10, 12, 16, 19, 24 go to Alameda Principal.

Málaga Bus Station

The bus station (tel: 952 35 00 61) is about 0.75km from Málaga city centre and adjacent to the railway station. There is a helpful **Municipal Tourism Office** in the bus station. For connections to city centre see Railway Station above.

Arriving in Almería

Almería Airport

Almería Airport (tel: 950 21 37 00 or 950 21 37 01) lies about 8km east of Almería city. **Bus** No 14 runs between the airport and the city centre approximately every half hour, from 7 am to 9 pm. A **taxi** to the Puerta de Purchena costs about €12.

Almería Railway Station and Bus Station

The railway station (Estación de Ferrocarril, tel: 950 25 11 35) and bus station (Estación de Autobuses) share the same arrival/departure concourse on Plaza de la Estación. It is a short walk of about 700m to the seaward end of Avenida Federico García Lorca (Rambla de Belén).

Arriving in Granada

Granada Airport
The airport (tel: 958 24 52 00), about 13km west of Granada city, is for internal flights only. **Buses** run from the airport to Plaza Isabel la Católica at the end of Gran Vía de Colón in the city centre. There are 5 buses a day at 9.05 am, 10 am, 2 pm, 3.05 pm, 7.35 pm (no 2 pm bus at weekends).

Granada Railway Station
The station (tel: 958 27 12 72), on Avenida de Andaluces, is about 1.5km from the city centre. City **buses** 1, 3, 4, 5, 6, 7, 9 and 11 run between the station and Gran Vía de Colón and Los Reyes Católicos at the city centre. **Taxis** cost about €3 to Los Reyes Católicos.

Granada Bus Station
Carretera de Jaén (tel: 958 18 58 10), about 3km from the city centre. City bus No 3 runs to city centre.

Arriving in Córdoba

Córdoba Railway Station
The station (tel: 957 40 02 02) is about 1.25km from central Córdoba. **Bus No 3** connects to Plaza de las Tendillas, about 0.5km north of the Mezquita, and continues to the riverside in front of the Mezquita. **Taxis** cost between €2 and €3 to the Mezquita area.

Córdoba Bus Station
Bus No 3 (see above) takes arrivals from the bus station (tel: 957 40 40 40) to the city centre.

Arriving in Seville

Seville Airport
The airport (tel: 954 44 90 00) handles internal flights and international flights from London, Amsterdam, Brussels, Düsseldorf, Geneva and Paris. It lies about 10km northeast of Seville city centre.
- **Bus** to city centre (Amarillos company) runs from about 6.45 am to 11.30 pm at least every hour, with a break in service between 3 and 5 pm.
- **Taxi** to the city centre costs between €14 and €15.

Seville Railway Station
Bus No C1 takes you from the station (tel: 954 54 02 02) to Avenida Carlos V, just a short walk from the cathedral area. **Taxis** to the cathedral area cost about €3, plus €2 for luggage. A **tourism information desk** can book hotels.

Seville Bus Station
Seville has two bus stations. International arrivals and arrivals from other Spanish cities outside Andalucía come in at Plaza de Armas (tel: 954 90 77 37/90 80 40). Buses from Andalucía's other main cities, including Granada, Málaga and Cordoba, arrive at Prado de San Sebastián (tel: 954 41 71 11).

Tourist Information Offices
In Andalucía's main cities there are two types of tourist office: the regional tourist office, the **Oficinas de Turismo de la Junta de Andalucía (J de A)**, which deals mainly with city tourism, and the city or municipal tourist office – **Oficina Municipale Turismo (OMT)**, which deals with city and regional tourism.

Getting Around

Public Transport

Train

RENFE (Red Nacional de Ferrocaril de España) is the national rail network. Services between main cities are generally fast, comfortable and efficient. Services to smaller towns and throughout rural areas are much slower, but are often scenic. Stations and halts in rural areas can be several kilometres from the main settlement that they serve; public transport is usually not available and you may need to phone for a taxi.

- For general enquiries about RENFE services throughout Andalucía, tel: 902 24 02 02. RENFE also has a Website in Spanish, www.renfe.es
- It is advisable to **reserve a seat** on mainline trains. You can buy **tickets** and reserve seats at city-centre travel agents that display the RENFE sign. Most city railway stations have a queuing system at ticket desks: you must first take a numbered slip from a machine signed "*Venta anticipada su turno*", then watch for your number to appear on indicators above the desks.
- For details of **railway stations** in Málaga, Almería, Granada and Seville, ➤ 34–5.

Types of Train
- **Cercanías** are city and suburban link trains, though services may extend to nearby provincial towns. They are fast and fairly cheap.
- **Regionales** are intercity links within Andalucía. They are being upgraded to what are known as TRDs (Trenes Regionales Diésel) and are fast and comfortable.
- **Larga Distancia**, known as AVE (Tren Alta Velocidad) is the national high-speed service into Andalucía from Madrid to Córdoba and Seville. .

Bus

Andalucía has an excellent regional bus service run by a number of companies. Buses, in general, are reliable and comfortable (with air conditioning on intercity buses) and fares are usually about 25 per cent less than for similar journeys by train. In rural areas bus travel is often faster than train or is the only option.

- For details of **bus stations** in main cities, including telephone information numbers, ➤ 34–5.
- Buy **tickets** as early as possible (preferably the day before) for bus journeys between main cities and towns. If you arrive within minutes of departure without a ticket, you will probably be given a ticket for a later bus. There can be long queues, especially in the mornings.
- Some bus stations sell all tickets from one desk, but at **Málaga bus station** the Alsina Graells company ticket office handles main services inland and the Automoviler Portillo company handles Costa del Sol, Cádiz and coastal routes to the east.
- Services are greatly reduced on Sundays and public holidays.
- Luggage goes in the hold, but there is room under the seat in front of you for a normal-size case or pack, if you want to keep an eye on your luggage.

Taxi

Taxis in Andalucian cities and towns have meters. Fares are much cheaper than in northern Europe. Make sure the meter is operating, but expect a change to an increased rate as soon as you leave city limits, or late at night, at weekends and during holidays. A surcharge is also likely for luggage carried.

Driving

Driving in Andalucía is fairly stress-free away from cities and towns, although the high speeds and congestion of the **N340** main road along the Costa del Sol can be daunting.

- Drive on the **right-hand side** of the road.
- **Seat belts** must be worn in front seats and in rear seats where fitted.
- **Fuel** (*gasolina*) is available in four grades: *normal*, *super*, *sin plomo* (unleaded) and *gasoleo/gasoil* (diesel). Most garages take credit cards, but rural garages often prefer cash.
- The **speed limit** on the *autopistas* (toll motorways) and *autovías* (free motorways) is 120 kph. On dual carriageways and roads with periodic overtaking lanes it is 100 kph and on rural roads 90 kph. The maximum speed on urban roads is 50 kph and 25 kph in residential areas.
- Breath testing is random. The legal limit if you are driving is 0.5gm alcohol per 1,000cu cm breath.
- In cities and larger towns always check whether you have parked in a **pay-for area**. Penalties for non-payment range from a fine to the towing away of your vehicle.
- You will find that traffic is much quieter, and that there are more parking spaces, if you arrive in towns and villages during the afternoon **siesta hours** (between 2 and 5 pm).

Hiring a Car

- **Book ahead** at peak holiday times. From the UK, try **Budget** (tel: 0800 181 181) or **Europcar** (tel: 0870 607 5000).
- **On-the-spot hiring** can be done at airports and at most city railway stations. If you can speak some Spanish you can get good deals and often friendlier service from local companies. A good hire company is **ATA. S.A Rent a Car** with offices in Seville (tel: 954 22 09 57/58) and Granada (tel: 958 22 40 04/22 56 65). These offices can also put you in contact with their regional outlets (in Cádiz and Marbella, for example).
- Always **check** bodywork, tyres, undercarriage and inside trimmings of your hire car and indicate any damage to the hirer before driving off.
- In the event of a **breakdown**, follow the instructions on your car-rental agreement. Make certain that there are portable warning symbols with your hire car and use these to warn other traffic no matter where you break down. Most hire companies have breakdown contingency schemes, but check that they do. If using your own car use the procedures outlined in your insurance or motoring association membership.
- You will be expected to return the car with the **petrol** tank at the same level as when you left. Clarify this situation with the hirer.

Admission Charges

The cost of admission for museums and places of interest mentioned in the text is indicated by the following price categories:

Inexpensive under €1.5
Moderate €1.5–€3
Expensive over €3

Accommodation

This guide recommends a carefully selected cross-section of places to stay, ranging from *paradores* (the state-owned chain of top-quality hotels) to small family-run *hostales* (modest hotels). In the more popular tourist destinations, such as the Costa del Sol, it is advisable to book ahead, particularly between May and October when most of the larger hotels have block bookings by charter tour companies. At the lower end of the range, there are bargains to be had, particularly away from the major resorts, with double rooms in an *hostal* or *pensión* costing as little as €18 a night.

Finding a Room
- If you have not reserved a room, the local tourist office will have a list of accommodation; most are prepared to call ahead to check if there is a room available. Note, most hotels are only required to retain a reserved room until 6 pm unless you have given your credit-card details in advance.
- If there is no tourist office, or it is closed, then look for the main plaza or the centre of town as the most likely area for hotels and *hostales*.
- If you are travelling with a pet or small child, the hotel should be informed at the time of booking.

Checking In and Out
- You will be asked to produce your passport when you check in; this will be used to complete a registration form.
- Check-out time is normally noon in hotels, although at some *hostales* and *pensiones* it is 11 am; always find out in advance, to avoid paying an extra day. If you are staying in cheaper accommodation and plan to leave early, advise the front desk.
- Hotels will normally store your luggage until the end of the day and arrange a taxi for you.

Types of Accommodation
Paradores
Paradores are an expensive but special option. They tend to be converted castles, palaces and monasteries and most successfully retain the historical character of the building, while incorporating modern bathrooms, air conditioning and all the luxurious trimmings that you'd expect from a 5-star hotel. They are often furnished with magnificent antiques and original works of art.

There are some 16 *paradores* in Andalucía. Advance booking is recommended; to reserve a room at any *parador*, contact: **Central de Reservas**, Calle Requena 3, 28013, Madrid, tel: 915 16 66 66, fax: 915 16 66 57.

Hotels
Spanish hotels are officially classified with one to five stars (*estrellas*) by the Ministry of Tourism, depending on the amenities such as en-suite bathrooms, lifts and air conditioning.

- A **5-star** hotel is truly luxurious with a price to match. You can expect facilities such as a mini-bar, tennis court, swimming pool and gym, as well as nightly entertainment.
- A **4-star** hotel is only slightly less deluxe and still offers first-class accommodation.
- A **3-star** hotel is considerably lower in price but the rooms are perfectly adequate and will include TV and air conditioning.

- A **1- or 2-star** hotel is more basic and relatively inexpensive. When booking such accommodation, enquire about the exact location and facilities provided, as standards can vary.
- Many hotels have family rooms with extra beds for children costing roughly 30 per cent more than the double room rate.

Hostales

Hostales often provide better accommodation and value for money than cheap hotels. Not to be confused with a youth hostel, a Spanish *hostal* is essentially a small hotel, often family-run and officially categorised from one to three stars. An *hostal* with **three stars** is roughly the equivalent of a two-star hotel. Although *hostales* can vary enormously, with few exceptions they provide straightforward accommodation at a reasonable price, with the option of en-suite bathroom.

There are some charming small *hostales* in Andalucía, particularly in the major cities where they are invariably situated in the historic quarter of town.

Pensiones

There is not a great deal of difference between an *hostal* and a *pensión*, except that the latter is more like a boarding house and will often have a shared bathroom. A *pensión* will usually require you to take either full board (three meals) or half board (breakfast, plus lunch or dinner). You can expect your room to be clean but spartan and you will have to supply your own soap and shampoo, although towels and extra blankets should be provided.

Budget Accommodation

Camas or **habitaciones** are the closest Spanish equivalent to a bed-and-breakfast, usually advertised in the windows of private houses and the upper floors of bars and *ventas* (▶ 41), perhaps with the phrase *"camas y comidas"* (bed and meals). Don't expect an en-suite bathroom. A **fonda** is a small inn offering basic no-frills accommodation.

Youth hostels (*albergues juveniles*) are only really worth considering if you are a die-hard youth-hosteller. Most are housed in old buildings that lack modern plumbing or air conditioning and possibly are unheated in winter. They are also usually situated out of town and packed with schoolchildren, and residents are subject to curfews.

Camping

Andalucía has some excellent campsites. These are routinely inspected and approved by the Spanish tourist authority, and classified under four categories: L (luxury), then 1st-, 2nd- and 3rd-class, according to their amenities. However, even the most basic campsite must have 24-hour surveillance, be within a fenced area, provide unlimited drinking water, have first-aid and fire-prevention facilities, and toilets and showers. There is usually an extra charge for hot water. Camping is forbidden on beaches and may result in a fine.

Seasonal Rates

Minimum and maximum rates are established according to the season, as well as the facilities provided. In popular summer resorts, such as those of the Costa del Sol, July and August are the high season (*temporada alta*) when room rates can increase by 25 per cent. In winter resorts, as in the Sierra Nevada (Granada), high season is, logically, winter. During national holidays and local fiestas such as Seville's Feria de Abril, accommodation costs more and is harder to find (▶ 19–21 for more information on festivals).

Outside the main season, many hotels offer discounts, and some will have reduced prices at weekends. *Paradores* can be particularly good value then.

Food and Drink

Andalucía has the climate, coast and terrain to produce a wonderful range of raw ingredients: swordfish (*pez espada*), mussels (*mejillones*), cockles (*coquinas* and *almejas*) and fresh anchovies (*boquerones*) for seafood lovers; baby goat (*choto*) and rabbit (*conejo*), both popular in this part of Spain, for meat-eaters; and beautiful fruit and vegetables according to season – purple figs, glossy red peppers, curly green chard or brilliant orange pumpkin.

The local Spanish love to eat out. Whether or not there is cause for celebration, they will usually invite friends and family to a favourite bar or restaurant, rather than cook at home.

Meal Timetable

■ **Breakfast** (*desayuno*) usually consists of coffee with toast (*tostada*) which locals prefer topped with olive oil instead of butter. Other toppings include pork lard (*manteca*), coloured a lurid orange by the addition of paprika, and crushed tomato with olive oil (*tomate y aceite*). Spiral-shaped *churros* and hot chocolate are another popular choice. However, most Spaniards drink coffee in the morning, either strong and black (*café solo*), with hot milk (*café con leche*), or black with a dash of milk (*café cortado*). If you find the coffee too strong, you may prefer the more diluted *americano*.

■ **Lunch** (*almuerzo*) is the most important meal of the day, eaten by the Spanish at 2 pm, although most restaurants will serve until 4 pm. There are usually three or four courses, starting with soup and/or salad, followed by a seafood or meat dish with vegetables. Vegetarians tend to be restricted to *gazpacho*, followed by a Spanish *tortilla* (see Andalucian Cuisine, below) or omelette with salad. Often the choice of desserts is limited to caramel custard (*flan*), ice cream or fresh fruit. Most average restaurants offer an economical menu of the day (*menú del día*), with several choices for each course and priced around €6.

■ **Tapas** are an integral part of the local culinary tradition (➤ 30–2).

■ **Dinner** (*cena*) is generally a lighter meal than lunch. Few restaurants offer their cut-price menu in the evening. The normal dinner hour is late compared to northern Europe, starting anywhere between 9 and 10.30 pm, although in the popular resorts you can usually dine at 8 pm.

Andalucian Cuisine

• **Soups** The best-known soup is *gazpacho*, served cold in summer and made from blended tomatoes, cucumbers, peppers, garlic, bread, vinegar and olive oil. A thicker version, known as *salmorejo* in Córdoba and *porra ante-querana* around Málaga, is also popular, while *ajo blanco*, a chilled soup made with almonds, garlic and grapes, is often found at better restaurants.

• **Eggs** Potatoes, onions and eggs are the simple ingredients for a Spanish omelette (*tortilla*), one of the most popular local dishes. A plain omelette is a *tortilla francesa*.

• **Seafood** *Chiringuitos* (➤ 41), located on beaches, are the best places to find economically priced fish such as fresh charcoal-grilled anchovies (*boquerones*) and sardines (*sardinas*). *Paella* is another all-time favourite, made with shellfish and garnished with red peppers and lemon wedges.

• **Meat** Popular meat dishes include loin of pork (*lomo de cerdo*), chops (*chuletas*), spicy sausage (*chorizo*) and roast suckling pig (*cochinillo*). Some of the best Spanish mountain ham (*jamón serrano*) originates from the Jaén region of Andalucía. Spit-roasted chicken is very popular and sold on the spot at small open-fronted shops (*asador*).

- **Vegetables** Salads are readily available, although they tend to be an unimaginative combination of lettuce, tomatoes and onion. Many vegetable dishes are seasonal, such as oyster mushrooms (*setas*) fried with garlic and parsley, and fresh asparagus prepared with scrambled eggs (*revuelto*).
- **Desserts** As well as caramel custard (*flan*) and ice cream (*helado*), you may find rice pudding (*arroz con leche*), vanilla whip (*natillas*), caramel custard with cream (*crema catalan*) and fresh fruit on the menu. Avoid commercial-brand frozen desserts, which are of poor quality and overpriced.

Where to Eat

- **Ventas**, rural restaurants that traditionally catered to farm workers and travellers, still serve hearty home-style cooking, though nowadays the clientele is a mix of construction workers, business people and, on Sundays, families. **Chiringuitos** are beachside restaurants serving fresh seafood.
- There's plenty of choice when it comes to **cafés and bars**, including *tascas* that specialise in *tapas*, and *bodegas* where you can sample wine or sherry straight from the barrel.
- **Restaurants**, ranging from sophisticated places serving international cuisine to ethnic and fast-food joints, are found in the Costa resorts. Spanish restaurants tend to specialise in seafood, game and meat dishes. Be aware that it's unusual to find a non-smoking section in a Spanish restaurant.
- **Teterías** are Moroccan-style tea shops serving a wide choice of herb teas (*infusiones*), accompanied by traditional Arab pastries.

Tipping

The Spanish tip an average of 5 per cent but there is rarely any arithmetic involved. It's more a matter of just leaving spare change. Most foreigners follow international practice and tip as they would in their own countries. Ten per cent should be the maximum.

What to Drink

- **Beer (*cerveza*)** is extremely popular – many Spaniards prefer it to wine. A *cervecería* is a bar that specialises in beer and usually has several brands on tap, plus a wide range of bottled and imported beers. Spanish beer is fairly strong, usually around 5 per cent alcohol by volume. For something lighter, try a shandy (*clara*).
- Rioja is perhaps the most famous of Spanish **wines**, but there are 40 other wine denominations in Spain. You may want to try a house wine (*vino de la casa*) or, for a refreshing alternative, a *tinto de verano*: red wine with lemonade (*gaseosa*). Red wine is *tinto*, white wine *blanco*. The sweet Málaga wine is made from muscat grapes grown in the Axarquia region east of Málaga.
- **Sherry** (*fino, manzanilla, amontillado, oloroso*) is produced in Andalucía and is a popular aperitif (➤ 28–9).
- A genuine **sangría** is a delicious red wine punch that combines wine, cognac, other liqueurs and *gaseosa* with slices of citrus fruit.
- **Cocktails and spirits** are much cheaper in Spain than in most other countries and the measures are generous. Many Andalucians will have a brandy (*coñac*) or *anís* with their morning coffee. Spanish spirits cost far less than international brands and there is little difference in quality. However, Spanish whisky is better avoided!
- The usual choice of fizzy soft drinks is available. Other **non-alcoholic drinks** include fruit juice (*zumo*) and *Bitter Kas*, the latter similar in flavour to Campari. For something different, try ice-cold *horchata*, a nutty milk-like beverage made from tiger nuts (*chufas*) and available at most cafés.

Shopping

In Andalucía's glitzy coastal resorts and major cities, top-name fashion salons exist side by side with shops selling traditional *flamenco* wear. In every region, you'll find *alfarerías* (pottery workshops) and *talleres* (craft studios) producing colourful ceramics and fabrics, leatherwork and silverware (craft traditions that have their origins in the region's Moorish past). You'll also find tempting delicatessens, wine shops and pâtisseries in every city, and colourful local markets, where you can buy a range of regional specialities.

Where to Shop

Fashion

All of Andalucía's main cities – Málaga, Granada, Seville, Córdoba and Cádiz – and the chic Costa del Sol resorts of Marbella and Puerto Banús, have a huge number of clothes and shoe shops. You can buy anything from top-of-the-range Armani or Gucci to affordable and bargain clothes and accessories.

There are many jewellery shops in the Costa del Sol resorts, although with some outlets you would be wise to know something about what you are buying. Long-established jewellers are also found in the main shopping areas of cities and larger towns.

Souvenirs

You can buy souvenirs that range from tacky T-shirts to traditional pottery in just about every city and large town in Andalucía. Most shops that are wholly dedicated to mass-produced souvenirs are concentrated around major attractions, such as Córdoba's Mezquita and Seville's Barrio Santa Cruz area. The more authentic outlets that sell fine pottery and other traditional Andalucian craftwork can still be found (the Where to…Shop sections throughout the guide give some suggestions). The main streets and seafront *paseos* of the major Costa del Sol resorts are lined with gift shops, and at peak season an additional layer of pavement stalls hawk cheap souvenirs. There's quality around as well, however, and you can often find entertaining items amid the relentless trash. (See also the sections below on antiques and art, crafts and village shops).

Antiques and Art

For interesting pieces with a genuine Spanish pedigree – a cut above the usual "souvenir" – search the antiques and fine-arts shops scattered through-out the centres of main cities like Granada and Seville. Most of the pieces on display may be too hefty to cart back home, but there are often worthwhile smaller items.

Crafts

Andalucian **ceramics** reach international standards, not least in such regional centres as Úbeda (► 126–7) and Níjar (► 100). Andalucía is particularly noted for vivid and colourful tile work in a tradition that goes back to the Moorish era. In Córdoba (► 114–19) you will find outstanding **leather-work** and **filigree silverware**, while Granada (► 82–91) is a centre for **marquetry**. The mountain areas of Andalucía, especially the Alpujarras (► 92–5) and the Sierra de Grazalema (► 66–7), are good places to find traditional fabrics and clothing such as ponchos, as well as small rugs and bedcovers, known as *jarapas*.

Food and Drink

The hill regions of the Alpujarras in Granada province and the Sierra Morena in Seville province are famous for their *jamón serrano* (cured ham); villages such as Trevélez (► 94–5) in the Alpujarras, and Aracena (► 157) and Jabugo (► 184) in the Sierra Morena, have shops devoted to *jamón* and other meats.

You can find own-label brands of **sherry** in the big-name *bodegas* of Jerez de la Frontera (► 56–8), El Puerto de Santa María (► 68) and Sanlúcar de Barrameda (► 67), while in specialist shops in the main towns and the wine-producing areas, you will find every kind of sherry, wine and liqueur on sale – and you can often sample before deciding what to buy.

Department Stores

There are other department stores, but Spain's shopping success story of recent years is the **El Corte Inglés** chain of mega-stores, which has branches in Seville, Granada, Córdoba, Málaga and on the Costa del Sol. Some, like Malaga's, are almost complete communities in themselves, crammed with departments that specialise in just about anything you could want.

Markets

Town and village markets are excellent sources of fresh food if you are self-catering or picnicking. Colourful, noisy, good-natured and, above all, bursting with life, they can be an entertainment in themselves.

> ### Best Markets
> **For fish:** Sanlúcar de Barrameda (► 74), Almería (► 107) and other coastal towns
> **For mixed fish, meat, fruit and vegetables:** Cádiz (► 75), Málaga (► 52)
> **For clothing and general goods:** Fuengirola (► 75), Córdoba (► 135)

Village Shops

Village hardware and general goods shops can sell anything from local pottery to straw hats, spices and condiments, colourful shawls and neckties. You'll pay a fraction of the price for such items that you would pay in town, while they have a far more authentic pedigree than a typical resort souvenir.

Opening Hours

Most shops in Andalucía open 9–1.30 and 4.30–8.30 Monday to Saturday, although there is individual flexibility at either end. Large department stores open all day from about 9.30 am to as late as 10 pm. Saturday afternoon and all-day Sunday closing is general outside coastal resorts.

Payment

In main cities and larger towns, credit cards are accepted in most shops and stores. In village shops and other rural outlets, cash payment is still expected.

Etiquette

Andalucians enjoy browsing in shops and you will have no problems about doing so as a visitor. To avoid any misunderstandings, shoppers should ask the assistant's permission before handling goods. However, in chic fashion salons you will be assumed to be serious about buying and here you may receive one-to-one attention as soon as you enter. In the wall-to-wall shopping of the resorts, shopkeepers and stallholders are sometimes overly attentive.

Entertainment

There is no lack of organised evening entertainment in Andalucía's towns
and villages, from nightclubbing to flamenco watching. Most cities have cinemas and the Costa del Sol has a number of casinos. For the outdoor
enthusiast there are plenty of activities, and children are more than catered
for on the Costa del Sol where there is a whole range of fun parks(➤ 62).

Nightlife

■ The main **clubbing circuit** is on the Costa del Sol. Most clubs **open** their
doors at 10 or 11 pm, but you'll have the place to yourself until at least
1 am, and things often don't really get going until 3 or 4 am.

■ **Cinemas** There are cinemas in all the major cities and in most large towns.
Many foreign-language films are dubbed into Spanish rather than subtitled.
If subtitled, the film listing will be marked v.o. – *versión original*.

■ There are plenty of opportunities to see **flamenco** throughout Andalucía
(➤ 16–8).

Special Events

■ **Festivals** are an essential and exuberant part of Andalucian life. The
calendar of events is fullest from Easter through to June (➤ 19–21).

■ The main **bullfight** season runs from Easter to October, but there are novice
fights into November on the Costa del Sol. Bullfights are advertised by
garish posters about three weeks before the event, and resort hotels often
organise bus pickups. For major rings, tickets are often booked well ahead
by locals. Prices can be as high as €120 and start at about €15. Even
Costa del Sol *novilladas* may cost you from €30 to €60, although they
should be much less. For more information ➤ 13–15.

Outdoor Activities

■ The windier Atlantic coast, especially at Tarifa (➤ 68–9), between Gibraltar
and Cádiz, is one of the world's best **windsurfing** venues, while the opportunities for **scuba diving**, **water-sking** and **paragliding** are increasing. Boat trips
are always an enjoyable option and in the Gibraltar and Tarifa area, there
are special **dolphin-watching** boat trips available.

■ Specialist "golf villages" proliferate on the Costa del Sol. On the Costa
courses in general you may find that you need to book well in advance for a
round, and provide a handicap certificate. Fees vary, but can be hefty on
some of the more upmarket courses where you may even have difficulty in
making a casual booking (➤ 76 for details). A good source of information
about golf in Andalucía is the **Federacíon Andaluza de Golf** (Calle Sierra de
Grazalema, Málaga, tel: 952 22 55 99).

■ Andalucía's magnificent mountains offer endless opportunities for adventure holidaying, whether it's basic **walking** along the numerous tracks and
paths in Las Alpujarras (➤ 92–5), the Sierra de Grazalema (➤ 66–7) and
the Sierras de Cazorla y Segura (➤ 124–5) or **horse riding** and **cycling** on
organised trips with expert guides. Ask at tourist offices. For information on
angling, a useful contact is the **Spanish Fishing Federation** (tel: 912 25 59
85). You can also go for the wilder edges of **adventure sport** and try rock
climbing, abseiling, canoeing, paragliding and hang-gliding.

Useful Publications

At most city tourist offices, you can pick up a copy of *Qué Hacer? - Guía de
Ocio de Andalucía*, a monthly entertainments guide, in Spanish and English.

Málaga and Cádiz

Getting Your Bearings 46–47
In Four Days 48–49
Don't Miss 50–64
At Your Leisure 65–69
Where to… 70–76

Getting Your Bearings

Málaga and Cádiz are Andalucía's most visited provinces, not only because of the popular appeal of Málaga's Costa del Sol, but for their spectacular landscapes, old Moorish villages and historic cities and towns.

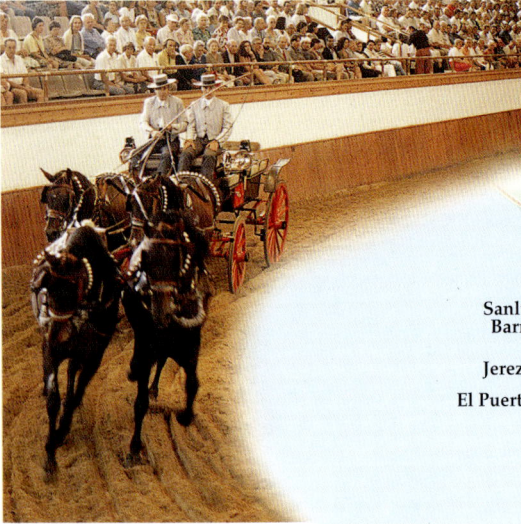

On track at Jerez de la Frontera's famous riding school

Parque Nacional de Doñana

Sanlúcar de Barrameda **8**

Jerez de la Frontera **7**

El Puerto de Santa María

Cádiz **10** **9**

San Fernando

Chiclana de la Frontera

Vejer de la Fron

Los Caños de Me

Costa de la Luz

Málaga province provides an ideal introduction to the extraordinary diversity of Andalucía. The vibrant, everyday life of its capital, Málaga, is a refreshing contrast to the conspicuous tourism of the neighbouring Costa del Sol's crowded resorts. North of Málaga and the Costa lie the forested valleys and rugged mountains of a different Andalucía, seen at its most dramatic in the bone-white limestone pinnacles and wooded ravines of the Parque Natural del Torcal near the historic town of Antequera. There is also dramatic scenery further west, in the Serranía de Ronda, especially at the clifftop town of Ronda. To the south and west of Ronda, where Málaga and Cádiz provinces meet, villages of whitewashed houses known as the *pueblos blancos* (white towns) dot the mountains of the Sierra de Grazalema and the wooded hills of the area known as El Alcornocales.

On the western border of Cádiz province, between Jerez de la Frontera, Sanlúcar de Barrameda and El Puerto de Santa María, lies a grape-growing area known as the "Sherry Triangle". The ancient, labyrinthine city of Cádiz lies on a promontory to the south. To its southeast are the undeveloped beaches of the Costa de la Luz and old Moorish towns such as hilltop Vejer de la Frontera and Spain's most southerly town, Tarifa. Further east again is the dramatic punctuation mark of the Rock of Gibraltar

★ Don't Miss

1 Málaga ➤ 50

4 Ronda ➤ 53

7 Jerez de la
Frontera ➤ 56

10 Cádiz ➤ 59

13 Costa del Sol ➤ 61

At Your Leisure

2 Nerja ➤ 65

3 Antequera ➤ 65

5 Parque Natural Sierra de
Grazalema ➤ 66

6 Arcos de la
Frontera ➤ 67

8 Sanlúcar de
Barrameda ➤ 67

9 El Puerto de Santa
María ➤ 68

11 Costa de la Luz ➤ 68

12 Gibraltar ➤ 69

Mock-
Moorish at
Benalmádena
Costa's harbour
complex

Right: The
dramatic
Puente Nuevo
in Ronda

Page 45:
Pueblo blanco,
north of Ronda,
in Málaga
province

From Málaga follow dramatic mountain roads to Ronda and the "white towns", then head for the sherry capital, Jerez, and historic Cádiz, before following the coast road back to Málaga.

Málaga and Cádiz in Four Days

Day One

Morning

Visit Málaga's colour-ful morning market, the **Mercado Atarazanas** (➤ 52), then stroll through narrow streets and sunlit plazas (right) to the Moorish citadel, the **Alcazaba** (➤ 50–1). Drop into the **cathedral** (➤ 51) to see its Renaissance interior before lunchtime *tapas* in the Bar Logüeno (➤ 71) .

Afternoon

Head through wooded, rocky mountains to **Ronda** (➤ 53–5), perched to either side of its stupendous gorge (left). Enjoy Ronda in the evening when the town is much less crowded than earlier in the day and you get the best views of the rocky walls of the gorge bathed in golden sunlight. Stay overnight.

Day Two

Morning

Visit **Iglesia de Santa María Mayor** (➤ 54) with its exquisite traces of the Moorish mosque it supplanted. Go on to the clifftop **Palacio de Mondragón** for its museum (➤ 54), decorative patios and spectacular views.

Afternoon

Drive through the **Sierra de Grazalema** (➤ 66), stopping at beautiful Grazalema itself or at Zahara de la Sierra. Continue through the mountains to reach **Jerez de la Frontera** (➤ 56–8) for an overnight stay.

Day Three

Morning
Visit the **Royal Andalucian School of Equestrian Art** (left, ➤ 57), then take a tour of one of the town's sherry *bodegas* (➤ 56–7) before a late lunch at a *tapas* bar.

Afternoon
Set off south for an overnight stay in **Cádiz**. See the city's great **cathedral**, then stroll through narrow streets full of early evening shoppers to the **Museo de Cádiz** (➤ 59) for absorbing displays (right) of Phoenician and Roman history, and paintings by Spanish masters. Wander along the seafront in the glorious evening light.

Day Four

Morning
Breakfast in the colourful **Plaza de las Flores** (left, ➤ 59), then drop into the adjoining market on your way to the **Torre Tavira** (➤ 59) for great views over the city. In the late morning, take the road east along the **Costa de la Luz** (➤ 68–9). If you have time, visit the old Moorish town of **Vejer de la Frontera** (➤ 68), then continue to **Tarifa** (➤ 68) over the coastal hills of the Sierra del Cabrito with dramatic views of Gibraltar's mighty rock. Aim for a late lunch at **Estepona** (➤ 61).

Afternoon
Relax on Estepona's splendid beach before heading for **Marbella** (➤ 61) and an evening at one of the Costa del Sol's many all-in-one food and entertainment venues. Or continue to Málaga to catch the evening *paseo* along Paseo del Parque (right), followed by a *tapas* and sherry crawl.

Málaga

Málaga's bustling provincial capital is often neglected by visitors to the Costa del Sol. The city may be known as the "Capital of the Costa" but it is geographically independent of the other Costa resorts and is an exciting and rewarding experience in its own right.

Málaga is the second city of Andalucía, after Seville. It has a busy port and a thriving financial sector, which underpins the mass tourism of its coastal hinterland as well as the city's textile and food-processing industries. This commercial success is reflected in the often featureless business and residential developments that cluster round the approaches to Málaga. Yet at its heart

lie 19th-century streets and squares, crammed with bars and cafés as well as many shops and art and craft galleries. Scattered throughout are historic monuments that reflect Málaga's long history as a port and trading centre. Most impressive is the Moorish Alcazaba on the lower slopes of Monte del Faro (Lighthouse Hill), so called because Roman colonists placed a night-time beacon on its summit to guide their ships to harbour.

Above: Panoramic view of Málaga from Monte del Faro

The Sights

The **Alcazaba** is a splendid example of the fortified palaces that were the focus of most Moorish cities. Begun in the 9th century and greatly expanded in the 11th century, the palace rises above the cramped streets in a series of buildings linked by cobbled ramps and archways and with terraces where elegant cypress trees stand beside fountains and pools. Alongside the entrance gateway are the impressive remains of a

Roman theatre uncovered in the 1950s; numerous marble columns and capitals from the Roman period are embedded in the red brickwork of the palace's Moorish walls.

As you climb higher into the Alcazaba, the views become spectacular. In the upper section of the complex, within the restored rooms of the main palace, is the **Museo Provincial de Arqueología** (Archaeological Museum); it details Málaga's history as a Mediterranean port and has a splendid collection of Moorish ceramics.

The renovated 14th-century **Castillo de Gibralfaro** (Gibralfaro Castle) occupies the summit of Monte del Faro, above the Alcazaba. There are magnificent views from the ramparts, but little else, and the stiff uphill walk to reach the castle, albeit through pleasant gardens, deters many visitors.

A short distance from the Alcazaba is Málaga's **cathedral**, begun in 1528 and completed in 1783. It is known locally as La Manquita, the "one-armed old woman", because its west front has only one tower. A second tower was planned, but the money for it went to help fund the American War of Independence. The cathedral is mainly baroque on the outside, a style suitably enhanced by the dark stone of its crumbling facades. The interior has rather gloomy Gothic and Renaissance features, but the carved mahogany stalls of the Coro (choir) are exquisite.

Above right: The Alcazaba and Castillo de Gibralfaro stand high above modern Málaga

Below: The main facade of the cathedral

Soaking up the Atmosphere

Málaga is a wonderful city in which to wander. The main street, Calle Marqués de Larios, lined with smart shops and cafés, leads to lively Plaza de la Constitución at the heart of

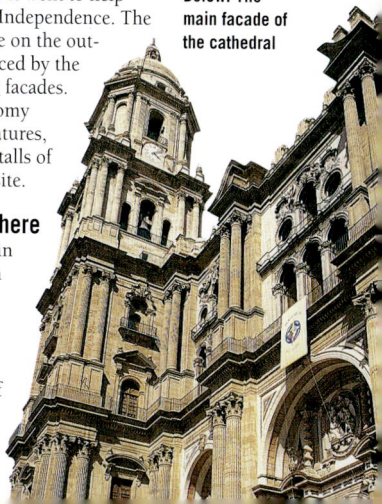

the old town. West of here, a tangle of narrow streets and squares is overlooked by tall, balconied buildings and historic churches. Between Calle Marqués de Larios and the cathedral are more alleyways – once the haunt of early 20th-century flamenco *aficionados* like the poet Federico García Lorca (► 25) – packed with tempting bars.

TAKING A BREAK

Stop for some lunchtime *tapas* at Bar Logüeno (► 71) or head for one of the city's *teterías*. These Arab-style tea houses, which serve practically every variety of tea, are becoming increasingly popular in Málaga. There are a couple on Calle San Agustín near the cathedral, but one of the best is **Tetería Barrakas** (10 Calle Horno, Málaga, tel: 952 21 47 38).

✠ 196 B1

Tourist Information
✉ Pasaje de Chinitas 4 (J de A) ☎ 952 21 34 45
✉ Municipal Office, Avenida de Cervantes 1 (OMT) ☎ 952 60 44 10

Parking
Underground car parks can be reached down ramps that lead from the Alameda Principal and the Plaza de la Marina.

Alcazaba and Museo Provincial de Arqueología
✉ Calle Alcazabilla ☎ 952 21 60 05
🕐 Wed–Mon 9.30–7 🎟 Free

Catedral
✉ Calle Molina Larios ☎ 952 21 59 17
🕐 Cathedral: Mon–Sat 9–6.45. Iglesia del Sagrario: daily 9.30–12.30 and 6–7.30
🎟 Inexpensive

Casa Natal de Picasso
✉ Plaza de la Merced 15 ☎ 952 06 02 15
🕐 Daily 11–2 (also Mon–Sat 5–8) 🎟 Free

MÁLAGA: INSIDE INFO

Top tips Join the locals at the morning market, **Mercado Atarazanas**, to the west of Calle Marqués de Larios – a cornucopia of fresh fish, meat, vegetables and fruit.
• See the **Iglesia del Sagrario** adjoining Málaga's cathedral (same ticket and times). It has a splendid Gothic portal and a beautiful altarpiece.
• Málaga's most famous son is the painter Pablo Ruiz y Picasso, whose birthplace in Plaza de la Merced is now the **Casa Natal de Picasso**, headquarters of the Picasso Foundation. Málaga has acquired more than 180 of Picasso's finest works, which will form the core of a new Museo Picasso due to open in 2003 in the Palacio de los Condes de Buenavista, Calle San Agustín (check tourist information centres for current details).
• Join the traditional evening stroll, the *paseo*, beneath the palm trees of Paseo del Parque.

Hidden gem The **Museo de Artes y Costumbres Populares**, in a restored 17th-century inn, displays traditional artefacts from the rural and seagoing life of old Málaga province (Pasillo de Santa Isabel 10, tel: 952 21 71 37, open Mon–Fri 10–1.30, 4–7, Sat 10–1.30. Closed public holidays. Admission inexpensive).

4

Ronda

Ronda is irresistible if only because of its spectacular position above the Río Guadalevín's rocky gorge, El Tajo, whose towering walls seem to be prised apart by the spectacular 18th-century Puente Nuevo. The town has been popular with tourists since the 19th century, when it became an essential destination on the itinerary of travellers from Northern Europe.

Ronda, perched on two sides of a rocky gorge, commands spectacular views of the surrounding countryside

The town can become very crowded during the middle part of the day as streams of coaches, packed with day visitors, arrive from the Costa del Sol, but by visiting the most popular sights during the early part of the morning, or in the evening, you can escape the worst of the overcrowding.

El Tajo is over 100m deep and splits the town into two parts. Where the Guadalevín enters and emerges from the depths of the gorge, the vast walls extend as escarpments to either side. Brown and white buildings cluster along the edges of the great cliffs like carved and painted extensions of the natural rock. The spectacular bridge, the **Puente Nuevo**, spans the gorge at its narrowest point and offers great views of the awesome walls, although you may have to jostle for position with crowds of camera-wielding fellow visitors. You can enjoy even better views of El Tajo and the escarpment by heading for the cliff-edge gardens of the Paseo Blas Infante, reached from Ronda's main square, Plaza de España, on the north side of the Puente Nuevo.

The Old Town

Ronda's most interesting sights lie on the south side of the gorge in the **Ciudad**, or Old Town, where you can discover mosques, churches and Renaissance palaces as you thread your way through the side streets. The focus of the Old Town is the Plaza Duquesa de Parcent, a leafy square surrounded by

handsome buildings and dominated by **Iglesia de Santa María
Mayor**. The church stands on the site of a mosque, and
Moorish features survive within the exquisite Gothic and
baroque fabric of the building. The belfry crowns a fragment of
an old minaret.

Just round the corner from the church, along Calle Manuel
Montero, is the 14th-century **Palacio de Mondragón**.
Originally a Moorish palace, it was altered after the
Reconquest, but some *mudéjar* (late Moorish) architecture
survives: there are three small patios that in their decoration
and style are superb examples of Islamic artistry. Take in the
stupendous views from the garden terraces; and as you climb
the main staircase, pause and look up at the brilliantly colourful cupola. Palacio de Mondragón doubles as the Municipal
Museum and there are imaginative displays outlining Ronda's
pre-Moorish history.

Nearby is the **Casa Juan Bosco**. The glory of this 19th-
century mansion is its ornamental garden, with mosaics,
fountains and clifftop views. In Calle Armiñán, the main street
of the Ciudad, is the **Museo del Bandolero** (Bandit Museum),
which tells the story of the 19th-century vagabonds who lived
by their wits in the surrounding mountains (▶ 10–12).

The Mercadillo

On the north side of the gorge is the **Mercadillo**, the Ronda of
smart hotels, restaurants, bars and souvenir shops. The **Plaza**

✚ 195 D2

Tourist Information
✉ Plaza de España 1 (J de A) ☎ 952 87 12 72
✉ Palacio de Mondragón, Plaza de
Mondragón, Calle Manuel Montero (OMT)
☎ 952 87 84 50

Parking
Central car park at Paseo de Blas Infante, just
off Virgen de la Paz and behind the bullring.
Multistorey car park just off Plaza de la
Merced at the west end of Virgen de la Paz.

Iglesia de Santa María Mayor
✉ Plaza Duquesa de Parcent ☎ 952 87 22
46 🕐 Daily 10–7.30 💶 Inexpensive

Left: Ronda's
18th-century
bullring, an
architectural
treasure

Below: A
dramatic view
of the Puente
Nuevo from the
lower gorge

Below right:
Palacio de
Mondragón,
noted for its
mudéjar
architecture

de Toros here is the second oldest bullring in Spain, and is where the legendary matador Pedro Romero established the rules and ornate moves of bullfighting in the mid-18th century. A museum within the handsome walls of the bullring is crammed with memorabilia of famous bullfighters and bulls and notable *aficionados*, such as American actor Orson Welles and writer Ernest Hemingway.

Opposite the bullring is the start of Ronda's main shopping street, the pedestrianised Carrera Espinel, flanked on either side by souvenir shops of varying quality, seductive delicatessens, and boutiques. Part-way up Espinel, on the left, is Plaza del Socorro with numerous restaurants, bars and cafés.

TAKING A BREAK

For a spectacular view of Ronda's dramatic gorge and the Puente Nuevo, stop for a drink or snack at **Don Miguel** (Calle Villanueva 4, tel: 952 87 10 90), a classic Spanish restaurant.

RONDA: INSIDE INFO

Top tips Stay **overnight in Ronda**. That way you can enjoy the town outside the very busy midday period.
• Stroll through the **Vista Panoramic Jardines Ciudad de Cuenca**. This cliffside terraced garden is on the north side of the gorge and can be reached from Plaza de España along Calle Nueva, turning right down Los Remedios and then right again down Calle Mina.

Hidden gems At the eastern entrance to the gorge of El Tajo are two other bridges, the medieval **Puente Viejo** and the Moorish **Puente de San Miguel**, with dramatic views along the bed of the gorge. Close to the Puente de San Miguel are the **Baños Arabes** (Arab Baths) dating from the 13th and 14th centuries (Calle San Miguel, open Wed–Sat 9.30–3.30, Tue 9.30–1.30 and 4–6. Admission free).

One to miss La Mina (The Mine), a series of 365 steps, descends from an 18th-century mansion, Casa del Rey Moro, through tunnels and caverns to the foot of the gorge. The steps are steep, poorly lit and wet in places (and should only be tackled if you're agile), and the bottom of the gorge dismal.

Palacio de Mondragón
✉ Plaza de Mondragón, Calle Manuel Montero ☎ 952 87 84 50 🕐 Mon–Fri 10–7, Sat–Sun and public holidays 10–3 💶 Inexpensive

Casa Juan Bosco
✉ Calle Tenorio 20 🕐 Daily 9–6 💶 Inexpensive

Museo del Bandolero
✉ Calle Armiñán 65 ☎ 952 87 77 85 🕐 Daily 10–6 💶 Inexpensive

Plaza de Toros and Museo Taurino
✉ Calle Virgen de la Paz ☎ 952 87 41 32 🕐 Daily 10–7 💶 Moderate

7

Jerez de la Frontera

Jerez has a touch of hauteur that befits the sherry capital of the world and a centre for stylish equestrianism and flamenco. However, it also has enough fine plazas, fashionable shops, and lively bars and restaurants to make it one of Andalucía's most enjoyable provincial towns.

A cathedral-like atmosphere pervades the city's sherry *bodegas*

The Sherry Experience

Wine production in Jerez goes back to Phoenician and Roman times, when the rich chalky soil of the surrounding area was found to be ideal for vine growing. Today, in the city's palatial sherry *bodegas*, fermented wine is transformed into sherry and fine Spanish brandy. A tour of one or other of the *bodegas* is *de rigueur* and you'll find it an enjoyable experience, even if you do feel a little like a captive as liveried guides march you through

From Xeres to Sherry

Jerez's very name reflects its most important industry. An original settlement was known to the Romans as Xeres. The Moors adapted the name to Sheriss, which, in turn, became Jerez ("de la Frontera" was added when Jerez became a border settlement of the Moorish kingdom of Granada in the late 14th century). Wine was produced in the area as early as Roman times, but it was only when the wines of the region became popular in the rest of Europe, during the 18th and 19th centuries, that the name sherry was used to describe them.

vast wine stores or decant you briskly from "road trains" at each stage of the tour. A tasting session at the end is a satisfying lesson in the differences between the types of sherry. The city's *bodegas* include such famous names as González Byass (Tío Pepe), Domecq, Harvey, Osborne, Sandeman and Williams & Humbert, but the tours of the González Byass and Domecq *bodegas* are the most lavish. Both are like self-contained villages with lush gardens, covered patios and cobbled streets. At the Williams & Humbert *bodega* you get flamenco and falconry too.

Horses and More

Jerez's association with horses dates from the 18th century, when the monks of the nearby La Cartuja

Displays at the Real Escuela Andaluza del Arte Ecuestre show equestrian skills of the highest calibre

monastery began the selective breeding of Cartujano horses, which were noted for their elegant lines and obedience. The Jerez area is still the premier horse-breeding district of Spain. At the **Real Escuela Andaluza del Arte Ecuestre** (Royal Andalucian School of Equestrian Art) you can watch the Sinfonía a Caballo displays of choreographed equestrianism that will enthral even those with little interest in horses. On days when there are no displays, you can visit the school's training area and stables.

If you have a little more time at your disposal, pay a visit to the 12th-century Moorish **Alcázar**, a walled complex of beautiful gardens that includes a restored mosque and bath house.

The acclaimed **Centro Andaluz de Flamenco**

Right: Skilled horsemen from the Real Escuela

(Andalucian Centre for Flamenco) is also worth a visit if you are interested in flamenco. The centre lies at the heart of the Barrio de Santiago, Jerez's old gypsy quarter and one of the acknowledged cradles of flamenco in its purest form. You can request showings of videos and there is an audiovisual theatre, which screens excellent films of flamenco greats such as the late Manolo Caracol (➤ 18). If you visit the barrio in the morning you may hear the evocative clatter of heels and the ripple of guitar music echoing from local flamenco schools.

For the best of modern Jerez, explore the busy streets to the west of the main street, pedestrianised Calle Larga, stopping at serene Plaza de la Asunción, known locally as Plaza San Dionisio after its handsome 15th-century church. The entire area is well supplied with excellent *tapas* bars.

Jerez's 18th-century Cathedral of San Salvador competes for attention with neighbouring sherry *bodegas*

TAKING A BREAK

At **La Maleta Bar** (27 Calle Lancería), a typical local bar but with more character than most, you can enjoy an ice-cold *fino* (sherry) accompanied by pickled mussels or a more substantial sandwich. Sit *al fresco* or in the bar – appropriately papered with sherry labels.

➕ 194 C2

Tourist Information
✉ Larga 39 (J de A)
☎ 956 33 11 50

Alcázar
✉ Alameda Vieja ☎ 956 31 97 98
🕐 Daily 10–8, May–Sep; 10–6, Oct–Apr 💶 Inexpensive

Real Escuela Andaluza del Arte Ecuestre
✉ Avenida Duque de Abrantes
☎ 956 31 80 08 (reservations)

🐎 Sinfonía a Caballo (riding displays): Thu noon, all year (also Tue noon, Mar–Oct). Training sessions and stable visits: non-show days 11–1 💶 Expensive (main show); moderate (training sessions)

Centro Andaluz de Flamenco
✉ Palacio Pemartín, Plaza de San Juan, Barrio de Santiago ☎ 956 34 92 65 🕐 Mon–Fri 9–2 (also Tue 5–7)
💶 Free

10

Cádiz

Cádiz has an intriguing air of genteel decay that seduces many visitors. The city's one-time wealth is reflected in the great cathedral and other baroque buildings and churches, but much of the pleasure of a visit comes from wandering through its narrow, cobbled streets and out to the brilliant light of seafront promenades.

Although Cádiz was an important port for Phoenicians, Romans and Visigoths, it declined under Moorish control and what you see today dates essentially from the 18th century, when the Spanish-American gold and silver trade revived the city's fortunes.

The **Museo de Cádiz** is a good place to start your exploration of the city. The museum, which is housed in a restored 18th-century mansion, is one of the best in Spain; the archaeological section includes superb Phoenician jewellery and glassware and a reconstruction of the wreck of a Roman trading vessel. The first floor contains the city's art treasures, including work by Murillo and Rubens and a series of 17th-century religious panels by Zurbarán (► 24).

The city's canyon-like streets are linked by pleasing squares such as the Plaza Topete, known also as **Plaza de las Flores**, site of a flower market and encircled by cafés and restaurants. Adjoining the plaza is Cádiz's food market. Narrow streets draw you on irresistibly, the shady labyrinth punctuated at intervals by suprises like the **Torre Tavira**, one of Cádiz's ancient watchtowers and now a maritime museum and camera obscura. The **Oratorio de San Felipe Neri** is also worth a visit. Its oval interior soars triumphantly to a sky-blue dome encircled by tiers of railed galleries that make your head spin as you look up

Above: The beautiful interior of the Oratorio de San Felipe Neri

Right: The massive cathedral dominates Cádiz's seafront promenades

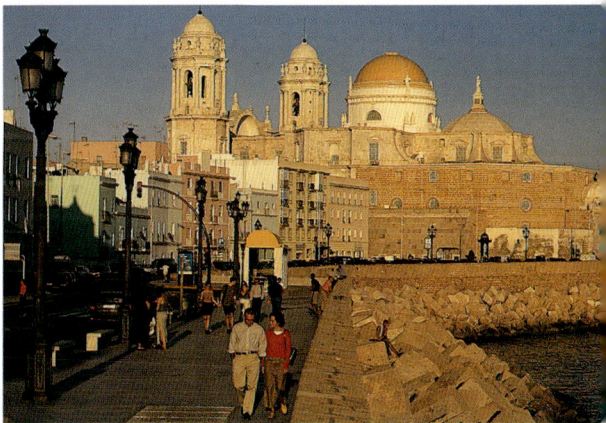

at them. Exuberant side chapels punctuate the walls and Murillo's luminous painting, *The Immaculate Conception*, graces the high altar.

The monumental **Catedral Nueva** (New Cathedral) is Spain's only completely baroque cathedral. Its main front dominates the broad **Plaza de la Catedral** and its interior is a vast arena of baroque architecture, all in plain stone and marble. The cathedral's central, so-called "gilded" dome is in fact faced with yellow tiles rather than precious metal, but the effect is still glorious, especially when you see it from the seafront promenades.

TAKING A BREAK

Stop off for a *café con leche* and a slice of *turrón de Cádiz* (wonderful home-made marzipan cake) at **Pastelería la Marina** (Plaza San Juan de Dios 3), in a bustling central square dominated by lofty palms and the city's magnificent town hall.

Sculpture at the Museo de Cádiz

✚ 194 C1

Tourist Information
✉ Avenida Ramón de Carranza s/n ☎ 956 25 86 46 ✉ Plaza San Juan de Dios (OMT) ☎ 956 24 10 01

Parking
Visitors are advised not to drive through the heart of Cádiz. There are car parks at the entrance to the old city, adjacent to the railway station and on the nearby Cuesta de las Calesas. Parking is also possible along parts of the seafront.

Museo de Cádiz
✉ Plaza de Mina 5 ☎ 956 21 22 81 🕐 Wed–Sat 9–8, Tue 2.30–8, Sun 9.30–2.30 💷 Inexpensive (free to EU passport holders)

Oratorio de San Felipe Neri
✉ Calle San José 🕐 Daily 10–1.30 💷 Inexpensive

Catedral Nueva
✉ Plaza de la Catedral 🕐 Tue–Fri 10–1 and 4.30–6.15, Sat 10–1 💷 Moderate. Free Mon–Fri 6.30–8 pm

CÁDIZ: INSIDE INFO

Top tips There is **free entry to the cathedral** Monday to Friday 6.30–8 pm. Ask for your own language edition of the leaflet describing the interior.
• Visit the **top floor of the Museo de Cádiz** where there are exhibitions of craftwork and an interesting display of antique marionettes representing the city's traditional puppet theatre.

Hidden gem The **Capilla** (chapel) in the former **Hospital de Mujeres** (Calle Hospital de Mujeres, open Mon–Fri 10–1) is a real treasure, though you may have to persevere before the porter finally relents and unlocks its door. Within its glorious baroque interior, you'll find El Greco's dramatic painting *The Ecstasy of St Francis*.

One to miss The cathedral museum (in Plaza de Fray Felíx not far from the cathedral) is included in the ticket price for the cathedral, but unless you are interested in vestments and church plate, paintings and relics, give it a miss.

🔞

Costa del Sol

The Costa del Sol is too easily dismissed as being an over-crowded, endless beach resort dominated by high-rise hotels in brutal concrete. Yet while high-density tourism dominates the Costa, individual resorts have distinctive and often endearing characters.

Above:
Estepona's
marina

Quiet streets
still exist in the
heart of
Estepona

Estepona, Marbella and Puerto Banús

The most westerly of the Costa del Sol's main resorts, **Estepona**, is in many ways the most appealing. The long seafront is entirely urban, but sensible planning has created a pleasant *cordón sanitaire* of aromatic flower beds, palm trees and shrubs between the main street, Avenida de España, and the broad promenade that runs alongside Estepona's fine beach. The old heart of the town is the Plaza de las Flores, a small jasmine-scented square that evokes 19th-century Andalucía. There are numerous bars, cafés and restaurants in the town centre, but few other diversions; Estepona's beach is the main attraction. At the west end of the resort are an old lighthouse, the fishing harbour, a yacht marina and– a few kilometres further west – Costa Natura, Spain's longest-established nudist beach.

East from Estepona the ubiquitous *urbanizaciones*, the "fill-in" residential estates of the Costa del Sol, cling to either side of the highway as far as Marbella, the next main resort. **Marbella** assiduously polishes its image as an upbeat, stylish resort. The town's generally subdued air by day is surprising, but you can expect lively nightlife, especially around the yacht harbour of Puerto Deportivo and in Plaza

Puente Ronda in the carefully manicured old town, the Casco Antiguo.

The Casco Antiguo has not been robbed entirely of its traditional character. At its heart is the Plaza de los Naranjos, created in the 14th century by demolishing the old Moorish quarter. Today it is an intimate tree-lined square with several pricey restaurants. The alleyways that radiate from the plaza are full of upmarket clothes shops and craft galleries. Just east of the square is Plaza de la Iglesia, where the handsome church of Nuestra Señora de la Encarnación rubs shoulders with part of Marbella's Moorish walls.

South of Plaza de los Naranjos the old town gives way to the busy through-road of Avenida Ramón Y Cajal, on the other side of which lies the Plaza de la Alameda with its big central fountain. From the far side of the plaza a walkway, the Avenida del Mar, descends to the seafront past a succession of eccentric Salvador Dalí sculptures. Marbella's beach offers the inevitable mix of churned-up sand and seafront *chiringuitos* (fish restaurants), souvenir shops, bars and cafés.

Keep heading west along the seafront for a few kilometres to reach the marina resort of **Puerto Banús**, with pseudo-Moorish apartment blocks, floating gin palaces, expensive shops and restaurants, and an often elusive celebrity circus.

Fuengirola and Torremolinos

About 25km east of Marbella is **Fuengirola**, perhaps the least favoured of the Costa resorts because of the high-rise hotels that crowd the seafront. This said, Fuengirola is a wholeheartedly fun resort, and you'll find a head-spinning

Right:
The chic shops are just one of Marbella's many attractions

Costa Fun Parks

There are innumerable theme parks and entertainment centres to keep youngsters happy when the beach life palls. These are the main ones.

Prado World, Estepona (tel: 952 79 11 74, open daily 10 until late, May–Oct; Sat–Sun and public holidays 11 until late, Sep–Apr). A water park and funfair on the coast between Marbella and Estepona.

Sea Life Park Submarino, Puerto Marina, Benalmádena Costa (tel: 952 44 50 00, open daily 10–6). Submarine view of Mediterranean sea life from tiny shrimps and shellfish to sharks.

Tivoli World, Arroyo de la Miel, Benalmádena Costa (tel: 952 57 70 16, open daily 6 pm– 3 am, Jun–Aug; daily 4 pm–1 am, Apr–May and Sep–Oct; Sat–Sun 1 pm–10 pm, Nov–Mar). Rides and amusements, Wild West shows and flamenco spectaculars.

Aquapark Torremolinos (tel: 952 38 88 88, open daily 10–5, May–Sep). A huge complex with lots of water slides and numerous other attractions.

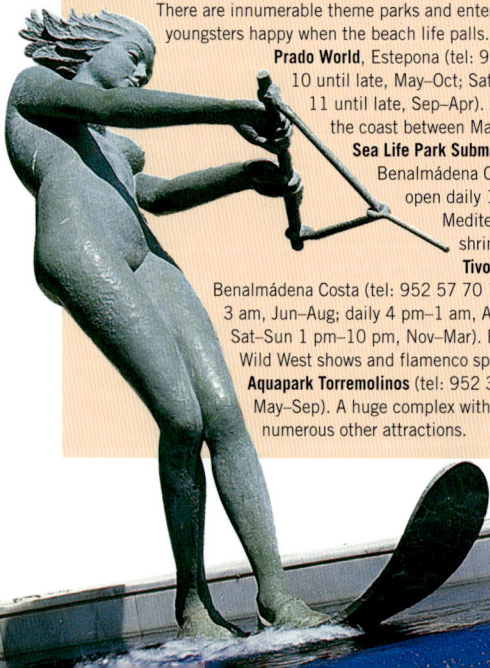

Costa Excursions

In the mountains behind the Costa del Sol are attractive hill villages. **Casares** lies in the Sierra Bermeja about 18km inland from Estepona, its whitewashed houses with orange-tiled roofs overlooked by a Moorish castle. The pretty village of **Mijas** lies 8km north of Fuengirola. Although touristy and very crowded during the day, it still retains much of its charm, especially on an evening visit. There are regular bus services to both villages from the main resorts.

Above: The beachfront at Marbella, one of the most stylish of the resorts on the Costa del Sol

sangria in the cheerful seafront bars: moderation is advised. The long, narrow beach is packed with sunbeds hired out, for a king's ransom, by adjoining bars and restaurants.

Torremolinos, probably the most visited (and developed) of the Costa resorts, is 20km northeast of Fuengirola. The place is a mass of souvenir shops, bars, cafés and restaurants, although fragments of an older Torremolinos survive. At peak season the main streets of the resort are dense with people, the beaches are carpeted with sunbeds, and the margins of the sea are mobbed. You can keep moving along the resort's delightful promenade, the Paseo Marítimo. It runs for about 5km, passing the pleasant beaches of La Carihuela and de Montemar, before reaching **Benalmádena Costa**'s kitsch Arabic harbour complex with layered terraces and whipped-cream domes. All the way along the Paseo Marítimo are tempting beachside *chiringuitos* sizzling with frying fish and glittering with cool, beaded glasses.

COSTA DEL SOL: INSIDE INFO

Top tips Torremolinos and Fuengirola are on the electric rail line to Málaga Airport and Málaga city. The train takes you right into the heart of both resorts, making car-free day visits an easy option.
● If you walk some distance to either side of the main beaches of the Costa resorts, you'll find less crowded sections of beach.

Hidden gem Marbella's **Museo del Grabado Contemporáneo** (Museum of Lithographic Art), housed in a pleasant Renaissance building, contains work by Joan Miró and Picasso as well as contemporary Spanish graphic artists. Hidden away among the exhibits is a wickedly erotic piece by Picasso, *Hombre Primitivo Celestina y Chica*.

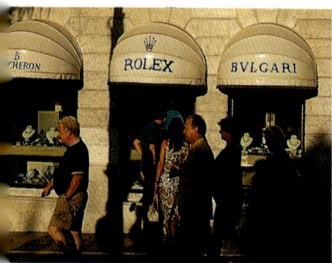

TAKING A BREAK

Splash out on a drink at the famous **Sinatra Bar** in Puerto Banús for a little celebrity spotting. This front-line bar is a traditional hang-out for the Marbella jet-set, and if you get tired of the poseurs you can admire the luxury yachts or do a little window shopping instead.

Above: Plaza de la Constitución in the centre of Fuengirola

Left: Exclusive shopping in Marbella

Estepona Tourist Information
✚ 195 E1 ✉ Avenida San Lorenzo 1 ☎ 952 80 09 13

Fuengirola Tourist Information
✚ 195 E1 ✉ Avenida Jesús Santos Rein 6 ☎ 952 46 74 57

Marbella Tourist Information
✚ 195 E1 ✉ Plaza de los Naranjos ☎ 952 82 35 50

Torremolinos Tourist Information
✚ 195 F2 ✉ Plaza Blas Infante 1 (main office) ☎ 952 37 95 12

At Your Leisure

Nerja's beaches are smaller and quieter than those on the neighbouring Costa del Sol

2 Nerja

Seaside Nerja, 56km east of Málaga, makes a refreshing change from the Costa del Sol's main resorts, although you will still share its pleasant beaches and whitewashed old quarter with crowds of other visitors. Nerja's best-known feature is the **Balcón de Europa**, a palm-fringed terrace overlooking the sea. The smallish beaches either side become crowded; the best

For Kids
- **Cuevas de Nerja** (➤ 65)
- **Parque Natural del Torcal** (➤ 66)
- **Tarifa**: dolphin/whale cruise (➤ 76)
- **Gibraltar**: cable car, Barbary apes, dolphin cruise (➤ 69 and 76)

and biggest beach is **Burriana**, reached by heading east from the Balcón along the Paseo de los Carabineros.

Three kilometres to the east of Nerja are the popular **Cuevas de Nerja**, a complex of limestone caverns. Tours are stagey affairs involving special lighting and piped music, but they provide an entertaining escape from the heat.

✚ 196 C1

Tourist Information
✉ Calle Puerta del Mar 2 (by Balcón de Europa) ☎ 952 52 15 31

Cuevas de Nerja
✚ 196 C1 ☎ 952 52 95 20 ◷ Daily 10–2 and 4–8 Jul–Aug; 10–2 and 4–6.30 Sep–Jun 🖑 Moderate

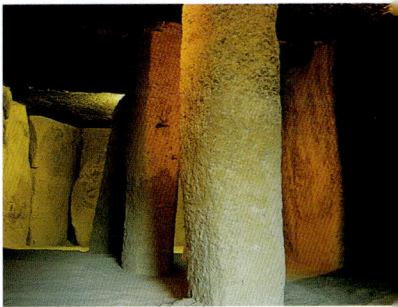

The Bronze Age Menga dolmens in Antequera

3 Antequera

Historic sights in Antequera range from prehistoric burial chambers to Moorish ruins and fine churches. Oldest of all are a remarkable group of neolithic to Bronze Age burial chambers: the **Menga** and **Viera** dolmens, off Camino del Cementerio on the northeastern outskirts. In the highest part of the town,

above central Plaza San Sebastián, stands the **Arco de Los Gigantes**, a 16th-century gateway incorporating Roman sculpture in its stonework. The dignified Renaissance facade of the **church of Santa María** dominates the adjoining plaza, and above it are the vestigial ruins of the town's Moorish **Alcazaba**, now a pine-scented, terraced garden. Just north of the Arco de Los Gigantes is the 17th-century church of **Nuestra Señora del Carmen**, its baroque altarpiece a feast of carved and painted figures.

About 14km south of Antequera is **Parque Natural del Torcal**, a natural park with a striking landscape of tall limestone pinnacles and wooded ravines. There is an easily followed waymarked walking route of 1.5km through the reserve. For longer, more rewarding walks you require an official guide, best booked in advance.

✚ 196 B2

Tourist Information

✉ Plaza de San Sebastián 7 ☎ 952 70 25 05

Menga and Viera Dolmens

✚ 196 B2 🕑 Wed–Sat 10–2 and 3–5.30, Tue 3–5.30, Sun and holidays 10–2. ✋ Free

Parque Natural del Torcal

✚ 196 A2 ☎ 952 03 13 89
🕑 Tue–Sun 10–2 and 4–6

Off the Beaten Track

If you have time to spare and crave peace, head for the Parque Natural de los Alcornocales, a region of hills and mountains clothed in cork oak forests north of Tarifa. The walking is good, and the area has some charming villages – Medina-Sidonia, Alcalá de los Gazules, Jimena de la Frontera...

5 Parque Natural Sierra de Grazalema

The Sierra de Grazalema is a range of craggy limestone peaks swathed in forests of oak and the rare Spanish fir, the pinsapo. Tortuous roads wind through the mountains and link villages such as Grazalema, Zahara de la Sierra and Benaocaz, classic examples of the *pueblos blancos*. Zahara de la Sierra (► 177), with its clifftop castle and sweeping views, is one of the most dramatic.

The village of Grazalema nestles beneath Peñon Grande, a dramatic limestone peak

The entire Sierra is a wildlife reserve, and you can sample horse riding, cycling, rock climbing, canoeing, and even paragliding, with experienced guides and instructors (► 76). There are numerous walking routes that you can tackle on your own or on a guided trip. The park information offices at El Bosque and Grazalema have route maps to the area. You need to obtain a permit from the El Bosque or Grazalema office if you wish to enter certain areas such as the Garganta Verde, a mighty river gorge near Zahara (➤ 178), and one of the main roosting sites of the magnificent griffin vulture.

✚ 195 D2

El Bosque Tourist Information
✉ Avenida de la Disputación ☎ 956 72 70 29

Grazalema Tourist Information
✉ Plaza de España ☎ 956 13 22 25

6 Arcos de la Frontera

Arcos de la Frontera tumbles downhill in a careless sprawl from the spectacular clifftop site of its old Moorish quarter. The old town's alleys surround the two main churches, San Pedro and Santa María de la Asunción. San Pedro is a quiet haven; it has some fine old paintings and, among other treasures, the atrophied body of a saint. Santa María dominates the central square, Plaza del Cabildo, and has a splendid Renaissance facade and a richly decorative interior full of pleasant gloom and Gothic extravagance. As you take in the vista across the plain from the plaza's viewpoint, look for the kestrels that drift along the cliff face. Then descend to mix with the boisterous life of the bars and restaurants of the lower town.

✚ 194 C2

Tourist Information
✉ Plaza del Cabildo ☎ 956 70 22 64

8 Sanlúcar de Barrameda

Great seafood restaurants and dry *manzanilla* wine, which has a different flavour from Jerez *fino* and is claimed to be of superior quality, are Sanlúcar de Barrameda's specialities. The town stands at the mouth of the Río Guadalquivir opposite the southern edge of the Doñana National Park (➤ 158–9), which is accessible from here by boat. The morning market in Calle Bretones, close to the main square, Plaza del Cabildo, is a colourful, raucous affair. Stroll uphill from the market for a look at Sanlúcar's town hall, located in the 19th-century Palacio de Orleáns y Bourbon, a showpiece of extravagant decoration in neo-Moorish style (open Mon–Fri 10–4). For background to the town's historic churches ask at the tourist office for their useful Spanish/English leaflet guide. For the *manzanilla* experience, visit the **Bodegas Barbadillo** in Calle Sevilla or, better still, the long-established **Bodegas La Cigarrera** in Plaza Madre de Dios near the market. In the old fishing district of Bajo de Guía, at the western end of the riverfront, you'll find numerous fish restaurants.

✚ 194 C2

Tourist Information
✉ Calle Calzada del Ejército ☎ 956 36 61 10

San Pedro church in Arcos de la Frontera stands on the site of a Moorish fortress

9 El Puerto de Santa María

The river port of El Puerto de Santa María is at the southernmost angle of the "Sherry Triangle", and has a reputation for excellent sherry and seafood. It is a useful base for exploring the region: Sanlúcar de Barrameda (► 67) is a short bus ride away, and Jerez de la Frontera (► 56–8) a mere 15 minutes by train, while Cádiz (► 59–60) is 10km across the estuary by the venerable ferry, *Motonave Adriano III*, known affectionately as *El Vapor* (The Steamer).

The finest of El Puerto's many churches is the **Iglesia Mayor Prioral** in Plaza de España, and there are several ornate 18th-century palaces

Fishing boats in Tarifa's harbour

Vejer de la Frontera is one of Andalucía's most vividly Moorish towns

scattered around the town. **Castillo de San Marcos** (Plaza de Alfonso, open Tue, Thu, Sat 10–2. Free Tue) is a 13th-century fortress built on the site of a mosque. The pedestrianised main street, Calle Luna, has a number of cheerful bars, and the waterfront area is full of life in the evenings. Sherry *bodegas* with famous names such as Osborne, Luis Caballero and Duff Gordon, are open to visitors; the tourist information centre has details of opening times.

✚ 194 C2

Tourist Information
✉ Calle Luna 22
☎ 956 54 24 13

11 Costa de la Luz (Cádiz)

Cádiz's Costa de la Luz, which means the "Coast of Light", is far less developed than the Costa del Sol. There are excellent beaches at **Los Caños de Meca** and **Zahara de los Atunes**, where broad stretches of golden sand still offer you room to breathe. This is an Atlantic coast, however, and the sea can be chillier and choppier than on the Mediterranean Costas. Inland from the coast the hilltop settlement of **Vejer de la Frontera** preserves its secretive Moorish character. The beaches at breezy **Tarifa**, the most southerly town in Spain, are a windsurfer's paradise. From Tarifa, the Rif Mountains of Morocco seem only a stone's throw away across the Strait of Gibraltar. You can take a one-day or two-day trip to Tangier from Tarifa; or try windsurfing, join a dolphin- and whale-watching cruise, or take a diving trip with experts (► 76).

✚ 194 B2

Vejer de la Frontera Tourist Information
✚ 194 C1 ✉ Marqués de Tamarón
☎ 956 45 01 91

Tarifa Tourist Information
✚ 195 D1 ✉ Paseo de la Alameda s/n
☎ 956 68 09 93

🔟 Gibraltar

A visit to Gibraltar, one of the UK's last remaining colonies, is like finding yourself in Britain at the heart of Mediterranean Spain. The vast Rock, one of the mythical Towers of Hercules, dominates the main settlement of **North Town**, whose busy, cramped Main Street is dully British in style and invariably packed with ex-pat Brits from the Costa del Sol in search of tax-free British goods. An exciting cable-car ride (Mon–Sat 9.30–6) whisks you away from the far end of Main Street to the Upper Rock, where you can visit the famous Barbary apes at the **Apes' Den**; but hang on to cameras and bags or the apes will have them. See too the vast **St Michael's Cave**, venue for occasional musicals and dance shows, and the **Upper Galleries** or "Great Siege Tunnels", a vast labyrinth excavated for military defence in the 18th century. You can explore the Upper Rock independently or settle for an all-inclusive taxi or minibus tour. Ignore touts offering trips round the Rock: the Gibraltar tourist information offices are the best sources for information about tours. Dolphin-watching trips and sightseeing cruises are also on offer.

It is inadvisable to take a car on to Gibraltar's extremely crowded streets.

✚ 195 D1

Tourist Information
✉ Duke of Kent House, Cathedral Square (main office) ☎ 350 74950

✉ The Piazza, Main Street ☎ 350 74982

✉ Customs Building, Frontier

The Rock of Gibraltar, a dramatic and contentious symbol of British presence in Spain

The Barbary Apes

Gibraltar's "apes" (right) are a breed of tailless monkey. They may have been brought over by Moorish settlers or introduced as pets by British colonists. There is a myth that Gibraltar will cease to be British if the apes ever leave the Rock. Fears of this happening during World War II prompted British officials to import more of the animals.

Where to... Stay

Prices
Expect to pay per person per night
£ up to €36   ££ €36–€96   £££ over €96

COSTA DEL SOL

Málaga
Finca La Mota ££

This delightful farmhouse-style hotel and restaurant, surrounded by olive groves, is ideal for families, with horse riding, miniature golf, children's pool, playground, and large terrace bar. The owner Majid, who runs the hotel with his English wife Sue, is from India, so the menu is appropriately spicy and varied and the restaurant gets packed out with foreign residents at weekends.

✛ 196 B1 ⊠ Alhaurín el Grande, Málaga ☎ 952 49 09 01, fax: 952 59 41 20 ⚆ Closed 1 Nov–1 Dec

Hotel Humaina ££

Away from the clamour of Málaga's coast, this is the perfect place to relax. The location is idyllic, in the centre of a natural park but just 16km from the city. Terracotta tiles, ochre walls and balconies in most rooms provide an authentic Andalucian feel. Food is prepared with organic vegetables grown in the garden.

✛ 196 B2 ⊠ Carretera del Colmenar s/n. Las Montes de Málaga ☎ 952 64 10 25, fax: 952 64 01 15

Larios £££

You get a top location in a swanky shopping street, yet from here it's just a short stroll to the cathedral and atmospheric old part of Málaga. Black-and-white tiles, soft beige furnishings and light wood make for an upbeat yet elegant look. Try for a room overlooking the attractive Plaza de la Constitución – though it can be noisy.

✛ 196 B1 ⊠ Marqués de Larios 2, Málaga ☎ 952 22 22 00, fax: 952 22 24 07, email: info@hotel_larios.com

Benalmádena
La Fonda ££

On a pretty pedestrian street in the centre of the relatively unspoilt town of Benalmádena, this hotel doubles as a cookery school – which means the added attraction of cut-price, top-quality fare. There are cool patios shaded by palms, pebbled floors and fountains, and the rooms are light and airy with terraces and views. The downstairs eating area is particularly quiet.

✛ 195 E2 ⊠ Calle Santo Domingo 7, Benalmádena ☎ 952 56 82 73, fax: 952 56 82 73

Alavera de Los Baños ££

Next to the 13th-century Baños Árabes (▶ 55), this German-run small hotel was featured as a backdrop for the film classic *Carmen*. It has super views of the Serranía de Ronda uplands and the city walls, plus facilities like a reading room, library and lounge. In the pleasant dining room, there is an emphasis on organically grown foods.

✛ 195 D2 ⊠ Hoyo de San Miguel, Ronda ☎ 95 287 91 43, email: alavera@ctv.es

Hotel Reina Victoria £££

Views from the Reina Victoria's cliff-top gardens, hanging over a 150-m precipice, are dramatic. The hotel (named after Queen Victoria by a patriot Brit) rose to fame in 1912 when Rainer Maria Rilke, the ailing German poet, came here to convalesce. His room is now a small museum. Though now slightly shabby, the rooms are well equipped and comfortable.

195 D2 Paseo Dr Fleming 25, Ronda 952 87 12 40, fax: 95 287 10 75

SIERRA DE GRAZALEMA

Molino del Santo ££

This century-old mill, on a running stream flanked by willows and olive trees, has books to borrow instead of TVs. Most rooms have fine views of the surrounding Grazalema park with a backdrop of mountains and pine trees. The hotel is popular with walkers; the British owner can give advice on local walks and will provide a packed lunch.

195 D2 Bda Estación s/n, Benaoján, Málaga 952 16 71 51, fax: 952 16 73 27, email: molino@logicontrol.es Closed 19 Nov–16 Feb

JEREZ DE LA FRONTERA

El Ancla Hotel £

El Ancla's architecture is classic Jerez, with yellow and white paintwork, wrought-iron balconies and wooden shutters. The hotel doubles as a popular local bar, which is good for atmosphere but means it can be noisy at night. Rooms are plainly furnished but comfortable, with TV and telephone. The underground car park across the street is a bonus.

194 C2 Plaza del Mamelón, Jerez de la Frontera 956 32 12 97, fax: 956 32 50 05

CÁDIZ

Hostal Bahía £

On a tree-lined pedestrian street just off the bustling Plaza de San Juan de Dios, this is a budget winner with firm beds, smart bathrooms, TV, air conditioning and small balconies in most of the rooms. The lack of a dining room is compensated by the choice and proximity of bars and restaurants, including the excellent Mesón La Nueva Marina which is right next door (➤ 73).

194 C1 Calle Plocia 5, Cádiz 956 25 90 61, fax: 956 25 42 08

Where to... Eat and Drink

Prices
Expect to pay per person for a meal, including wine and service
£ up to €12 **££** €12–€30 **£££** over €30

COSTA DEL SOL

Málaga

Restaurante Chinitas £–££

Expect traditional Andaluz décor in this century-old building with paintings of local bullfighters lining the walls. Cuisine is predictably macho, with oxtail a speciality, plus *serrano* hams and calf sirloin. Several dishes include Málaga sweet wine, including *solomillo al vino de Málaga* (fillet steak in a wine sauce). The *tapas* bar next door is equally popular, offering a good selection.

195 F2 El Moreno Monroy 4, Málaga 952 21 09 72 Daily 1–4, 7–midnight. Closed 24 and 31 Dec

Bar Logüeno £

Shoehorned into a deceptively small space, this well-loved traditional *tapas* bar is tucked down a side street near Calle Larios. The L-shaped wooden bar is crammed with a tantalising 75-plus choice of *tapas*, including many Logüeno originals, like sautéed oyster mushrooms (*setas*) with garlic, parsley and goat's cheese. There is an excellent range of Rioja wines, and the service is fast and good, despite the lack of elbow room.

195 F2 Calle Marín García s/n, Málaga No phone Mon–Sat 1–4, 7–late

Tetería Barrakas £

Tetería Barrakas is a tea shop of sorts, although the atmosphere is more souk than shopping mall, with background music a combination of New Age and ethnic. Low tables are surrounded by Oriental carpets with piles of cushions just made for lounging. Originally a 14th-century Arab bakery, this traditional *tetería* serves more than 40 types of tea, including passionfruit, hibiscus and mint, accompanied by sticky Arab sweets.

🖰 **195 F2** ✉ **Calle Horno, 10, Málaga** ☎ **952 21 47 38** ⊘ **Daily 5.30 pm– midnight**

Estepona

Restaurante El Lido £££

El Lido, 3km east of Estepona, is known for its award-winning cuisine and sumptuous elegance; try for a table overlooking the glorious gardens with ocean backdrop. The dishes are broad-spectrum Mediterranean with an emphasis on seafood and Italian specialities – like a delicious deep-sea prawn ravioli in a spicy curry sauce. There's a ten-page wine list with prices that start at an acceptable level.

🖰 **195 E1** ✉ **Las Dunas Beach Hotel and Spa, Boladilla Baja, Carretera de Cádiz, Km 163.5, Estepona** ☎ **952 79 43 45, fax: 952 79 48 25** ⊘ **Daily 12.30–3, 8–11**

Marbella

Tai Pan £££

This Marbella Chinese is certainly not an inexpensive choice, but if you like your food to taste authentic it won't disappoint. The food is perfectly spiced, and dishes include such classics as Szechuan prawns and crispy duck. The chic bamboo-and-cream furnishings are suitably "feng shui", and the view over the restaurant's gardens and beautifully lit pool is stunning. The service is, of course, exemplary.

🖰 **195 E1** ✉ **Hotel Puente Romano, Carretera de Cádiz, Km 177, Marbella** ☎ **952 77 78 93** ⊘ **Daily 8 pm–late**

Fuengirola

Moocher's Jazz Café and Restaurant ££

This has a great location, on a pedestrian street right off Fuengirola's main plaza, a pebble's throw from the beach. There's live music nightly, ranging from blues to lightweight rock, and former Londoners Andy and Yvonne are super-friendly hosts. The menu is international; particularly recommended are the giant pancakes with every imaginable filling, both savoury and sweet. There are vegetarian choices, plus a ten per cent discount before 7.30 pm.

🖰 **195 E1** ✉ **Calle de la Cruz 17, Fuengirola** ☎ **952 47 71 54** ⊘ **Daily 6 pm–1 am**

Mijas

Restaurante La Alcababa ££

You get the best views in hilltop Mijas from this glass-fronted restaurant that overlooks the coastline. You can even spy Africa on a clear day. The menu is more Spanish than most in this popular tourist town, with a fabulous *ajo blanco* (almond and garlic soup) and a good choice of salads and seafood. The prices are only slightly above average, given the smart waiter service and the superb location.

🖰 **195 E2** ✉ **Plaza de la Constitución, Mijas** ☎ **952 59 02 53** ⊘ **Tue–Sun noon–4, 7–11**

Torremolinos

La Chacha £

Wedged incongruously in between Torremolinos's fashionable boutiques, this is one of the few original seafood bars dating from the town's days as a fishing village. Make your selection from the glass display cases, perhaps mussels, giant prawns or octopus, all best washed down with ice-cold *cerveza* (beer). There's a scrubbed wooden bar with stools and the service is friendly and swift.

🖰 **195 F2** ✉ **Palma de Mallorca 3, Torremolinos** ☎ **No phone** ⊘ **Daily 11.30–3, 8–11.30**

RONDA

El Navasillo £-££

This unassuming-looking, long whitewashed building with a columned front terrace is 11km outside Ronda. Inside, *jamónes serranos* hang over the long wooden bar gently curing in cigarette smoke, while the dining room looks over craggy mountainous country. The food is unadventurous but good with an emphasis on fresh game and barbecued meat.

➕ **195 D2** ☒ **Carretera Ronda San Pedro, Km 11, Ronda** ☎ **952 11 42 35** ⏰ **Daily 7 am–midnight**

THE SHERRY TRIANGLE

Las Bóvedas Restaurant ££-£££

This is a fabulous restaurant in a gracious baroque building, now a hotel, on a narrow cobbled back street in El Puerto de Santa María. Formerly a monastery, Las Bóvedas was once the laundry room for the nuns, although it's hard to believe

that such mundane pursuits took place beneath the fine vaulted ceiling. Chef Joaquín Ramírez has won several awards for his innovative cuisine, which includes an excellent variety of seafood dishes.

➕ **194 C2** ☒ **Hotel Monasterio San Miguel, Calle Larga 27, El Puerto de Santa María, Cádiz** ☎ **956 54 04 40** ⏰ **Daily 9 pm–late**

El Convento ££

The restaurant is in the same ownership as the exquisite small hotel of the same name on Arcos de la Frontera's Calle Maldonado. The dining room, in the glorious colonnaded patio of a 16th-century palace, is appropriately spacious and decorated with palms, sculptures and paintings. The food is some of the best in the province, with many familiar Spanish dishes given an original twist.

➕ **194 C2** ☒ **Calle Marqués de Torresto 7, Arcos de la Frontera** ☎ **956 70 32 22** ⏰ **Daily 1–4, 7–10. Closed 24 and 31 Dec**

El Mirador de las Almenas £-££

The décor here, one of several attractive restaurants on this small cobbled side street in the older part of Jerez, is typical Andalucían, with gaily painted chairs, pots of geraniums and a flamenco music background. The waiters are charming and the menu more varied than most, with filled baked potatoes a welcome change from chips. This is a particularly good warm-weather choice as the terrace seating is shady and quiet yet with plenty of ¡Olé! atmosphere.

➕ **194 C2** ☒ **Calle Pescadería Vieja, Jerez de la Frontera** ☎ **No phone** ⏰ **Daily noon–4.30, 7.30–late**

CÁDIZ

El Faro ££-£££

El Faro, in the city's shabby, onetime fishermen's quarter, is deservedly famous. You can opt for seafood *tapas* at the bar or really splash out in the restaurant on innovative dishes like Parmesan

grilled peppers stuffed with crabmeat, or the relatively pricey *menú del día*. The décor is understated Andalucían with ceramic wall tiles, marble and mahogany bar, and lots of photos of Cádiz past and present.

➕ **194 C1** ☒ **Calle San Félix, Cádiz** ☎ **956 21 10 68** ⏰ **Daily 1–4, 8.30–11.30. Closed 24 Dec**

Mesón La Nueva Marina £-££

Jamón serrano hams jostle for space with strings of garlic, dried peppers and black-and-white photos of the port in this welcoming restaurant and *tapas* bar. *Manzanilla* from nearby Sanlúcar is available on tap and the small adjoining restaurant gets packed at weekends. The menu is varied, in particular the 24-plus choice of starters which can be doubled up for a main course, and includes some mouth-watering specialities like *cazón en adobo* (marinated deep-fried white fish).

➕ **194 C1** ☒ **Calle Plocia 2, Cádiz** ☎ **956 28 93 81** ⏰ **Daily 1–4, 8–late. Closed 24, 25, 31 Dec, 1 Jan**

Where to... Shop

MÁLAGA

Málaga's Calle Marqués de Larios is the heart of the city's fashion shopping. Try the branch of the smart Spanish fashion chain **Mango** (Larios 1, tel: 952 22 31 02), and **Boutique Azulay** (Larios 10, tel: 952 21 75 39) for ultra-chic clothes, and **Agatha Paris** (Larios 5, tel: 952 60 36 27) for smart jewellery too.

West of Marqués de Larios is a more traditional shopping area in the streets around Plaza Flores, Plaza de Félix Sáenz and Calle Puerta del Mar and Calle Nueva. Here you'll find shops of all kinds. Don't miss **La Mallorquina** (Plaza de Félix Sáenz), a delicatessen with a terrific selection of cured meats and other delicacies. Diagonally opposite is **La Mallorquina Regalos** run by the same company, a *licorería* (liquor shop) with a superb selection of drink including some of Málaga's distinctive sweet wines.

Málaga's branch of the department store chain of **El Corte Inglés** is at Avenida de Andalucía 4–6 and is enormous. It carries a big range of foreign-language newspapers and is a good source of maps and books.

RONDA AND SIERRA DE GRAZALEMA

Ronda (▶ 53–5) has many – sometimes tacky – souvenir shops, a good number in the town's main shopping street, Carrera Espinal. Scattered among them, however, are some excellent shops selling *productos artesanos*, local produce of all kinds. Look for **Márquez** (Espinel 13, tel: 952 87 29 86) for everything from cured meats to wine, herbs and honey. For more upmarket craftwork and souvenirs you'll find a sprinkling of outlets in Ronda's old town, although prices can be high.

In the mountains of the Sierra de Grazalema (▶ 66–7), **Artesanía Grazalema** in Grazalema's tourist office (Plaza de España, tel: 956 13 22 25) has a range of local clothing, carpets, pottery, and produce that includes cheeses, honey, and pears in wine. Another pleasant place to browse in Grazalema is **La Jara Cerámica Artesanal** (Calle Agua 19, tel: 956 13 20 75) for quality craftwork and gifts. On the Grazalema to Zahara de la Sierra road, stop off at **El Vínculo Molino de Aceite Alojamiento Rural** (tel: 956 12 30 02) for a chance to buy some very fine olive oil, wine and cheeses (▶ 178).

THE SHERRY TRIANGLE

Pedestrianised Calle Larga and its surrounding streets are where you'll find the best shopping in **Jerez de la Frontera** (▶ 56–8), with shops selling fashion, crafts, ceramics, leatherware and jewellery. If it's sherry you want, you'll find that, although every *bodega* sells its own product exclusively, **La Casa del Jerez** (The Sherry Shop, Divina Pastora 1, tel: 956 33 51 84) stocks all brands and you can sample happily. It is opposite the **Royal Andalucían School of Equestrian Art** (▶ 57), where there is a souvenir shop for all things equestrian. For flamenco clothes, tapes, videos and accessories visit **Calle del Flamenco** (Calle Francos 49, tel: 956 34 01 39) at the heart of the Barrio de Santiago (▶ 58).

The *manzanilla* and sherry *bodegas* in **El Puerto de Santa María** (▶ 68) and **Sanlúcar de Barrameda** (▶ 67) all sell their own products. For the area's food specialities, don't miss Sanlúcar's busy morning **market** off Plaza de San Roque, or the **fresh shellfish shop** attached to the Romerijo fish restaurants in Ribera del Marisco, in El Puerto de Santa María.

Where to...
Be Entertained

Andalucía's most visited provinces offer a huge variety of entertainment, from the club scene on the Costa del Sol and in the larger cities, to the more traditional cultural pursuits of flamenco, bullfighting and fiesta. The energetic can enjoy water sports in the coastal resorts and dry-land adventure in the mountainous interior.

The *Guía Marbella – Día y Noche*, a Spanish/English listings guide, and the weekly *Sur* newspaper, which has a useful entertainment section, are available from tourist offices. Another free publication, with entertainment listings and a golf page, is *The Entertainer*.

NIGHTLIFE

The club scene in Malaga province is at its most intense on the **Costa del Sol**.

In Puerto Banús, the waterfront **Sinatra Bar** (Muelle Ribera 2, tel: 952 81 09 50) is a top spot for stars and celebrity wannabees.

In neighbouring Marbella the hottest scene is in the seafront area of Puerto Deportivo with its massed discos and bars. Fuengirola is a relentless nightlife zone, with scores of clubs; for total clubbers there's **Ministry** (Paseo Marítimo, tel: mobile tel: 600 02 48 23, open Wed–Sat) – foam-engulfed midnight-to-dawn dancing. Benalmádena Costa's big **Kiu Club** (Plaza Solymar, tel: 952 44 05 18) and the **Palladium** (Avenida Palma

CÁDIZ AND BEYOND

Cádiz has a superb morning **market**, located just next to Plaza de las Flores with its colourful flower stalls. The pedestrianised Calle Francisco, Calle Rosario and Calle Ancha, together with their linking streets, form Cádiz's main shopping district, where there is a good mix of shops.

Further along the coast to the east, **Gibraltar** (▶ 69) is famous for its VAT-free shopping, and the town's Main Street is packed with shops of every kind. Prices are cheaper than in Britain and northern Europe, but you won't necessarily find that special Andalucían gift or memento.

COSTA DEL SOL

All the main resorts confront you with ranks of souvenir outlets: you take your pick of everything from jewellery to leather accessories, but with little variation in quality or

prices. For big fashion names, such as Versace, Armani, Donna Karan, Gucci, go for the smart main shopping drag **Ramón y Cajal** and **Casco Antiguo** (Old Town) in Marbella (▶ 61–2), or the waterfront **Muelle Ribera** in nearby **Puerto Banús** (▶ 62). **El Corte Inglés** department store chain has a branch on the outskirts of Puerto Banús at Carretera N340, Km 174.

Markets in this prosperous area are always worth browsing through. There are often good antiques and objets d'art lurking among the pottery, clothing and kitsch buys in **Puerto Banús's Saturday morning market** at Centro Plaza in the Nueva Andalucía district, near the bullring, or – biggest and best of all – **Fuengirola's Tuesday morning market** on Avenida Jesús Santos Rein, which deals in everything from fruit and vegetables to local crafts. For Spanish food and wine, try the big **BRC Hypermarket** in Benalmádena at Avenida Salvador Vicente 2.

de Mallorca, tel: 952 38 42 89) in Torremolinos are also popular.

Visit Marbella's **Casino Marbella** (Bajos del Hotel, Plaza de Andalucía, tel: 952 81 40 00) for a stab at blackjack, roulette, poker, and slot machines in plenty. Alternatively, try your luck at **Casino Torrequebrada and Fortuna Night Club** (N340, Km 220, tel: 952 44 60 00). Passports need to be shown at reception for both casinos.

Málaga's nightlife is concentrated on the area to the northeast of the cathedral around Plaza de Uncibay and the nearby streets of Granada and Beatas. In **Jerez de la Frontera**, you'll find discos and music bars in Calle Divina Pastora and around. In **Cádiz** city, head for the streets round Plaza de España.

FLAMENCO

In Málaga there are regular flamenco shows at the **Teatro Miguel de Cervantes** (Calle Ramos Marín, tel: 952 22 41 00). In Ronda there is

flamenco at **Casa Santa Pola** (Calle Santo Domingo 3, tel: 952 87 92 08, Fri and Sat evenings). Jerez de la Frontera has a strong flamenco tradition (➤ 16–18) and there are worthwhile flamenco shows at **El Laga** (Plaza del Mercado, tel: 956 33 83 34). In Cádiz try **La Cava** (Calle Antonio López, tel: 956 21 18 66) to experience flamenco in relaxed surroundings.

THEATRE

Theatre lovers will find excellent programmes of music, drama and dance at Málaga's **Teatro Miguel de Cervantes** (Calle Ramos Marín, tel: 952 22 41 00) and at Cádiz's **Gran Teatro Falla** (Plaza de Falla, tel: 956 22 08 28). Ask at tourist offices for current programmes.

BULLFIGHTING

All the main resorts have bullrings where *novilladas*, fights with young bulls and novice bullfighters, are

staged, usually on Sunday evenings. These are advertised, and hotels often have details. The bigger rings at Málaga, Ronda and Jerez stage major fights; booking for these is advised.

GOLF

Most golf courses are on the Costa del Sol. Many require a handicap certificate and forward booking is heavy. **Estepona Golf**, Estepona (Apartado 532, tel: 952 11 30 81), and **Golf Torrequebrada**, Benalmádena Costa (Carretera de Cádiz, N340, tel: 952 44 27 42) are moderately priced

HORSE RIDING

You can ride in the hills around Ronda with **Picador La Granja** (Camino de los Molinos, Ronda, tel: 952 87 59 56), or explore the Sierra de Grazalema with **Al-hazan** (Carretera CA-5311, Km 3, tel: 956 23 42 35).

OUTDOOR ACTION

For hang-gliding and paragliding try **Club Escuela de Parapente Abdalajís** (Valle de Abdalajís, tel: 952 48 91 80). In the spectacular Sierra de Grazalema, **Horizon** (Calle Agua 5, tel: 956 13 23 63) in Grazalema (➤ 66) offers caving, rock climbing, mountain biking, paragliding and trekking.

WATER SPORTS

For scuba diving, contact the **Club Nautico Diving Centre** (Puerta Marina, Benalmádena, tel: 952 56 07 69) or **Centro Buceo Tarifa** (Calle Alcalde Juan Núñez 10, Tarifa, tel: 956 68 16 48). For windsurfing try **Club Mistral** (Hotel Hurricane, Carretera Cádiz–Málaga, tel: 956 68 49 19) near Tarifa. You can also arrange dolphin-watching trips through **Dolphin Safari** (Marina Bay Complex, Gibraltar, tel: 956 77 19 14), or **Whale Watch** (Paseo de la Alameda, Tarifa, tel: 956 68 47 76).

Granada and Almería

Getting Your Bearings 78–79
In Four Days 80–81
Don't Miss 82–98
At Your Leisure 99–103
Where to... 104–108

Getting Your Bearings

Andalucía's eastern provinces of Granada and Almería contain spectacular and diverse landscapes. In Granada, the mighty mountains of the Sierra Nevada range contrast with deeply wooded river valleys, while in Almería you'll find strange desert hills and arid coastal plains that seem more suited to North Africa than to Europe.

Such diversity extends to the towns and cities of the region. Granada city's main treasure is the Alhambra Palace, one of the world's great buildings and the most hauntingly beautiful symbol of Moorish Andalucía, but it also has a medieval quarter, the Albaicín, that seems more like a Moorish village in the heart of the Andalucian hills than a city enclave.

Granada has neither the exuberant sunny nature of Seville nor the easygoing atmosphere of Málaga and Cádiz, a character due in part to the city's Christian conquerors, who extinguished Moorish influence here more thoroughly than anywhere else in Andalucía. Their successors imposed a more austere Northern European style upon Granada's buildings and streets and on the habits of its citizens. It is a style reflected today in the city's generally sober approach to life.

Southeast of Granada, the rugged slopes of the Sierra Nevada soar to the highest peaks in Spain, and then descend in great waves to the foothills of the beautiful Alpujarras, where you can sample superb regional food and wine.

In inland Almería province, parched desert buttes and gulches – Hollywood stand-ins for the Wild West – lie seared by the wind, while the arid, treeless

Moreda

N323

Sierra Harana

N432

A92

Guadix **9**

Parque Nat
de la Sie
de E

A92N

1 Granada

A92

Parque Natural
Sierra Nevada

S i e r r a   N e v a d a

Capileira

Trevélez

Yegen

Sie

Lanjarón

Orgiva

N323

2
Las
Alpujarras

El

Motril

N340

Adra

Left: Terraced hillsides in the Alpujarras

Previous page: Patio de los Leones (Hall of the Lions), in the Alhambra, Granada

★ **Don't Miss**
1 Granada ➤ 82
2 Las Alpujarras ➤ 92
3 Almería ➤ 96

At Your Leisure
4 Cabo de Gata ➤ 99
5 Níjar ➤ 100
6 Mojácar ➤ 100
7 Sorbas ➤ 101
8 Mini Hollywood ➤ 102
9 Guadix ➤ 102

coast offers strange lunar landscapes. The capital, Almería city, once surpassed Granada as a Moorish stronghold, and its formidable hilltop fortress, the Alcazaba, is a dramatic reminder of medieval al-Andalus in its heyday.

The narrow Cuesta de Gomérez provides a steep approach to the Alhambra palace in Granada

0 | 50 km
0 | 30 miles

Huércal Overa
Serón
Sierra de los Filabres
Baza
Gérgal
A92
Sorbas 7
Mini Hollywood 8 Tabernas
Sierra de Alhamilla
Níjar 5
Gador
3 Almería
Parque Natural de Cabo de Gata-Níjar
4 Cabo de Gata
Mojácar 6
Carboneras

Views of the Alhambra from the Mirador de San Nicolás

Enjoy the splendours of Granada city before heading south into the timeless wooded hills of the Alpujarras. For dramatic contrast, explore Almería city, its scorched desert hinterland, and its coast, Spain's sunniest.

Granada and Almería in Four Days

Day One

Morning

Breakfast in one of the cafés in Granada's bustling **Plaza Nueva**, then take the Alhambrabus (➤ 91) from the stop on the south side of the square to the **Alhambra** entrance. After exploring the complex (right, ➤ 83–6), treat yourself to lunch in the Parador de San Francisco, the plush hotel at the Alhambra's very heart.

Afternoon

Linger in the gardens of the **Generalife** (left, ➤ 86), then walk back down to Plaza Nueva through the cool woods of the Bosques y Paseos. Go through the Gate of the Pomegranates and continue down Cuesta de Gomerez, where you'll find plenty of marquetry and souvenir shops.

Day Two

Morning

Stroll through the old Moorish quarter of the **Albaicín** (right) in the fresh morning light (➤ 87). Stop for coffee in **Plaza San Miguel el Bajo** (➤ 87). Back in central Granada visit the **Capilla Real** (➤ 88–9) and the adjoining **cathedral** (➤ 88–9).

Afternoon

Drive south from the city along the Motril road, the N323, and turn off along the A348 to Lanjarón. Continue to Órgiva, then follow the winding mountain road into **Las Alpujarras** (➤ 92–5), the foothills of the Sierra Nevada. Stay overnight in any one of the three lovely villages clinging to the sides of the **Poqueira Gorge** – Pampaneira, Bubión or Capileira (➤ 92–4).

Day Three

Morning

Make an early start and set off east along the high road of the Alpujarras to **Trevélez** (right, ➤ 94–5), famous for its *jamón serrano* (cured ham). Enjoy a slice or two for lunch at one of the cafés in the village.

Afternoon

Continue east, past a string of typical Alpujarran villages – Juviles, Bérchules, Yegen…Continue to **Almería** city (➤ 96–8) and an overnight stay. Go on an evening *tapas* tour, starting in the Puerta de Purchena area (➤ 98).

Day Four

Morning

Visit Almería's Moorish fortress, the **Alcazaba**, before the sun gets too hot, then stroll back through tranquil **Plaza Vieja** (➤ 98) and enjoy an early lunch at Bar Bahía de la Palma in Calle Mariana just north of the plaza.

Afternoon

Take the Granada road north, calling in at **Mini Hollywood** (➤ 102) if you have the time; or continue to **Guadix** (➤ 102–3) and visit its cave district and intriguing museum before heading back to Granada.

Granada

Granada's hilltop Alhambra Palace is the greatest relic of Islamic Spain. As one of the most seductive monuments in the world, the Alhambra is a hard act to follow, but this compelling city has much else of beauty and interest, including the Albaicín (the old Moorish quarter), the Capilla Real (Royal Chapel) and cathedral, and some outstanding churches and museums. Beyond the modern city's traffic-bound main thoroughfares lies a leisurely world of colourful plazas and pedestrianised streets with their relaxed café life and mix of fashionable shops, galleries and markets.

Granada was the last stronghold of the Moors in Andalucía. It was ruled from Córdoba, and then from Seville, before emerging in the 1230s as the capital of the kingdom of the gifted Nasrid dynasty founded by Muhammad ibn Yusuf ibn Nasr. In 1246, the Nasrids became vassals of the Christian kingdom of Castile, an arrangement that helped to ensure the survival of Granada as a Moorish kingdom until the late 15th century. A succession of Nasrid sultans did much over 200 years to create the Alhambra's most beautiful buildings and their exquisitely decorated chambers, scented patios and lush gardens. In 1492, the Christian rulers Fernando and Isabel (➤ 23), driven by their desire to return all of Spain to the Catholic fold, "conquered" Granada and evicted Abur Abd Allah, known to the Spanish as Boabdil, the last Nasrid sultan. The Catholic monarchs preserved much of the Alhambra's Islamic beauty, however, and they left the Moorish Albaicín intact. Today the Alhambra stands triumphantly above its densely wooded lower slopes against the stunning backdrop of the often snow-capped Sierra Nevada.

Tourist Information

➕ 200 C2 ✉ Corral del Carbón s/n (J de A) ☎ 958 22 59 90
➕ 200 C1 ✉ Turismo Municipal, Plaza Mariana Pineda 10 (OMT)
☎ 958 22 66 88

Parking

There are underground car parks in La Caleta at the western end of Avenida de la Constitución near the railway station and in Calle San Agustín, just north of the cathedral and off Gran Vía de Colón; also one near the central post office in Puerta Real at the junction of Calle Reyes Católicos and Acero del Darro. There are car parks adjacent to the Alhambra ticket office.

The Alhambra

The Alhambra's hilltop complex is the essential and irresistible starting point of a visit to Granada. Within its large area are four main groups of buildings and gardens: the Alcazaba, the original fortress; the Palacio Nazaríes, which served as the sultans' administrative, judicial and diplomatic headquarters as well as their private home; the Palacio de Carlos V, an early 16th-century addition; and the Generalife, the sultans' summer palace and gardens, where they could escape from the pressures of court life.

The Generalife is immediately to the right of the main entrance to the Alhambra, while the Alcazaba and the Palacio Nazaríes lie close to each other at the far western end of the site. Given the Alhambra's size and complexity, one of the best ways of organising a visit is to head straight for the most westerly section of the site and begin by visiting the Alcazaba. From there you can work your way back via the Palacio Nazaríes and the Palacio de Carlos V to finish at the Generalife, a relaxing finale amid flowers and cooling fountains.

The Alcazaba

The Alcazaba today is essentially the shell of the 13th-century Moorish fortress, but its mighty walls and towers survive. The great tower at the western end is the **Torre de la Vela**, the Alhambra's belfry, from whose airy summit there are magnificent views over Granada, the Albaicín and the surrounding countryside known as the Vega. The poet García Lorca, a native of Granada, imagined the misty Vega as a bay of the sea, and once teased a friend by asking him if he had not seen boats bobbing below the Alhambra's towers.

On the southern edge of the Alcazaba are the lush, aromatic garden terraces of the **Jardín de los Ardaves**, with the green woods of elms and cypresses on the Alhambra hill sweeping away below, and the great massif of the Sierra Nevada rising in the distance.

The distant peaks of the Sierra Nevada provide a magnificent backdrop to the Alhambra

The northern arcade of the Patio de los Arrayanes (Patio of the Myrtles)

Palacio Nazaríes

The Palacio Nazaries, a decorative treasurehouse of Islamic craftsmanship in brick, wood and stucco, is the crowning glory of the Alhambra. The entire complex reflects the subtle use of space, light and cool water that was the great gift of Islamic arts and crafts. You enter through a modest doorway and first come to the **Mexuar** (Audience Hall), the public rooms of the Islamic palaces, where superb tiling and stucco work are a foretaste of what is to come.

Beyond the Mexuar lies the **Serallo**, a complex of chambers that opens off the **Patio de los Arrayanes** (Patio of the Myrtles), a rectangular courtyard with a central pool, gently splashing fountains and a border of myrtle hedges. The patio's northern arcade leads to the **Sala de la Barca** (Hall of the Boat), named for its boat-shaped ceiling, and the magnificent **Salón del Trono**, or Salón de los Embajadores (Throne Room or Hall of the Ambassadors), where the sultan received emissaries. The tiled and stuccoed walls soar to a ceiling dome that is a dazzling masterpiece of carved woodwork depicting the star-speckled heavens.

The next section of the palace was built as an inner sanctum for the sultans, and is where the rooms of the harem were located. The focus is the **Patio de los Leones** (Hall of the Lions), enclosed by pillared arcades of marble columns and with a fountain at its centre surrounded by 12 stone lions. On the southern side of the patio is the beautiful **Sala de los Abencerrajes**, a small room which contains some of the complex's most breathtaking craftsmanship. The ravishing dome, composed of a mass of tiny stalactites like star-bursts, and the 16-sided ceiling frieze are reflected in a fountain on the floor beneath it. The dark stains in the fountain bowl are said to represent the blood from the severed heads of 16 slaughtered princes of the Abencerraj family (after whom the room is named), whose chief had coveted Sultan Abu al-Hassan's favourite concubine, Zoraya. Rust is probably the more likely source of the stains, but black deeds and acts of cruelty certainly did take place amid these exquisite surroundings.

Near Ruin

From its early days, the Alhambra was plundered of its valuables. Vandalism took many forms. Nineteenth-century collectors from Northern Europe often came armed with small hammers with which they surreptitiously removed parts of the exquisite stucco work. In the 1820s, the American writer Washington Irving set up home in the abandoned Palacio Nazaríes, where he wrote the romantic *Tales of the Alhambra*, a book that triggered huge interest in the Alhambra and prompted the Spanish authorities to protect and restore the site.

The exquisite Sala de las Dos Hermanas

At the far end of the Patio de los Leones is a long narrow room, the **Sala de los Reyes** (Hall of the Kings), where recessed chambers retain paintings on their leather-covered ceilings. These are believed to depict tales of chivalry and are possibly the work of later Christian artists. The hall was used for summer entertainment, and the recesses may have served the same purpose as boxes at the theatre.

Opposite the Sala de los Abencerrajes is the **Sala de las Dos Hermanas** (Hall of the Two Sisters), named for two large slabs of marble in the chamber floor. The stuccowork on the room's roof is dazzling, like an explosion of shattered crystals. Beyond lies the romantic **Sala de los Ajimeces** (Hall of the Arched Windows), the private quarters of the sultan's favourite, where a gazebo overlooks a lush patio below.

Palacio de Carlos V

From the Sala de los Ajimeces a series of rooms and passageways leads into terraced gardens interspersed with patios and Moorish towers. You leave the gardens alongside the Renaissance **Palacio de Carlos V**, a grandiose intrusion on the Moorish complex by the Spanish monarch, who ripped out part of the Palacio Nazaríes to accommodate it. This is a building that would stand as a splendid structure in any other context. The core of the palace

is a vast circular courtyard, open to the sky. It was used at one time as a bullring. The surrounding rooms contain the **Museo Hispano-Musulmán** with outstanding artefacts from the Islamic era, finest of which is the great Jarrón de las Gacelas (Gazelle Vase), elegantly decorated in enamel. The building's upper floors house the **Museo de Bellas Artes** (► 91).

The cool green gardens of the Generalife are a real delight

The Generalife

On the Cerro del Sol (Hill of the Sun), at the eastern end of the Alhambra complex, is the luxurious Generalife, a world of cool fountains and pools, of garden patios and flower-filled terraces. This was the extravagant pleasure palace of the Nasrids, where banquets and theatrical performances were staged. Today you can wander through the **Patio de los Cipreses,** a walled garden containing a cypress tree that is hundreds of years old, and dip your hands in the **Camino de las Cascades**, a stone stairway where water pours down the channelled balustrades.

🔢 201 E2 ✉ Alhambra Hill ☎ 958 22 09 12; fax: 958 21 05 84 🕐 Daily 8.30–8, Mar–Oct (also floodlit visits Tue–Sat 10–11.30 pm); 8.30–6, Nov–Feb (also floodlit visits Fri–Sat 8–9.30 pm). Closed Dec 25 and Jan 1

🍴 Restaurants (£££); drinks and snack kiosks (£–££) 🚌 Alhambrabus (► 91). Every ten minutes from Plaza Isabel la Católica and Plaza Nueva 💰 Expensive (senior citizens moderate; disabled and under-8s free)

Entry to the Alhambra

Entry to the Alhambra is limited to 7,700 visitors daily. A main ticket to the entire complex is stamped with a half-hour time slot for entrance to the Palacio Nazaríes and you must enter within that half-hour. You can remain inside for as long as you like. Tickets can be purchased at the Alhambra Entrance Pavilion, but expect long queues. If you purchase a ticket at the Entrance Pavilion late in the day, all the Palacio Nazaríes time slots may be taken up. You are strongly advised to pre-book your visit. This can be done directly through the Spanish bank, the Banco Bilbao Vizcaya (BBV) at any of its 2,829 branches throughout Spain or at its offices in Paris, London, Milan and New York. Tickets can be reserved up to a maximum of one year ahead by phoning from within Spain (tel: 902 22 44 60) or from abroad (tel: 003 413 745 420). Payment is by Visa or MasterCard only. In Granada you can purchase a ticket from the BBV branch in Plaza Isabel la Católica, although advance purchase is again advised. For updated information, check the excellent official Website www.alhambra-patronato.es.

The Albaicín

Granada's old Moorish quarter, the Albaicín, stands on the slopes of Sacromonte hill and faces the lofty Alhambra across the valley of the Río Darro. Its roughly cobbled streets and alleyways wriggle to and fro, punctuated by tall palm trees, between whitewashed walls splashed with bougainvillaea and geraniums. Scattered throughout are leafy plazas buzzing with local life. At sudden junctions you catch glimpses of the Alhambra painted against the backdrop of the Sierra Nevada and at popular viewpoints, such as the Mirador de San Nicolás (► 172), you can experience a glorious view of the floodlit palace at dusk.

The southern edge of the Albaicín is flanked by the Carrera del Darro, the narrow street that leads alongside the Río Darro, its line of buildings pierced at intervals by the steep and narrow alleyways that lead upwards into the heart of the Albaicín. In the Carrera del Darro, you'll find the 11th-century **Baños Árabes** (Arab Baths). You enter through a minuscule patio garden, an enchanting prelude to the brick-vaulted chambers of the baths themselves, with their starred and octagonal skylights. Nearby is Granada's excellent **Museo Arqueológico** (Archaeological Museum), with a fine collection of prehistoric, Phoenician, Roman, Visigothic and Moorish exhibits, housed in a Renaissance palace, the Casa de Castril. Its arcaded patio balcony has a view of the Alhambra above.

Other highlights of the Albaicín include **Plaza Larga**, where everyday life is focused on surrounding shops and bars, and **Plaza San Miguel el Bajo**, to the west of the Mirador de San Nicolás; here amid whispering plane trees you can linger over drinks and *tapas* at the popular

Bar Lara or Bar El Yunque. Nearby is another fine viewpoint, the **Mirador de Cruz de Quirós**. The eastern heights of Sacromonte hill contain the caves where a vibrant gypsy community once lived. Now the former dwellings only house a few establishments offering expensive flamenco shows.

The Albaicín can be explored by a planned itinerary (► 170–2) or by wandering at random. Heading downhill will usually lead you back to central Granada. Don't wander in this area at night, and watch for bag snatchers during the day.

Away from the clamour of the crowds – the Calderería Nueva in the Albaicín

---

Baños Árabes
✚ 201 D3
✉ Carrera del Darro 31
☎ 958 22 23 39
🕐 Tue–Sat 10–2
🚌 Alhambrabus (► 91)
🎫 Free

Museo Arqueológico
✚ 201 D3
✉ Carrera del Darro 41
☎ 958 22 56 40
🕐 Wed–Sat 9–8, Sun 9–3, Tue 3–8
🚌 Alhambrabus (► 91)
🎫 Inexpensive (free to EU passport holders)

Capilla Real and Catedral

In the centre of modern Granada, just off the busy main Gran Vía de Colón, you'll find two important post-Moorish buildings, the catedral (cathedral) and adjoining Capilla Real (Royal Chapel).

The **Capilla Real** is an impressive Gothic building that, in many ways, steals the thunder of the adjoining cathedral. It was built in the early 16th century as the resting place of the Catholic Monarchs, Isabel and Fernando, who drove the last of the Moors from power in Spain (➤ 23). The royal couple's original wish was to be buried in Toledo, but the triumphalism of their conquest of the Moors encouraged them to build a burial chapel for themselves beside the cathedral that would replace Granada's Great Mosque.

The chapel is richly endowed with elegant columns and arches and superb altarpieces. A splendid grille encloses the lavish mausoleum of Isabel and Fernando, whose likenesses are depicted in Carrera marble. To its right are the figures of their daughter Joana ("the Mad") and her husband Felipe. Narrow steps descend to a crypt where the lead coffins of all four lie in grim display. Whether the remains within the coffins are those of the royal family is open to question, as they were vandalised by Napoleon's troops (always irreverent) during their short stay in the city during the Napoleonic Wars.

The chapel's sacristy is an absolute joy and includes in its collection of royal artefacts Isabel's personal treasury of Italian and Flemish paintings, the latter including fine works by Hans Memling and Rogier Van der Weyden.

Granada's Renaissance **cathedral** adjoins the Capilla Real. Its tiled turrets, gables and buttresses rise out of a clutter of other buildings towards a central dome that is a fleeting reminder of the Great Mosque that the cathedral supplanted. The cathedral seems always to have taken second place to the Capilla Real. It was begun in the 1520s as work on the chapel was almost finished, but was not completed until the 18th century. The high central dome gives the interior of the cathedral a wonderful airiness, and there are a number of impressive chapels that light up sporadically as visitors feed coins into switch boxes. There are fine paintings and sculptures within the cathedral, several by the

A detail of the elaborate organ of Granada cathedral and of the roof of the nave

A relief of Joana the Mad and Felipe the Handsome

The Capilla Real, Granada's finest Christian Gothic building, attracts many visitors

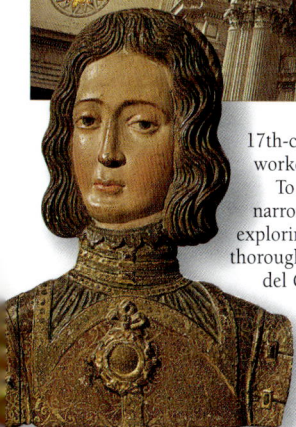

17th-century Granada-born artist Alonso Cano, who worked on the cathedral's main west facade.

To the southwest of the cathedral lies an area of narrow streets and attractive plazas that is worth exploring. On its east side, across the main thoroughfare of Calle Reyes Católicos from the Corral del Carbón tourist office (itself a finely preserved 14th-century merchants' inn), is the entrance to the **Alcaicería**, a mock-Arab souk or arcade, crammed with souvenir shops. Just beyond is Calle Zacatín, a pedestrianised shopping street that leads into **Plaza Bib-Rambla**, a huge square ringed by tall buildings and well supplied with café-bars and restaurants and with a swathe of flower stalls. The streets beyond the plaza are the heart of Granada's shopping district.

TAKING A BREAK

Try the **Vía Colona** bar-restaurant at Gran Vía de Colón 13, close to the Capilla Real and cathedral. It's busy, but friendly, and great for everything including breakfasts. Don't mind the full-size baroque angel and harp that stand on the bar.

Capilla Real
✚ 200 B2 ✉ Oficios 3 ☎ 958 22 92 39
🕐 Mon–Sat 10.30–1 and 4–7, Sun and public holidays 11–1 and 4–7 🚌 Buses 1, 3, 4, 6, 7, 8, 9 💶 Inexpensive

Catedral
✚ 200 B2 ✉ Gran Vía de Colón ☎ 958 22 29 59 🕐 Mon–Sat 10.30–1.30 and 4–7, Sun and public holidays 4–7 🚌 Buses 1, 3, 4, 6, 7, 8, 9 💶 Inexpensive

Monasterio de la Cartuja

Try to fit in a visit to the **Monasterio de la Cartuja** (Carthusian Monastery) on the northern outskirts of the city, one of Spain's most extravagant baroque buildings. The 16th-century monastery seems austere from outside, as do its central patio and its chapels, which are full of bloodcurdling paintings. None of this prepares you for the sanctuary and sacristy of the adjoining church, where eruptions of stucco, marble, jasper, and gilded wood define the elaborate altars, walls and domed ceilings. In the main body of the church, pigeons flit to and fro below the central cupola from whose shining apex exquisite angels peer down at you.

Right: Moorish plasterwork in La Madraza, the old Muslim college, located opposite the Capilla Real

Left: The sacristy of the Monasterio de la Cartuja is a baroque masterpiece

Parque de las Ciencias

A visit to the city's science museum provides a modern, and futuristic, perspective of Granada. It is a treat for youngsters, who can get interactive with various hands-on installations, as well as with giant chess and water games, and there's a planetarium, a butterfly house and a plant labyrinth. The museum is about 2km from the city centre but there are regular buses.

Monasterio de la Cartuja
✚ 200 off B5 ✉ Calle Real de Cartuja
☎ 958 16 19 32 ⏰ Mon–Sat 10–1 and 4–8, Sun and public holidays 10–noon and 4–8
🚌 Bus 8, Bus C 💷 Inexpensive

Parque de las Ciencias (Science Museum)
✚ 200 off A1 ✉ Avenida del Mediterráneo s/n ☎ 958 13 19 00 ⏰ Tue–Sat 10–7, Sun and public holidays 10–3. Planetarium: hourly shows 🚌 Buses 4, 5, 10, 11 💷 Moderate

GRANADA: INSIDE INFO

Top tips Granada's main **tourist office** is usually very busy. The Municipal Tourist Office on Plaza Mariana Pineda is a useful alternative.
• Take an early evening stroll through the **university district** to the northwest of the cathedral. There is a youthful bustle in the streets and you may hear the strains of music emanating from buildings as you pass by. Look out for some splendid churches (see Hidden gem below) and other buildings with spectacular baroque features scattered through the area.
• The **Alhambrabus** (Linea 32) is a very useful circular bus service that links Plaza Nueva with the Alhambra and the Albaicín. The service runs every 10 minutes between 7 am and 10 pm. The Plaza Nueva terminus, where buses for both the Alhambra and the Albaicín depart, is near the entrance to Cuesta de Gomérez, the narrow lane that leads up to the Alhambra. Every hour the Albaicín service has an extension into the Sacromonte area.

Hidden gem Enjoy the peace of a visit to the restored 16th-century **Monasterio de San Jerónimo** in the university district (Rector López Argüeta 9, open daily 10–1, 4–7). The church contains superb frescoes and a classical central altarpiece rising to a barrel vault through a series of niches crammed with magnificent sculptures and reliefs. There's a tranquil central cloister, and if you go in the evening you might hear the subdued chanting of the Sisters of St Jerome, who now live in the former monastery buildings.

One to miss Unless you are a devoted art lover, you may find the **Museo de Bellas Artes** in the upper rooms of the Alhambra's Palacio de Carlos V (▶ 85–6) a museum too far, considering the wealth of things to see within the Alhambra. The museum holds some fine paintings, but nothing to take what's left of your breath away.

❷

Las Alpujarras

The Alpujarras, a beautiful area of wooded hills and valleys, descends in green waves from the bare uplands of the Sierra Nevada. Prehistoric settlers first cultivated these terraced slopes, but it was the Moors, banished by the Christian conquerors of Granada in the 1490s, who brought unsurpassed skills of irrigation to the area and who built the flat-roofed Moroccan-style houses that give today's Alpujarran villages such charm. In the loveliest section, the western High Alpujarras, narrow roads wind between villages of white-washed houses that cling to the wooded slopes in the clear mountain air.

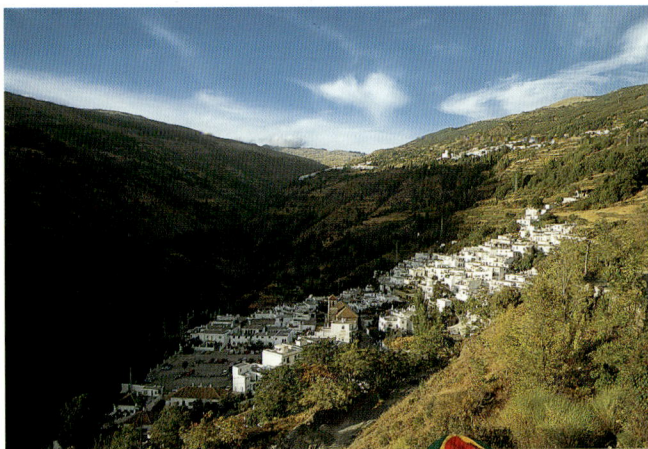

The approach from Granada to the Western Alpujarras is through the spa town of **Lanjarón**, where spring water is bottled and where the local *balneario* (spa) offers everything from mud baths to massage. Eighteen kilometres east of Lanjarón, at the market town of Órgiva, turn off north to follow an exhila-rating mountain road that takes you into the heart of the formidable Poqueira Gorge. This is the best of the High Alpujarras.

The Poqueira Villages

The Poqueira Gorge, a broad but steep-sided wooded valley, slices into the hills towards the second

A taste of the Alpujarras – roasted chestnuts bought from a street vendor

Typical flat-roofed houses at the hidden heart of Bubión, one of the most appealing villages in the Poqueira Gorge

highest summit of the Sierra Nevada, Pico Veleta (3,398m), with the highest summit Mulhacén (3,481m) just out of sight to the east. The white houses of a chain of three villages climb up the terraced slopes of the valley. The first village is **Pampaneira**, a compact jumble of houses that rises above the rugged old church of Santa Cruz in the central square, Plaza de la Libertad. On the square, you'll find Nevadensis, an excellent information centre for the Alpujarras and Sierra Nevada, along with several bars and plenty of souvenir shops selling local pottery, rugs and blankets that reflect Pampaneira's popularity with coach parties. Head down the narrow alleyway with a central water channel that runs under an arcade to the left of the square, to find the Bodega Moralea, a crafts shop and delicatessen with a wonderful assortment of enticing products.

Left: The villages of Pampaneira, Bubión and Capileira cling to the terraced slopes of the Poqueira Gorge

Above Pampaneira is the village of **Bubión**, the most tranquil and least visited of the Poqueira villages, with narrow streets spilling down the slopes below the main road to the flower-hung church square, Plaza Iglesia. On the corner of the square is the **Casa Tradicional Alpujarreña**, an outstanding museum of Alpujarran life. It occupies a traditional village

Walking in the Alpujarras

At the Nevadensis information office in Pampaneira (▶ 95) you will find a number of leaflets that outline short circular walking routes in the Poqueira Gorge area. However, they rely too often on sections of road walking in order to fit the "circular" style.

There is a delightful path of about 2km that climbs the valley side from Pampaneira to Bubión's Plaza Iglesia. You can do this walk less strenuously from Bubión, then catch a bus back uphill.

Most of the villages along the southern slopes of the Alpujarras are linked by the waymarked long-distance path GR-7. With careful planning you can walk sections of the route between villages and return to your starting point by bus.

Autumn foliage
in the valleys
above Trevélez

house, left unchanged since its occupant moved away in the
1950s. On the way down to the square is the **Taller del Telar**
(Weaver's Workshop, ➤ 107), where fine woollen cloth is
produced on a loom that belonged to the last master weaver of
Granada. The cloth, of superb quality, comes in subtle colours;
it is for sale, as are other artefacts such as textile lampshades.

The highest of the Poqueira villages is **Capileira**. It is
extremely popular and gets very crowded in summer. Away
from the main road, however, you can wander between classic
Alpujarran flat-roofed houses on narrow alleyways with
covered roofs of twisted branches packed with clay. Then, as
the lower houses of Capileira thin out, you can follow tracks
that lead higher into the wooded gorge, where the Poqueira
river gushes across polished boulders amid scented pinewoods.

Trevélez and Beyond

The road east from the Poqueira Gorge runs in delectable
twists and turns along the great wooded shelf of hills and
passes through the less visited villages of Pitres, Pórtugos and
Busquístar, before turning north once more along the slopes of
another deep valley to the town of **Trevélez**. This is the highest settlement in Spain and is famed for its production of
cured ham, *jamón serrano*. The houses of Trevélez climb the

All About the Alpujarras
The English writer Gerald Brenan lived in the village of Yegen
during the 1920s and wrote of his experiences in his book
South From Granada, an enthralling account of Alpujarran life.
A plaque commemorating Brenan is fixed to the wall of the
house in which he lived, now called the Casa de Brenan, near
the village's main square. Another popular Alpujarran book,
Driving Over Lemons, was published in 1999. It was written by
Chris Stewart, ex-drummer of the band Genesis, who set up as
a small farmer near Órgiva.

LAS ALPUJARRAS: INSIDE INFO

Top tips Driving in the Alpujarras takes much longer than you think, so plan accordingly. It may take you the best part of a morning to drive 50km along the area's winding roads, and with all the spectacular scenery, the temptation to stop and admire the view is irresistible.

• If you have time to spare, why not be adventurous? You can enjoy plant and birdwatching walks or longer treks, horse riding, cycling, four-wheel drive trips, and even hang-gliding throughout the area, all with experienced local guides. Ask for details at Nevadensis in Pampaneira (➤ Tourist Information, below).

One to miss Solynieve (Sun and Snow) is Granada province's winter sports resort, reached from Granada. It stands on the upper slopes of the Sierra Nevada and in summer is fairly desolate. If you ski, you could catch some late seasonal runs – with the aid of numerous snow-making machines.

upper slopes of the valley in a succession of *barrios*, separate quarters that have quite distinct characters. The lowest of these, the *barrio bajo*, pays the price of Trevélez's popularity. Its main square is not much more than a large car-parking area where souvenir shops, cafés, restaurants and *jamón serrano* outlets clamour for attention. A steep zigzagging road leads up to middle Trevélez, the *barrio medio*, then continues to the upper village, the *barrio alto*, where traffic fades away and lanes grow ever narrower as they climb towards the steepening mountain slopes above.

Continuing east from Trevélez takes you deeper into the Alpujarras, through a landscape of woods and streams, dense with chestnut, poplar, evergreen oak and pine. The road takes you past old Moorish settlements, such as **Bérchules** and **Yegen** (➤ panel, page 94), unspoiled villages that cling to the tumbling slopes of the hills and captivate with their slow pace of life. Beyond Yegen the road continues east until the landscape begins slowly to lose its green mantle as it gives way to the arid hills of Almería province.

TAKING A BREAK

In Pampaneira, the **Alegrías** bar-restaurant makes use of a pleasant little terrace just below the preserved public washhouse. Head uphill from the church square of Plaza de la Libertad on a cobbled lane with a central water channel. For one of the most spectacular views of the Alpujarras, stop for a drink at **Bar Albuxarra** at the end of Capileira's main street.

Visitors to the Alpujarras can buy a variety of local crafts

✛ 197 D2

Tourist Information
✉ Nevadensis, Plaza de la Libertad, Pampaneira   ☎ 958 76 31 27
✉ Rustic Blue (private), Bubión   ☎ 958 76 33 81

Casa Tradicional Alpujarreña
✉ Plaza Iglesia, Bubión   ☎ 958 76 30 32   🕓 Mon–Fri 11–2, Sat–Sun and public holidays 11–2 and 5–7   💶 Inexpensive

3

Almería

According to an old saying, "When Almería was Almería, Granada was but a farmstead", an expression of pride justified, not least, by the city's dramatically sited Moorish fortress. Below it, the older, western part of the city, characterised by narrow streets and crumbling buildings, lies side by side with the busy shopping streets and recently refurbished boulevards of the modern city. In Almería you move easily between Moorish and medieval Andalucía and the busy world of 21st-century Spain.

From the 8th century, Almería was the chief port of al-Andalus and grew rich on two-way trade with North Africa and the eastern Mediterranean. The city fell to the Christians in 1490, and the break with North Africa led to a decline exacerbated by destructive earthquakes in the 16th century. By the 19th century Almería was beginning to prosper once more. Today *plasticultura*, greenhouse farming (► 181), and increased tourism, have brought much development to the city.

The Alcazaba

The Alcazaba's 10th-century builders took advantage of the craggy edges of their hilltop site, and even today the restored walls and towers of the fortress look like natural extensions of the encircling cliffs. The approach ramp to the **Alcazaba** complex winds steeply up to the **Puerta de la Justicia** (Justice Gate), a perfect example of a Moorish entrance archway. The double horseshoe arch has a staggered inner gate that was designed to disorientate an attacker. Beyond is the **Primer**

Below: A harbour view of Almería's Alcazaba. The city's Moorish name translates as "mirror of the sea"

Steps lead
down from
Almería's
Alcazaba into
the old Moorish
part of the city

Recinto (First Precinct), the lowest level of the Alcazaba, used as a camp by the Moorish garrison and as a refuge for citizens during sieges. It has been transformed into a series of terraced gardens. From here you climb gently to a cool oasis of trees that shades the high wall of the **Segundo Recinto** (Second Precinct), a large area filled with the poignant ruins of the sumptuous living quarters that reflected the wealth and importance of Almería in the 10th and 11th centuries, first under the Córdoban Caliphate, then as an independent principality, and later as part of Muslim Granada. The **Tercer Recinto** (Third Precinct) contains the formidable inner fortress built by the Christian conquerors after 1492 on the site of a previous keep. From its walls there are breathtaking views to the sea.

Immediately below lies the **Barrio de Chanca**, Almería's old cave district with the often brightly painted facades of the flat-roofed houses and of the cave dwellings that punctuate the rocky escarpments above them. The houses, and a few of the caves, are occupied by the poorest citizens of Almería.

Other Sights

The city's **cathedral** was built in the 1520s on the site of a ruined mosque; its fortress-like walls were intended to protect the building from pirates. The interior of the building is gloomily Gothic, but the carving of the choir stalls is exquisite and the 18th-century altar has superb features in red and black jasper. A door in the south wall leads to a leafy little patio.

The **Museo Arqueológico** (Archaeological Museum) is currently closed and destined for relocation (check with the tourist information office for the latest details). Meanwhile items from the Los Millares early Bronze Age site (▶ panel, page 103), along with material from the Roman and Moorish periods, are on display in Almería's public library, a short walk east of the cathedral. The **Centro de Artes** (Art Gallery), a bone-white rotunda near the railway and bus station, opened in 2000 and exhibits traditional and contemporary art.

Central Almería is divided east and west by the Rambla de Belén, a wide boulevard that slopes gently down towards the harbour and is dotted with palm trees and fountains. To the west is the city's main street, the sleekly refurbished Paseo de Almería lined with shops and café-bars. At its north end is Puerta de Purchena, a busy junction, groaning and fuming with traffic, its pavements thronged with voluble Almerians. The pedestrianised Plaza Manuel Pérez García leads from the western end of Puerta de Purchena into the attractive shopping street of Calle de las Tiendas and thence into other streets crammed with shops, bars and restaurants.

TAKING A BREAK

For great *jamón* and fish *tapas* and meals, and a terrific selection of sherries, don't miss **Bodega las Botas** (Calle Fructuosa Pérez 3), a high-roofed bar with traditional upturned sherry barrels for tables.

✚ 197 E2

Tourist Information
✉ Parque Nicolás Salmerón s/n (J de A)
☎ 950 27 43 55 ✉ Avenida Federico García Lorca (OMT) ☎ 950 28 07 48

Parking
There is an excellent underground car park on the east side of the Rambla de Belén just off the main roundabout at its seaward end.

Alcazaba
✉ Almanzor s/n ☎ 950 27 16 17 🕐 Daily 9–6.30 🎫 Inexpensive (free to EU passport holders)

Catedral
✉ Plaza de la Catedral 🕐 Mon–Fri 10–4.30, Sat 10–1 🎫 Inexpensive

Museo Arqueológico
✉ Biblioteca Pública (temporary exhibition), Calle Hermanos Machado 1 ☎ 950 62 10 21
🕐 Tue–Fri 9–2, Sat 9.30–1.30
🎫 Inexpensive (free to EU passport holders)

Centro de Artes (Museo Almería)
✉ Plaza Barcelona s/n ☎ 950 26 96 80
🕐 Mon–Fri 11–2 and 6–9, Sat 6–9, Sun and public holidays 11–2 🎫 Free

---

ALMERÍA: INSIDE INFO

Top tips The sun can be blisteringly hot here, so **use sunscreen and wear a hat**, especially when visiting the Alcazaba where there is not much shelter.
• Try to take in Almería's lively **morning market**. It's held in Calle Aguilar de Campo, an alleyway reached from halfway down Paseo de Almería.

Hidden gem The 17th-century **Plaza Vieja** (Old Square) is a tranquil place to relax. Palm trees encircle a white monument, which commemorates the execution in 1824 of Almerians who defied the repressive rule of King Ferdando VII.

One to miss Almeria's old cave district, the **Barrio de la Chanca**, is best viewed from the Alcazaba (see above). A close-quarters visit to this deprived part of the city, especially at night, is not advised.

At Your Leisure

4 Cabo de Gata

This peninsula on the eastern side of the Gulf of Almería is believed to be the driest and possibly the hottest place in Europe, a landscape of long empty beaches, salt pans and raw volcanic hills. On the southern tip of the peninsula, at the actual cape (*cabo*), stands a lonely lighthouse from where there are dramatic views of rugged cliffs and offshore pinnacles. Cabo de Gata's attractions lie in its often empty beaches, its plant and bird life and the remoteness of the cliffs and lonely coves of the wild coast to the northeast of the cape. The most accessible beaches lie on

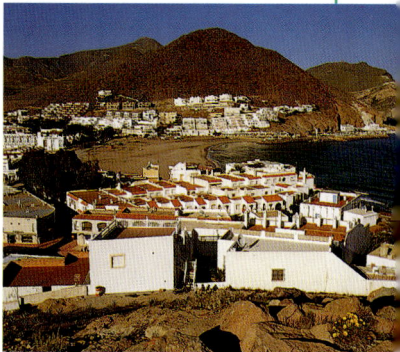

The charming village of San José, northeast of Cabo de Gata lighthouse

Wildlife of the Cabo de Gata

The **Parque Natural de Cabo de Gata-Níjar** is an area of special protection for plants and birds. Plants that can cope with the desert-like conditions include the Zizyphus, or jujube, a shrub whose thorny leaves and branches form an umbrella over the soil to preserve moisture and Europe's only indigenous palm, the dwarf fan palm. Behind the village of San Miguel de Cabo de Gata lies **Las Salinas**, a large area of salt marshes, where you may spot flamingos, avocets, storks and egrets among the many resident and migrant birds. The Natural Park information centre, **Los Amoladeros Centro de Interpretación** (tel: 950 16 04 35,open daily 10–2, 5.30–9 in summer; Tue–Sun 10–3 in winter), between Almería and San Miguel, has exhibitions on the local wildlife, as well as a gift shop.

the shores of the Gulf of Almería alongside the road between the village of San Miguel de Cabo de Gata and the lighthouse. They are marred only by the occasional winds that blow up by midday. Just before

the lighthouse, a narrow road, signed *Acceso Sendero Vela Blanca*, leads off north for a few kilometres to a final headland crowned by a radio station and by the old Moorish watchtower of Vela Blanca. Beyond here a dirt track winds along the side of wild mountain slopes and gives access on foot to some small, secluded beaches.

➕ 197 E1 🍴 El Naranjero Restaurant at San Miguel de Cabo de Gata (moderate). Seasonal café at lighthouse (inexpensive)

Tourist Information

✉ Los Amoladeros Centro de Interpretación
✉ Cabo de Gata lighthouse (seasonal information kiosk)

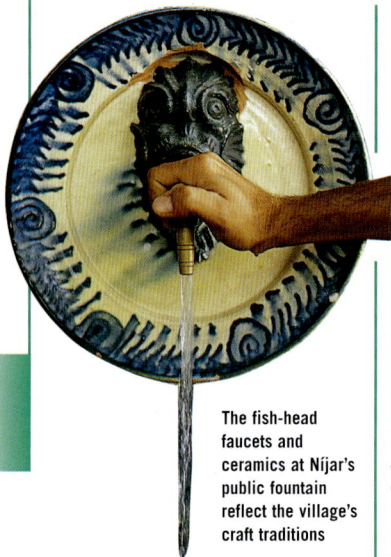

The fish-head faucets and ceramics at Níjar's public fountain reflect the village's craft traditions

Further Afield
The sea coasts of Granada and Almería provinces, known collectively as the Costa Tropical, have only a few resorts. Almería's western Costa is almost wholly given over to *plasticultura* (right, ➤ 181), its flat coastal plain a glaring expanse of shining polythene greenhouses. Granada's coast is a mere 60km in length and has been saved from the creeping plastic because of its rugged cliffs. The best resorts along the Granada coast are Almuñécar and Salobreña.

5 Níjar
The village of Níjar, centre of a ceramics industry dating from Moorish times, sits in the foothills of the Sierra de Alhamilla 30km northeast of Almería. Below is the arid plain of the Campo de Níjar, carpeted with the glistening sheets of *plasticultura* greenhouses (➤ panel, page 181). Níjar's potters specialise in vivid colours created from mineral dyes; you can buy their wares in the main street, **Avenida García Lorca**, which is lined with pottery and craft shops. However, the main workshops and showroom are in the adjoining **Barrio Alfarero**, which leads off from the top of García Lorca. The craft shops also sell brightly coloured carpets and blankets. Beyond Avenida García Lorca is the old town with tree-lined **Plaza la Glorieta** and the 16th-century church of Santa María de la Anunciación, noted for its *mudéjar* ceiling. Continue beyond the church to the **Plaza del Mercado** with its huge central tree and blue-tiled public fountain. For excellent Níjar ceramics look for La Tienda de los Milagros (➤ 107) in Calle Lavadero, just beyond the plaza.

➕ 197 E1

Tourist Information
✉ Calle Maestros 🍴 Café-Bar La Glorieta

6 Mojácar
Mojácar is the main beach resort in Almería province and can become extremely busy in high season. If you want easily accessible beaches with modern conveniences, however, this is the place to find them. There are two Mojácars. The long, straggling coastal resort of **Mojácar Playa** makes the most of a narrow stretch of excellent beach alongside the rather busy main road. Beachfront development runs for several kilometres and there are numerous hotels, shops, cafés, restaurants and lively bars. Just 2km inland is old Mojácar, known as **Mojácar**

Pueblo, a settlement of sugar-cube houses clustered round a rocky hilltop. Moorish influence lingered well into the 20th century here and women in Mojácar were said to wear veiled dress until about 50 years ago. The village can still charm in spite of the crowds of summer visitors who throng the souvenir shops and amble down sunlit alleyways.

➕ 197 F2

Tourist Information
✉ Calle Glorieta 1, Mojácar
☎ 950 47 51 62
✉ Avenida de Andalucía s/n, Mojácar Playa ☎ 950 61 50 25

🄻 Sorbas

The village of Sorbas, 40km north-east of Almería, is noted for its pottery and you can visit workshops and salerooms in its Barrio Alfarero (➤ 107). As you wander through the village's winding streets you will come across the occasional decaying, but still elegant facade of a 17th-century mansion. In the Castilian architectural tradition, they reflect the conscious rejection by wealthy landowners of the *mudéjar* style.

Signposted to the south of the village are the **Cuevas de Sorbas**, at the heart of the limestone hills. You can take two-hour guided trips through the cave systems. These are mildly adventurous, but even young children can cope with the occasional scrambling and clambering. Helmets and headlamps are supplied, but be prepared to get muddy.

➕ 197 E2

Tourist Information
✉ Calle Terraplén 9 ☎ 950 36 44 76

Cuevas de Sorbas
➕ 197 F2 ☎ 950 36 47 04.
Booking a day ahead is advised.
🄲 Open daily every hour on the hour 10–8 in summer; 10–1 and 3–6 in winter 🄳 Expensive

Traditional Andalucía can still be found in the sun-scorched lanes of Mojácar

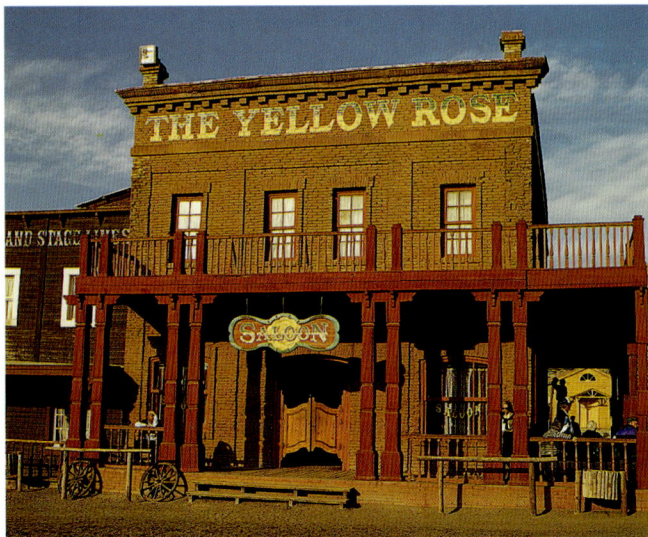

8 Mini Hollywood

The extraordinary Arizona-style "Badlands" of Tabernas to the north of Almería city is where such Western classics as *The Magnificent Seven*, *A Fistful of Dollars* and *The Good, the Bad and the Ugly* were filmed. The mock Wild West towns that were built for these movies amid drystone gulches and treeless wastes remain as tourist attractions. Of the three theme towns currently operating, Mini Hollywood is the largest and the best managed. It lies just off the Carretera Nacional, about 10km west of the village of Tabernas. The main street has saloons, sheriff's office, typical Western shops and the essential funeral parlour and boot hill cemetery. You can have yourself

Playing the cowboy card at Mini Hollywood, near Tabernas

photographed wearing gunfighter gear or other Western outfits. Special cowboy shows are staged at set times outside the sheriff's office, with jail breaks, gunfights and hangings. Youngsters love every minute of it. Adjoining the town is the Reserva Zoológica, a well-kept zoo with big cats and an extended area of hillside stockades that contain a range of animals including deer, zebra, bison, lions and hippos.

✠ 197 E2 ☎ 950 36 52 36 (Mini Hollywood), 950 36 29 31 (Reserva Zoológica) ⏰ Daily 10–9, Jul–Sep; 10–7, Oct–Jun. Western show: daily at noon and 5 (extra show at 8, Jun–Sep); cancan dance show: daily at 1 and 4 (extra show at 7, Jun–Sep); parrot show: daily 11, 3, 6 🍴 Restaurant and café (£–££) 💰 Inexpensive (dogs are not admitted)

9 Guadix

The bustling country town of Guadix, 60km east of Granada, contains a remarkable "suburb" of cave dwellings that have been carved out of soft sandstone rock. Cave dwellings are said to have become popular in the 16th century when dispossessed Muslims, expelled from the towns by their Christian conquerors, found refuge in natural caves. At Guadix, the soft rock of the surrounding hills lent itself to further excavation of chambers and passage-ways. The caves here comprise entire dwellings with all the modern conveniences, and the windowless rooms maintain a constantly equable temperature. Many caves have whitewashed extensions and well-tended gardens.

In the **Cueva Museo** (Cave Museum), which can be reached by road train from the town centre, a series of domestic rooms have been beautifully preserved and furnished in traditional manner.

Off the Beaten Track

If you have time for a very different experience, head for the **Cueva de los Millares**, a few kilometres north of Almería amid remote hills (🔢 197 E2, open Wed–Sat 9.30–2 and 4–6, Sun 9–2.30, Apr–Sep. For winter times check with Almería tourist office or tel: 608 95 70 65). Dating from the early Bronze Age, the site contains the remains of defensive walls, circular stone huts and beehive-shaped tombs, one of which has been imaginatively reconstructed. You have to walk about one kilometre to the site from the roadside entrance and it can be very hot by midday.

A unique suburbia: cave houses at Guadix

The main town of Guadix is dominated by a magnificent Renaissance cathedral in rich red sandstone. Opposite its main door is an archway that leads to the attractive Renaissance square of Plaza de la Constitución, known also as Plaza Mayor. From the square, cobbled alleyways lead to a clutch of handsome Renaissance buildings in the upper town.

🔢 197 D2

Tourist Information
✉ Carretera de Granada ☎ 958 66 26 65

Cueva Museo
✉ Plaza del Padre Poveda ☎ 616 35 48 29 🕐 Mon–Sat 10–2, 5–7, Sun 10–2, Jul–Sep; Mon– Sat 10–2, 4–8, Sun 10–2, Oct–Jun 💰 Expensive

Where to... Stay

Prices

Expect to pay per person per night
£ up to €36   ££ €36–€96   £££ over €96

Casa del Aljarife ££

The views of the Alhambra from this pension, set in a tiny square at the heart of the Albaicín, are splendid. The 17th-century house has been sensitively restored, and has a delightful shady central courtyard and rooftop terrace typical of the area. The rooms (there are just four) are small but have plenty of character with interesting angles and use of space.

➕ 200 C3 ✉ Placeta de la Cruz Verde 2, Albaicín, Granada ☎ 958 22 24 25, email: most@wanadoo.es

Hostal Britz £

The Britz, just within walking distance of the Alhambra, offers great value. Rooms are basic but comfortable, and some have terraces and brightly tiled en-suite bathrooms. The location on the bustling Plaza Nueva means it can be noisy, but also has a choice of pavement cafés is just a short stroll away.

➕ 200 C2 ✉ Cuesta de Gomérez 1, Granada ☎ 958 22 36 52

Hotel Los Tilos ££

This good-value, no-frills hotel has a comfortable, modern interior, and is about as central as you can get, overlooking a pleasant square where there is a daily flower market. Best of all is the fourth-floor terrace where you can sip a drink, read a book or just enjoy a fabulous panoramic view of the city skyline.

➕ 200 B2 ✉ Plaza Bib-Rambla 4, Granada ☎ 958 26 67 12, fax: 958 26 68 01

Las Terrazas £

As the name implies, Las Terrazas is perched atop a terraced hillside with three large terraces for eagle's-nest views of the stupendous mountainous surroundings. There's a delightful homey feel to the place, with parrot and other pets around; and there are mountain bikes to borrow and very helpful hosts. The rooms are simple, with locally woven bedspreads and terracotta floors, and breakfast is included in the extremely reasonable price.

➕ 196 C2 ✉ Plaza del Sol 7, Bubión ☎ 958 76 30 34, fax: 958 76 32 52 ☒ Closed Jan

Villa Turística de Bubión ££

It sounds contrived, but this carefully designed "village" actually works. The 43 houses are replicas of traditional Alpujarran dwellings, set amid lush landscaping with cool seating areas. They all have a terrace or private garden and dreamy views. There is a restaurant on site.

➕ 196 C2 ✉ Barrio Alto s/n, Bubión ☎ 958 76 31 12, fax: 958 76 31 36

Hotel La Perla ££

The oldest hotel in town and still family-run, La Perla was favoured by the stars in Almería's "spaghetti western" days. It has been expanded to several more floors but still exudes a certain old-world charm. The rooms are pleasant – ask for one overlooking the plaza – and the facilities, including air conditioning, satellite TV and parking, good

➕ 197 E2 ✉ Plaza del Carmen 7, Almería ☎ 950 23 88 77, fax: 950 27 58 16

Where to...
Eat and Drink

Prices

Expect to pay per person for a meal, including wine and service

£ up to €12   ££ €12–€30   £££ over €30

El Acebreche £–££

Hop off the Alhambrabus (▶ 91) and head for a table outside in the Plaza San Miguel el Bajo, a pretty square in the Albaicín lined with chestnut trees. Moroccan María Jiménez prepares healthy, tasty dishes with no preservatives and plenty of vegetarian choice. Try her delicious cous-cous for a real taste-bud treat or come early for a healthy high-energy breakfast.

✚ 200 C4 ☒ Plaza San Miguel el Bajo 6, Albaicín, Granada ☎ 958 27 31 01 ◉ Daily 9–late

La Gran Taberna £

The interior of this town-centre *tapas* bar is typical, with stools around barrels, and hams, strings of garlic and red peppers hanging above the bar. If you want a quiet drink, forget it, especially if it's a football night when the TV will be blaring. The *tapas* here are terrific. You can choose from a vast selection, including trout with cottage cheese, Roquefort with beets and goat's cheese canapés as well as the more standard selection.

✚ 200 C2 ☒ Plaza Nueva 12, Granada ☎ 958 22 88 46 ◉ Daily 9–3, 7–midnight

El Jardín de los Sueños £

A typical *tetería* (tea house) in a fascinating street lined with Moroccan cafés, bakeries, shops and restaurants, this is the sort of laid-back place where you sit on the floor on large cushions and play a game or two of backgammon. As well as a long list of teas, there are some delicious milkshakes; try the banana, almond and pistachio. Even if you can't stop for a drink, then buy one of the sticky almond cakes. They taste as good as they look.

✚ 200 C3 ☒ Calderería Nueva 23, Granada ☎ 958 22 70 50 ◉ Tue–Sun 3–midnight

Rabo de Nube £

Popular with students and strollers, Rabo de Nube is the best-value bar of several on this scenic stretch with its neck-craning view of the Alhambra. Order a drink for a complimentary *tapa* of *jamón serrano* or crumbly aged Manchego cheese. Alternatively, you can select from an extensive sandwich menu.

Best value of all are the groaning plates of pasta with surprisingly innovative sauces, including creamy Roquefort.

✚ 201 E3 ☒ Paseo de Los Tristes 1, Granada ☎ 958 22 04 21 ◉ Daily noon–late

San Nicolás £££

Head straight for a table by the window for the fabulous views of the Alhambra (particularly recommended at sunset). The restaurant's decor is sumptuous and elegant, with exquisite marble, pale pistachio-coloured walls and linen-clad tables. The menu includes such nouvelle-Andaluz dishes as leg of pork filled with lavender and honey, and there's an outside terrace for *al fresco* lunches and a little candlelit romance. It's a pricy option, but the views alone justify the expense.

✚ 201 D4 ☒ Calle San Nicolás 3, Albaicín, Granada ☎ 958 80 42 62 ◉ Wed–Mon, 1–4, 8 pm–2 am. Closed all day Tue and Sun dinner

LAS ALPUJARRAS

La Artesa Restaurante £–££

This charming small bar and restaurant serves some unusual local dishes, such as *gacás pimentonas* (a vegetable pepper stew with dumplings) and *migas con chicharrones* (fried breadcrumbs with pork), as well as more traditional fare. Dark wood and bright tiles are typically Andaluz; a small dining room upstairs takes on the overflow at weekends.

⊞ 196 C2 ⊠ Calle Carretera. Bubión ☎ 958 76 30 82 **ⓒ** Daily 1.30–4, 8–11. Closed 24 and 31 Dec

La Fragua ££

You can enjoy blissful views over the rooftops to the valley beyond from the pine-clad dining room in this old village house. Dishes are simple and regional, like delicious locally cured ham or pork loin with mixed herbs. There's wonderful bread from the local baker and the puddings are superb. A couple of doors away is the hotel of the same name – useful if you overindulge.

⊞ 197 D2 ⊠ Calle San Antonio 4, Trevélez ☎ 958 85 86 26, fax: 958 85 86 14 **ⓒ** Daily noon–5, 8–11. Closed 10 Jan–10 Feb

Restaurant Ruta de Las Nieves £–££

The setting is rustic, with a traditionally furnished beamed dining room. Step out onto the terrace for a great valley view. There are good-value *raciones*, such as spicy chicken (*pollo en salsa*), ham and chicken croquettes (*croquetas*), as well as a well-priced daily menu including trout, ham and a traditional fry-up of local sausages, ham and eggs with *patatas pobres* (fried potatoes with onion and garlic) on the side. Several popular hikes start from Capileira, so you can expect to see plenty of walkers fuelling up here before they set off.

⊞ 196 C2 ⊠ Carretera de la Sierra s/n, Capileira ☎ 958 76 31 06 **ⓒ** Daily 1.30–4, 8.30–10.30

ALMERÍA

Asador Torreluz £££

One of the city's most sophisticated restaurants, Asador Torreluz is ideal for a special occasion. The décor is more French baronial than southern Spain, with elaborate brocade chairs, light brick walls and plenty of stained glass and gilt. The service is discreet and attentive, the ingredients fresh, and the dishes flavourful. Specialities include suckling pig (*cochinillo*) slowly roasted in a wood-burning oven, grilled meats, and fresh fish.

⊞ 197 E2 ⊠ Plaza Flores 1, Almería ☎ 950 23 45 45 **ⓒ** Mon–Sat 1.30–4, 8.30–midnight

El Alcázar £

This *marisquera* (seafood restaurant) is one of many in the street, but is clearly the most popular with locals. The food is simple but exceptionally fresh, and the choice is excellent. Try the *gambas pil pil* if you like your prawns with a chilli kick, or the *sopa de pescado* (fish soup), another speciality. There are a few tables inside, but most spill out onto the pavement. Otherwise, you can get your seafood to go.

⊞ 197 E2 ⊠ Calle Tenor Iribarne 2, Almería ☎ 950 23 89 95 **ⓒ** Mon–Sat noon–4.30, 7–midnight

Salsitas & Beach Restaurante £–££

Right in the centre of the city's smartest shopping street, this restaurant couples good value with a great choice. The menu includes snack-size sandwiches made on pitta-style bread (*tortas*), paella, pizza and burgers, so is particularly good for fussy families. The theme is maritime and modern with lots of blue and white paintwork, fountains and ferns, and the bar is popular for a quick *tapa* – try the fried potatoes with onions and garlic (*patatas pobres*).

⊞ 197 E2 ⊠ Calle Conde Ofalia 5, Almería ☎ 950 24 64 24 **ⓒ** Tue–Sun 11–4, 8–midnight

Where to...
Shop

Both Granada and Almería provinces have rich craftwork traditions, ranging from Granada's inlaid woodwork to the vividly coloured pottery of Níjar and the textiles and clothing of Las Alpujarras.

GRANADA CITY

Granada city's main shopping area is the streets between the arms of its two main thoroughfares, Calle Reyes Católicos and Gran Vía de Colón. In **Reyes Católicos** are a number of small, but very stylish fashion shops. A few metres in from here is the **Alcaicería**, a mock-Arab souk or arcade, crammed with souvenir shops full of Granadine crafts including brass and copper-work, embossed leather and pottery. Nearby is the narrow, pedestrianised **Zacatín** with a good range of clothes and gift shops. A Granada speciality is *taracea* (marquetry), and there are several shops selling it in **Cuesta de Gomérez**, the narrow street leading steeply uphill from Plaza Nueva to the Alhambra. One of the best is **González Ramos Taller de Taracea** (Cuesta Gomérez 16, tel: 958 22 70 62). The street also contains plenty of souvenir shops, as well as some of the best guitar makers in Andalucía. Try **Casa Ferrer** (Cuesta de Gomérez 30, tel: 958 22 18 32), a highly rated music shop, founded in the late 19th-century by a member of the same family that still runs it.

For the full range of shopping there's the department store **El Corte Inglés** in Acero del Darro, the broad continuation of Reyes Católicos. One of the best food and drink shops in the city is the well-stocked **Mantequería Castellano** (Calle Almireceros 6, tel: 958 22 48 40) just off Gran Vía de Colón and opposite the cathedral. In nearby **Calderería Vieja and Calderería Nueva**, in the heart of the Albaicín, there are a number of shops selling "Arabic" spices, perfumes, food and souvenirs. One of the best for leatherwork is **Artesenía Albaicín** (Calle del Agua 19, tel: 958 27 90 56), which has a good selection of tooled leather goods, including bags, purses, wallets and coasters.

LAS ALPUJARRAS

In the High Alpujarras, shops in villages such as Pampaneira (▶ 93) sell souvenirs, pottery and traditional *jarapas* (rugs and bedcovers). Worth seeking out in Pampaneira is **Bodega La Moralea** (Calle Veronica, tel: 958 76 32 25), which carries a vast stock of local food products and artefacts. In Bubión (▶ 93) follow shops for **Taller del Telar** (tel: 958 76 31 71) for superb textiles and fabrics. For the celebrated *jamón serrano*, the cured ham of the region, Trevélez (▶ 94) is the best bet.

ALMERÍA CITY AND PROVINCE

Almería city's main shopping area is **Calle de las Tiendas** and its surrounding alleyways that lie to the south of Puerta de Purchena and west of the top end of Paseo de Almería. The morning **market** in Calle Aguilar de Campo, off Paseo de Almería, is lively and colourful. For fine pottery, head for **Níjar** (▶ 100), where you can also buy brightly coloured *jarapas*. Look for **La Tienda de los Milagros** (Calle Lavadero 2, tel: 950 36 03 59) for an imaginative approach to pottery. Another good source of ceramics is **Sorbas** (▶ 101), where workshops in the Barrio Alfarero (the Potter's Quarter) produce more functional wares than those of Níjar in such family-run workshops as **Alfarería Juan Simón** (Calle Alfarerías 25, tel: 950 36 40 83).

Where to...
Be Entertained

Ask at tourist offices in Granada city for *Guía de Granada*, a free monthly listings guide. The city's daily newspaper *Ideal* also has an entertainment section in Spanish. The English-language free weekly newspaper *The Entertainer* has some information on entertainment in Almería city.

NIGHTLIFE

Many clubs and music bars in Granada cater to the city's lively student population. For something a little more sophisticated, try **Granada 10** (Cárcel Baja, tel: 958 22 40 01) just off Gran Vía de Colón near the cathedral. This doubles as a cinema, but the music starts about midnight. It attracts a smarter set, and is consequently more expensive than many places. The mainstream **El Camborio** (Camino del Sacromonte) is a less expensive choice. It has several dance floors and a garden terrace with views of the Alhambra. Again, midnight is the earliest time for things to start happening.

Almería has some lively music bars in the Calle San Pedro area, and during the summer months **disco-marquees** are set up on the Paseo Marítimo to the east of the seaward end of the Rambla de Belén. These can be fairly noisy and youth-orientated, but Spanish youngsters are not ageist, so, whatever your age, you can do it...

DANCE

The **Teatro Alhambra** (Calle de Molinos 56, tel: 958 22 04 47) stages flamenco, ballet and modern dance, as well as Spanish-language plays. Musical performances include chamber music, orchestral and jazz.

There are a number of flamenco venues in Granada city. One of the most popular is **Jardines Neptuno** (Calle Arabial, tel: 958 52 25 33), though the show is more cabaret than pure flamenco and organised as part of an all-in-one restaurant experience. Something closer to the real thing can be seen at **El Corral del Príncipe** (Campo del Príncipe, tel: 958 22 80 88) and **Tarantos** (Camino del Sacromonte 9, tel: 958 22 45 25).

OUTDOOR ACTION

The Sierra Nevada and Las Alpujarras (▶ 92–5) have much to offer outdoor enthusiasts. Las Alpujarras offers ideal **walking** conditions and, if you are experienced and well equipped, there's high-level walking on the Sierra Nevada peaks. Enquire about maps and guide books at **Nevadensis** (Plaza de la Libertad, Pampaneira, tel: 958 76 31 27), the friendly and helpful Parque Natural Sierra Nevada information office.

For **horse riding**, contact **Rutas a Caballo** (Bubión, tel: 958 76 30 38) or **Cabalgar Rutas Alternativas** (Bubión, tel: 958 76 31 35), who organise anything from a few hours' riding to nine-day treks. They also organise day-long four-wheel-drive tours through the mountains. For a range of adventure activities including walking, riding, rock climbing and paragliding, contact Nevadensis (see above) or **Rustic Blue** (Barrio la Ermita, Bubión, tel: 958 76 33 81).

For **water sports** enthusiasts there is diving in the Cabo de Gata area (▶ 99). For information, contact Puerto Deportivo de San José, San José, tel: 950 38 00 41).

Córdoba
and Jaén

Getting Your Bearings 110–111
In Five Days 112–113
Don't Miss 114–127
At Your Leisure 128–130
Where to... 131–136

Getting Your Bearings

Andalucía's northern provinces of Córdoba and Jaén, rich in Moorish and Renaissance monuments and with relatively quiet towns and unhurried village communities, can be a relief after the crowded Costa resorts and the sometimes frenetic pace of Seville and Granada.

The city of Córdoba is the most accessible and popular destination in the two provinces, not least because of the magnetic appeal of the Mezquita, the Great Mosque. This lovely city has many other attractions, from the old Moorish palace – the Alcázar – with its restful fountains and gardens, to handsome Renaissance churches and

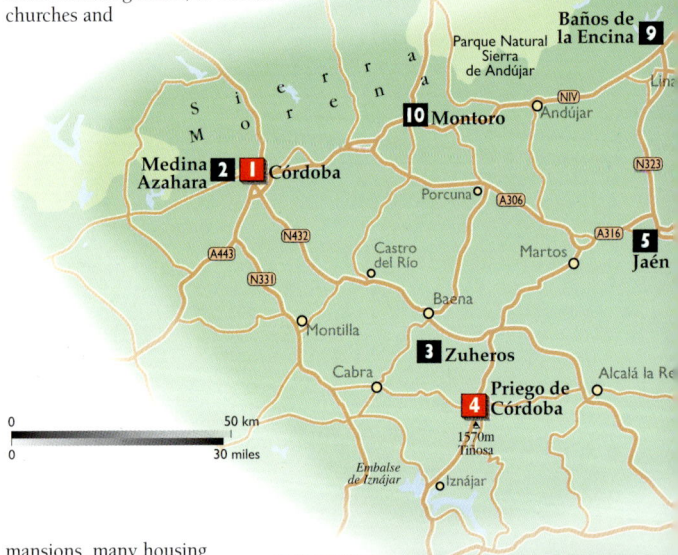

Parque Natural
Sierra
de Andújar

Baños de
la Encina **9**

Lin

10 Montoro

NIV
Andújar

Medina
Azahara **2** **1** Córdoba

N323

Porcuna

A306

A316

5
Jaén

N432

Castro
del Río

Martos

A443

N331

Baena

Montilla

3 Zuheros

Cabra

Priego de
4 Córdoba

Alcalá la Re

1570m
Tiñosa

0 ————— 50 km
0 ————— 30 miles

Embalse
de Iznájar

Iznájar

mansions, many housing museums and art galleries.

For a mix of the Moorish and Renaissance on a more intimate scale, go south from Córdoba, through olive groves and vineyards, to see pretty hill villages, in particular Priego de Córdoba, crammed with handsome buildings and elegant monuments.

Previous page: Cazorla and the olive fields of Jaén province

★ Don't Miss

1 Córdoba ➤ 114
4 Priego de
  Córdoba ➤ 120
6 Baeza ➤ 122
7 Parque Natural de
  Cazorla y Segura ➤ 124
8 Úbeda ➤ 126

At Your Leisure

2 Medina Azahara ➤ 128
3 Zuheros ➤ 128
5 Jaén ➤ 129
9 Baños de la
  Encina ➤ 130
10 Montoro ➤ 130

The province of Jaén, less accessible and less immediately rewarding than its neighbour, also contains treasures. Jaén city has a monumental cathedral and a bustling commercial and social life but is surpassed for overall charm by its smaller neighbours, Baeza and Úbeda. Both contain superb Renaissance buildings in honey-coloured stone, yet remain country towns with the easygoing atmosphere of provincial Spain. For lovers of the outdoors, there are the magnificent mountains of the Sierra de Cazorla on Jaén's eastern border, ideal for the peace and quiet of woodland walks or for visits to isolated villages.

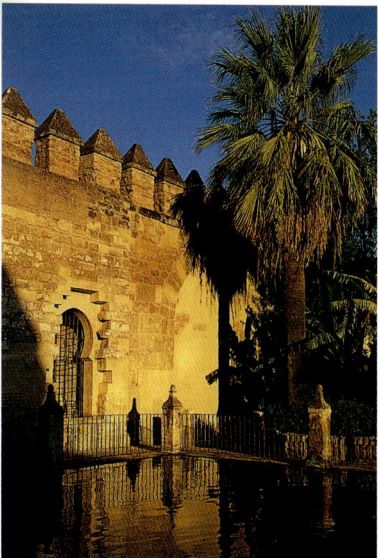

Segura de
la Sierra

N322

8 **Úbeda**

eza   Cazorla

7 **Parque
Natural de
Cazorla y
Segura**

Jódar

ra
ina

Pozo
Alcón

Guadahortuna

l Harana

Left: Narrow streets and jumbled houses in the mountain village of Zuheros

Right: Córdoba's Alcázar, a haven of peace and quiet

Explore Moorish Córdoba, then drive through wine country to the baroque treasures of Priego de Córdoba. Move on through the olive groves of Jaén province to Renaissance Baeza and Úbeda, taking in the mountain landscapes of the Sierra de Cazorla.

Córdoba and Jaén in Five Days

Day One

Morning

Visit Córdoba's **Mezquita** (right, ➤ 115–16), then stroll round the streets of the **Judería** (➤ 117), visiting the old **synagogue** (➤ 117) on the way. Lunch in the bar of Pepé de la Judería or of El Rincón de Carmen, both in Calle Romero.

Afternoon

Visit the palace and gardens of the **Alcázar de los Reyes Cristianos** (➤ 117), then enjoy a short siesta. Take an early *tapas* tour followed by a late evening meal before rounding off the day with a feast of classical flamenco at the Tablao Cardenal (➤ 136) opposite the Mezquita.

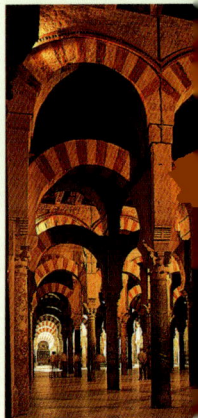

Day Two

Morning

Explore the quieter streets to the east of the Mezquita, or visit one of Córdoba's lesser-known attractions, such as the **Museo Arqueológico** (➤ 118) or the **Palacio Museo de Viana** (➤ 119).

Afternoon

Head southeast through the Montilla wine-producing country to **Priego de Córdoba** (➤ 120), perhaps visiting the charming hill village of **Zuheros** (left, ➤ 128) on the way. Stay overnight in Priego and enjoy the town's baroque churches and fountains and its charming old quarter, the Barrio de la Villa, in the mellow light of the late afternoon and early evening.

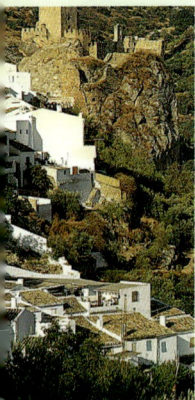

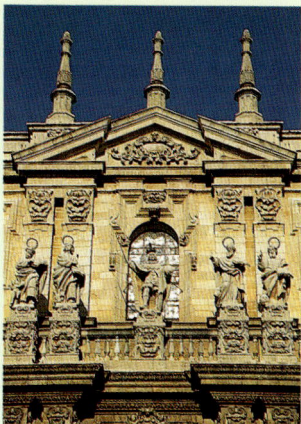

Day Three

Morning
Take the scenic road north from Priego, then follow the A316 east, calling in at **Jaén** (➤ 129–30), if you have time, to see the cathedral (left) and the Arab baths. Continue to **Baeza** (➤ 122).

Afternoon
After exploring Baeza's Renaissance buildings, such as the **Palacio de Jabalquinto** and the **cathedral**, take in the evening scene in the central Paseo de la Constitución. Stay overnight.

Day Four

Morning
Enjoy breakfast with the locals at the Bar Cafetería Mercantil on the corner of Plaza de España. Then drive some 50km to **Cazorla** (➤ 124), on the western edge of the Sierra de Cazorla, for an overnight stay.

Afternoon
Make for the nearby mountains after lunch for a scenic drive, or a stroll amid the pinewoods of the **Parque Natural de Cazorla y Segura** (➤ 124–5).

Day Five

Morning
Head west to **Úbeda** (➤ 126–7) and visit the remarkable buildings that enclose the Plaza de Vázquez de Molina. Make time to visit the Museo de Alfarería (Pottery Museum) and, if possible, Calle de Valencia (➤ 135), where Úbeda's potters produce some of the finest ceramics in Spain.

Afternoon
After lunch, set off back to Córdoba. On the way, if there's time, visit the hilltop village of **Baños de la Encina** and its magnificent Moorish castle (right, ➤ 130).

Córdoba

One of the greatest Islamic buildings of all time, the Mezquita (the Great Mosque) stands at the heart of Córdoba's old quarter on the banks of the Río Guadalquivir. There are always crowds there, of course, but you can find yourself alone just a few streets away, on the trail of some of the city's other fine buildings, monuments and museums, its fashionable shops and craft galleries, or some of the best bars in Andalucía.

Once a Roman city, Córdoba was occupied by Visigoths, and then in the 8th century by the Moors. The city became the capital of Muslim Spain, and for 200 years a succession of gifted rulers turned it into a glittering rival to Baghdad and Damascus. In 1236, Córdoba fell to the Christians who, through neglect, made the city a byword for decay. It was only in the 20th century that the city revived as a centre for light industry, agriculture and tourism.

Above: The Mezquita dominates Córdoba's skyline

Below: Córdoban carriage driver at rest

➕ 198–199

Tourist Information
➕ 198 B2 ✉ Calle de Torrijos 10 (J de A) ☎ 957 47 12 35
➕ 198 B2 ✉ Plaza Judá Levi (OMT) ☎ 957 20 05 22

The Mezquita

Much of Islamic Córdoba survives and nowhere more triumphantly than in the Mezquita. The main body of the Mezquita dates from between the 8th and 12th centuries, but what makes it remarkable is the presence of a cathedral choir and high altar at the heart of the mosque, added in the 16th century after the Christian Reconquest.

The famous clustered arches of the Mezquita

The blank, massive exterior walls of the Mezquita are typical of Moorish style; external decoration was of little importance to Islam and public buildings were always constructed with potential defence in mind. Only the splendid carvings on the arched entrance gateways hint at the marvels within.

Go through the Puerto del Perdón, beside the Torre del Alminar, into the **Patio de los Naranjos** (Courtyard of the Orange Trees), where Muslim worshippers once carried out their ritual ablutions. A stall in the back wall of the courtyard sells entrance tickets to the mosque, which you enter through the modest doors of the Puerta de las Palmas (directly opposite the Puerta del Perdón). Once inside, thickets of pillars stretch away in all directions. Over 1,000 pillars – some plain, others multicoloured columns of marble, jasper and onyx – support semicircular and horseshoe arches composed of alternating stripes of red brick and white stone. The impression created is of great depth, intimacy and mysteriousness. In Moorish times, light would have flooded in from the Patio de los Naranjos through open doorways at prayer time; these doors are now permanently closed.

The finest example of Islamic design is on the far side of the building. At the end of the widest aisle is the *maksura* (the area where the ruling caliphs prayed), with the *mihrab* (prayer

Royal Disapproval

The intrusion of the cathedral into the Mezquita was condemned by the Emperor Charles V; he had supported the idea initially, but was horrified when he saw what had been done and accused the Archbishop of Córdoba of having "destroyed what was unique in the world".

niche, indicating the direction of Mecca). Far more than a simple niche, the Mezquita's *mihrab* is a distinct chamber, its entrance framed by a beautiful horseshoe arch. Even from behind the barrier that keeps the public at a distance you are aware of the brilliant light that reflects off the coloured mosaics cladding the walls and roof.

The central dome in front of the *mihrab* is supported by intersecting ribs that form a star shape, a design new for its time that was copied by later Christian architects in churches throughout Europe. It was this remarkable merging of structural forms with decorativeness that distinguished Muslim architecture and that is seen so superbly in the Mezquita.

At the centre of the Mezquita, implanted within the mosque in 1523 by the Christian rulers of Córdoba, is the open-sided **cathedral** *coro* (choir) and *capilla mayor* (high altar chapel). Although they are undoubtedly ill-judged intrusions in terms of the Mezquita as a whole, choir and chapel have no enclosing walls and are masked in part by the Islamic columns that crowd round them. Looked at in isolation, their Gothic and Renaissance elements, the superbly carved choir stalls and slim, twisted pillars, are of great beauty. More fitting post-Muslim additions are the **Capilla Real** of 1258 and the 14th-century **Capilla de Villaviciosa**, the latter incorporating a *mihrab* of the early 9th century. Both chapels display the glazed panels and elegant arches typical of the *mudéjar* style (➤ 8).

The 10th-century *maksura* and *mihrab* are some of the finest examples of Islamic architecture in the Mezquita

---

✚ 198 B2 ✉ Calle Torrijos 10 ☎ 957 47 05 12 🕐 Mon–Sat 10–7, Apr–Sep; 10–5, Oct–Mar; Sun and holidays 3.30–7 💰 Expensive

Mass is celebrated in the cathedral each morning. Entrance to the rest of the Mezquita is free during this time (Mon–Sat 9–10, Sun 9–11). You cannot enter the cathedral itself unless you intend staying for the duration of the service.

The Judería and Alcázar

Spreading out to the west of the Mezquita is a warren of narrow streets. This area is the Judería, Córdoba's medieval Jewish quarter.

Close to the Mezquita, the streets of the Judería are awash with souvenir shops, but you can still find some enchanting corners such as the flower-filled Callejón de las Flores, a narrow cul-de-sac whose walls neatly frame the Mezquita's belfry. At the heart of the Judería, in Plaza Maimónides, you come to the **Museo Taurino** (Museum of Bullfighting), all bulls' heads and gloomy bravado.

To the left of the Museo Taurino is Calle Judíos, where there is an impressive statue of Moses Maimonides, the great 12th-century Jewish philosopher and theologian, who was born in Córdoba. Further up the street is the small, well-preserved 14th-century **synagogue**, sole Andalucian survivor of the Jewish expulsion in 1492. Nearby is a modern reconstruction of a **Zoco**, an Arab souk or market; craft shops and a bar overlook a charming patio. Calle Judíos leads to the **Puerta de Almodóvar**, a 14th-century gateway in Córdoba's ancient walls.

Beyond the Judería, on the banks of the river, stands the **Alcázar de los Reyes Cristianos** (Palace of the Christian Kings). It was built in the late 13th century by the Christian conquerors of al-Andalus as a replacement for a Moorish Alcázar that stood alongside the Mezquita. For many years it was the headquarters of the Inquisition and became a prison in the 19th century, though today its glorious gardens, filled with colourful flowers and shrubs and shimmering pools and fountains, barely hint at its grim past. The surviving buildings are somewhat stark, but contain superb Roman mosaics recovered from various parts of the city.

A statue in the Judería commemorates the 12th-century Córdoban philosopher Moses Maimonides

Alcázar de los Reyes Cristianos
✚ 198 B1
✉ Plaza Campo Santo de los Mártires
☎ 957 42 01 51
🕐 Tue–Sat 10–2 and 4.30–6.30, Sun and holidays 9.30–3
✋ Moderate (free Fri)

Museo Taurino
✚ 198 B2
✉ Plaza Maimónides 5
☎ 957 20 10 56
🕐 Tue–Sat 10–2 and 4.30–6.30, Sun and holidays 9.30–3
✋ Moderate (free Fri)

Sinagoga (Synagogue)
✚ 198 A2
✉ Calle Judíos
☎ 957 20 29 28
🕐 Tue–Sat 10–1.30 and 3.30–5.30, Sun 10–1.30
✋ Inexpensive (free with EU passport)

Other Sights

Left: Keeping cool in the Plaza de las Tendillas

North of the Mezquita, in an area of narrow streets far less visited than the Judería (➤ 117), is Córdoba's **Museo Arqueológico** (Archaeological Museum) in a Renaissance mansion, the Palacio de los Páez, on tree-shaded Plaza Jerónimo Páez. The palace has coffered ceilings and elegant staircases, and displays prehistoric, Roman and Moorish exhibits. Highlights include Roman mosaics and an exquisite miniature of a bronze stag, found at the ruined 10th-century palace-city of Medina Azahara 6km west of Córdoba (➤ 128).

Just inland from the river is **Plaza del Potro** (Square of the Colt), with a statue of a rearing horse on the central fountain. The plaza was once a livestock market surrounded by medieval brothels and drinking dens, the haunt of such Cordoban characters as the celebrated poet Luis de Góngora (1561–1627). On the plaza's western side is the old Posada del Potro Inn, mentioned in Cervantes's *Don Quijote*, and now a cultural centre. Opposite is the Hospital de la Caridad, housing the **Museo de Bellas Artes** (Museum of Fine Arts). The decorated ceilings of the ground-floor rooms are as fine as some of the paintings; the collection includes work by Zurbarán, Goya and Murillo. On the other side of the central patio is a museum dedicated to Cordoban artist Julio Romero de Torres, most of whose paintings feature sultry nudes.

The heart of the modern city is **Plaza de las Tendillas**, where fountains spout sparkling jets of water from ground level – irresistible to local youngsters in hot weather. As you relax at a café table, you may hear the plaza's clock chiming flamenco phrases. From Plaza de las Tendillas, you can walk west down the shopping street of Conde de Gondomar to the pedestrianised Avenida del Gran Capitán, scene of Córdoba's evening *paseo*.

Right: Julio Romero de Torres's painting *El Pecado* (The Sin) is full of erotic symbolism

TAKING A BREAK

Begin your evening with a sherry in the popular bar or cool leafy patio of **El Caballo Rojo** (Calle Cardenal Herrero 28), reputed to be the oldest restaurant in Córdoba.

CÓRDOBA: INSIDE INFO

Top tips Many attractions have free entry on Fridays. These include the Alcázar, the Museo Taurino and the Museo Julio Romero de Torres. EU citizens also have free entrance to a number of museums and other attractions, but you must show your passport.
• Opening times of Córdoba's sights and museums change frequently. Check with the tourist office for the latest timetables before planning visits.

Hidden gems Córdoba stages a **Fiesta de los Patios** (Festival of the Patios) during the first week of May each year, when flower-filled patios normally hidden within private houses are open for visits, often to the accompaniment of music, including flamenco.
• The 14th-century **Palacio Museo de Viana** (✚ 199 D5, Rejas de Don Gome 2, tel: 957 48 01 34, admission moderate) has 12 patios, each with its fountain and with roses, jasmine, wisteria and bougainvillaea woven together with geraniums. Be warned, though, the Spanish-language guided tours of the palace's rooms are rather regimented.

One to miss Crossing the much renovated **Puente Romano** (Roman Bridge) over the sluggish Río Guadalquivir offers fine views of the Mezquita, but the walkways are very narrow and the traffic is constant.

Museo Arqueológico
✚ 198 C3 ✉ Plaza Jerónimo Páez ☎ 957 47 40 11 🕐 Wed–Sat 9–8, Tue 3–8, Sun and holidays 9–3 💶 Inexpensive (free with EU passport)

Museo de Bellas Artes
✚ 199 D3 ✉ Plaza del Potro 1 ☎ 957 47 33 45 🕐 Wed–Sat 9–8, Tue 3–8, Sun and holidays 9–3 💶 Inexpensive (free with EU passport)

Museo Julio Romero de Torres
✚ 199 D3 ✉ Plaza del Potro 1 ☎ 957 49 19 09 🕐 Tue–Sat 10–2 and 4.30–6.30, Sun and holidays 9.30–2.30 💶 Moderate (free Fri)

4

Priego de Córdoba

The quiet provincial town of Priego de Córdoba is
distinguished by its many baroque churches and a
magnificent Renaissance fountain. In the Moorish quarter,
the Barrio de la Villa, alleyways wind between whitewashed
houses, dripping with flowers.

Priego stands at the edge of an escarpment beneath the highest
mountain in Córdoba province, La Tiñosa (1,570m). The town
dates from at least Roman times and was fought over by
Moorish and Christian forces during the 13th and 14th
centuries; but it was the 18th-century boom in silk production
that produced Priego's legacy of outstanding buildings.

At the centre of Priego is the busy **Plaza de Andalucía** and
adjoining **Plaza de la Constitución**, where the life of the
town is gossiped over each morning. Historic Priego lies to the
east of Plaza de Andalucía. Here, among other fine buildings,
is the **Iglesia de la Asunción** (Church of the Ascension),
Priego's most famous monument. Behind the church's plain,
whitewashed exterior lie two of Spain's finest baroque
treasures: a superb carved *retablo* (altarpiece) and an amazing
sagrario (sacristy). The latter is a froth of white stucco
erupting into a cupola.

From Plaza de Santa Anna, alongside the church, the Calle
Real leads into the **Barrio de la Villa**, where the white walls
of the houses are hung with baskets of geraniums and draped

The Fuente del
Rey (below and
right), an 18th-
century baroque
extravaganza,
lies at the heart
of a peaceful
plaza

The flower-
bedecked heart
of Priego de
Córdoba's
Barrio de la
Villa

PRIEGO DE CÓRDOBA: INSIDE INFO

Top tips Priego's **churches** are usually open 11–1, and are often open for services in the evenings.
• The tourist office can organise **tours of Priego's finest sights** – a good idea if your time is short. You should make a prior arrangement for such a tour.

Hidden gem The **Carnicerías Reales** (near San Pedro Church) is a 16th-century slaughterhouse and market, now shorn of its original associations and preserved for its architectural value. The arcaded and cobbled patio of the old market, with mullioned windows framing a view over olive groves, stages occasional exhibitions by local artists.

with bougainvillaea. The quarter is free of cars, but unfortunately not of scooters and motorcycles. At the barrio's eastern edge is the **Paseo de Adarve**, a promenade giving great views of the surrounding countryside. Northwest of the barrio is the **Iglesia de San Pedro** (Church of St Peter), with a splendidly painted main altar.

Don't miss the elegant **Fuente del Rey** in a peaceful square at the west end of town (reached from Plaza de Andalucía by following the broad Calle del Río). Water pours from dozens of faucets in the form of grinning masks into the fountain's sequence of stepped basins. At the centre of all this glittering water are statues of sea deities Neptune and Amphitrite. Behind the Fuente del Rey, in dappled shade, is a second fountain, the Italianate, late 16th-century **Fuente de la Virgen de la Salud**.

TAKING A BREAK

After you've ogled the lavish confection of white stucco in the Iglesia de la Asunción, enjoy a glass of wine at **El Alijibe** (➤ 134) across the square.

✚ 195 F3

Tourist Information
✉ Calle del Río 33 ☎ 957 70 06 25

Parking
Car park in Plaza Palenque, at the west end of

Carrera de las Monjas. Busy in the mornings.

Iglesia de la Asunción
✉ Plaza de Abad Palomino ⊙ Daily 11–1.30 and 5.30–7

6

Baeza

In Baeza you step back into a more leisured Andalucía. This is a genial town that has been spared too much modern encroachment on its Renaissance and Gothic buildings and its delightful central plazas and streets.

Baeza sits on the edge of an escarpment overlooking olive groves and wheatfields. The best place to begin your exploration is in the **Plaza del Pópulo.** This exquisite Renaissance square, known also as Plaza de los Leones because of the ancient stone lions adorning its weatherworn fountain, is enclosed by the handsome facade of an old slaughterhouse and the twin archways of the Moorish Puerta de Jaén and the 16th-century Arco de Villalar. At the top end of the square is the elegant Casa de Pópulo, once a court-house and now Baeza's tourist office.

To the left of the tourist office, a flight of steps, the Escalerillas de la Audiencia, leads to a narrow lane, Calle Romanones, that takes you to Plaza Santa Cruz and the **Palacio de Jabalquinto**, whose Gothic facade is studded with diamond-shaped bosses. The interior courtyard of the palace has a fountain and is surrounded by a double tier of arcades from which a fine baroque staircase leads to the upper floor. Directly opposite the palace is the little Romanesque **Iglesia de Santa Cruz** with traces of Visigothic arches and of the mosque the church replaced.

Just up from Plaza Santa Cruz is quiet Plaza de Santa María with its central fountain in the form of a triumphal arch. The square is dominated by Baeza's **Catedral de Santa María**, which has a spacious Renaissance nave designed by Andrés de Vandelvira, the architect of many of Úbeda's buildings (▶ 126–7). The main altar has an exuberant altarpiece and there are a number of splendid *rejas* – wrought-iron grilles that screen side chapels. The cathedral was built on the site of a mosque and some remains of the earlier building have been uncovered in the Gothic cloister.

On low ground below Baeza's historical quarter is the town centre, busy Plaza de España and tree-lined Paseo de la Constitución, where youngsters play football and cycle madly around the central concourse. The Paseo is lined by arcaded buildings and numerous bars and cafés. Stroll west from here for a look at the ornate 16th-century facade of the town hall in Calle Benavides.

The stone lions in the central fountain in the Plaza del Pópulo have given the square its popular name, Plaza de los Leones

TAKING A BREAK

Join the locals at the friendly **La Góndola** (▶ 134), one of Baeza's most atmospheric bars, and indulge in their delicious *patatas baezanas.*

Baeza stands on a lofty escarpment overlooking the great central plain of Jaén province

➕ 196 C3

Tourist Information
✉ Plaza del Pópulo (Plaza de los Leones)
☎ 953 74 04 44

Parking
There is convenient parking round the Paseo de la Constitución but spaces are limited during the morning and evening.

Palacio de Jabalquinto
✉ Plaza Santa Cruz
🕐 Tue–Sun 10–1 and 4–6
✋ Free

Iglesia de Santa Cruz
✉ Plaza Santa Cruz
🕐 Mon–Sat 11–1 and 4–6
✋ Free

Catedral de Santa María
✉ Plaza de Santa María
🕐 Daily 10.30–1 and 4–6
✋ Free

BAEZA: INSIDE INFO

Top tips Make sure you have change when you visit the cathedral. At the west end of the church is an uninteresting painting of St Peter. But pop a coin in a slot and the painting rumbles aside to reveal, to musical accompaniment, the **silver monstrance** used in Baeza's holy processions.

• Don't be alarmed by the number of uniformed Civil Guards strolling around Baeza in the evening. Most of the Guards are students from the nearby Academia de Guardias de la Guardia Civil.

Hidden gem Halfway along Calle Romanones, the narrow side street of Calle Arcos de las Escuelas leads down left. At No 2 is the shop and **studio of sculptor Diego Lozano Jiminéz**, where remarkable marble replicas of several of Baeza's buildings are on display.

7

Parque Natural de Cazorla y Segura

In the Parque Natural de Cazorla y Segura, rugged mountains rise to over 2,000m, with deep rocky gorges and thickly forested valleys, and tiny hilltop villages scattered throughout. The gateway to the park and the main settlement is the attractive town of Cazorla.

Cazorla stands at the western edge of the Sierra de Cazorla directly below the great cliff faces of the mountain of Peña de los Halcones (Crag of the Falcons). The town straggles along the base of the mountain beginning at its busy main square, Plaza Constitución, from where the main street, Calle Dr Muñoz, leads to the far older Plaza de la Corredera, a lively square lined by cafés and shops. Beyond here, winding lanes take you past a lookout point, **Balcón del Pintor Zabaletato**, with glorious views of the ruined church of Santa María and the partially ruined castle, **La Yedra** (or Las Cuatro Esquinas, the Four Corners) that rises above. Below the church and castle is the heart of local life, Plaza Santa María with its Renaissance fountain.

The infant Río Guadalquivir flows through the Sierra de Cazorla wilderness

The Natural Park

The Sierras de Cazorla y Segura, together with lesser ranges, make up the largest natural park in Andalucía, covering an area of 214,000 hectares. The mountains of the park support forests of introduced evergreen oaks and pines as well as native species such as elder, maple and juniper. There are over 1,200 species of plants, and the animals of the Sierras include red deer, fox, wild cat, Spanish ibex and wild boar. You may also see some of the birds of prey that congregate in the Sierras, including griffon vultures, golden eagles and peregrine falcons (sometimes visible from roadside vantage points).

A network of good roads makes driving within the park area a pleasure. There is good walking in the area around Cazorla, but deeper into the mountains there are only a few waymarked paths. Local companies organise day walks, horse riding, mountain biking and four-wheel-drive trips into more remote areas (► 136). You can book such activities at agencies in Cazorla town.

You enter the park about 2km east of Cazorla, just beyond the village of Iruela with its tiny castle perched on a pinnacle of rock. A 34-km drive north-

The Sierra de Cazorla's wildlife includes magnificent peregrine falcons

PARQUE NATURAL DE CAZORLA Y SEGURA: INSIDE INFO

Top tips Try to get hold of a copy of the *Mapa y Guía Excursionista*, a map and (Spanish only) booklet about the park. The map gives the best available details on roads, paths and tracks. The informative booklet gives information on the park's wildlife and describes a few walking routes.

• If you set off along an unwaymarked path or track in the heart of the Sierras, make a note of any junctions so that you can retrace your steps.

• Cazorla has a daily **market** in Plaza del Mercado, between the car park and the main shopping street, with local produce and crafts.

Hidden gem The restored tower of the castle of La Yedra in Cazorla houses a **folklore museum** displaying farming artefacts, olive-oil presses and reconstructions of traditional rural life (Plaza de Santa María, Cazorla, open Mon–Sat 9–2.30, Sun 10–12.30, Jun–Sep, admission free).

Looking down on Cazorla from the high crags above the town east through the mountains will take you from Cazorla to the Centro de Interpretación Torre del Vinagre. The interpretation centre can be very busy in summer but it has excellent displays outlining the park's ecology. Nearby is a botanical garden with specimens of Sierra plant life.

✚ 197 E4

Parque Natural de Cazorla y Segura Tourist Information
✉ Parque Natural Information Centre: Calle Martínez Falero 11, Cazorla ☎ 953 72 01 25 or 953 71 30 40

Cazorla Tourist Information
✉ Paseo del Santo Cristo 17 ☎ 953 71 01 02

Parking
There is a car park just down from the Plaza de la Constitución

🔴 8

Úbeda

Úbeda hides an architectural treasure at its heart. Plaza de Vázquez de Molina is an enclave of exquisite Renaissance buildings, claimed to be the finest such complex in Spain.

The plaza was created by medieval Úbeda's leading families, the Cobos and the Molinas, who acquired great wealth from a 16th-century boom in textile production. Both families employed the best architects and artists to immortalise their names in stone, among them the finest architect of the time, Andrés de Vandelvira.

The enthralling **Capilla del Salvador** (Chapel of the Holy Saviour) was one of Vandelvira's creations, based on designs by architect Diego de Siloé. Its main facade combines classical features with lingering touches of earlier Gothic motifs; the whole is a magnificent example of the plateresque style (so called because of its resemblance to *platería*, the intricate work of medieval silversmiths). The chapel's cool interior provides a display of Gothic vaulting, gilded retables and Renaissance carving. The chancel has a coffered vault and is separated from the nave by an exquisite grille. The altarpiece is a beautifully restored representation of the Transfiguration of Christ. Built for Francisco de los Cobos as a private place of worship, the chapel is still privately owned.

The Palacio de las Cadenas, one of the notable buildings on Plaza de Vázquez de Molina

Other notable buildings in the plaza include the **Palacio de las Cadenas** (Palace of the Chains) designed with an elegant classical facade for Juan Vázquez de Molina by Vandelvira, and now Úbeda's town hall. The **Museo de Alfarería** (Pottery Museum) in the cellars of the palace displays many examples of the green-glaze pottery for which Úbeda is noted. Directly opposite is the church of

---

🔲 196 C4

Tourist Information
✉ Palacio del Contadero, Calle Baja del Marqués ☎ 953 75 08 97

Capilla del Salvador
✉ Plaza de Vázquez de Molina ☎ Daily 10–2 and 5–7.30

Museo de Alfarería (Pottery Museum)
✉ Plaza de Vázquez de Molina ☎ 953 75 04 40 🕐 Mon–Sat 10.30–2.30 and 4.30–7

The Hills of Úbeda

In medieval times Úbeda became synonymous with absentmindedness and the phrase "wandering across the hills of Úbeda" is still used to describe those who are forgetful. Its origins lie in a romantic tale. A young Christian knight missed a crucial battle because he was with his lover, a beautiful Muslim girl. When asked by King Ferdinand III where he had been, he replied, "Sire. On those hills...".

Santa María de las Reales Alcázares, whose Gothic cloister stands on the foundations of the mosque of Islamic Úbeda.

Just north of the plaza is the old market square, **Plaza del Primero de Mayo**, scene of bullfights and horrifying *autos da fé* (trials by fire) during the Inquisition. It contains the old town hall with elegant arcades, and the church of **San Pablo** with a fine Gothic portal and balcony. Narrow lanes lead off north through a splendid 13th-century gateway with double horseshoe arches, the Puerta de Losal. Beyond here is Calle de Valencia and the workshops of potters still making Úbeda's distinctive ceramics (➤ 135).

TAKING A BREAK

Take a step back in time and stop off for coffee at Úbeda's 16th-century *parador* on Plaza de Vázquez de Molina (➤ 134).

Above: The 18th-century Iglesia de la Trinidad, one of Úbeda's few baroque buildings

ÚBEDA: INSIDE INFO

Top tips You will have to find your way through Úbeda's everyday streets to reach Plaza de Vázquez de Molina. Look for signs that read *Zona Monumental*.
• Calle Real, the long narrow street between the main square, Plaza de España, and Plaza de Vázquez de Molina, has craft shops selling the **esparto grass artefacts** traditional to Úbeda.

Hidden gem Walk down the right-hand side of the Capilla del Salvador to reach Plaza de Santa Lucia and a viewpoint that looks out over olive groves to the hazy mountain wall of the Sierra de Cazorla.

At Your Leisure

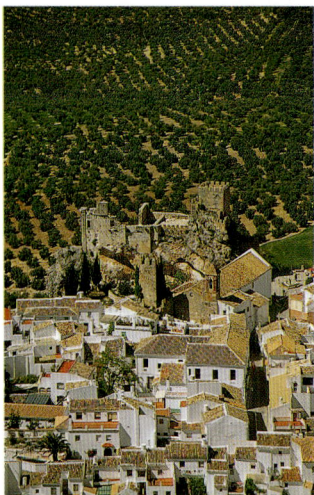

Zuheros and its Moorish castle, set against a backdrop of olive groves

2 Medina Azahara

The ruins of the 10th-century palace-city of Medina Azahara lie about 7km west from Córdoba. The complex was begun in 936 and in its heyday reflected some of the most sumptuous architecture and design of Moorish al-Andalus. Much of the site is still being restored, and work on recreating the luxurious gardens is ongoing. The main attraction of the complex is the superb Hall of Abd al-Rahman III, where the lavish marble carvings have been carefully restored. The best way of reaching the site is by car, though a bus service from Córdoba also operates. Organsied tours are also run from Córdoba.

🚹 196 A3 ✉ 7km west of Córdoba
☎ 957 32 91 30 🕒 Tue–Sat 10–2,
6–8.30, Sun and public holidays 10–2,
Apr–Sep; Tue–Sat 10–2, 4–6.30, Sun
and public holidays 10–2, Oct–Mar
💲 Inexpensive

3 Zuheros

The narrow streets of Zuheros are a delight to explore; their charm reflects the village's situation on a rocky hillside amid the Sierra Subbética hills near Priego de Córdoba. Built into the rocks above the houses are the remains of a Moorish castle. In Plaza de la Paz are the handsome 18th-century **Iglesia de la Virgen de los Remedios** and the village **museum** displaying artefacts from the prehistoric, Roman and Moorish periods. Zuheros is noted for its cheeses and olive oil, which you can buy from the tourist centre at the entrance to the village. The **Cueva del Cerro de los Murciélagos** (Cave of the Bats), with fascinating rock formations, lies about 4km east of Zuheros. Archaeological finds here during the mid-19th century included mummified bodies and wall paintings that indicate use by neolithic people.

🚹 196 B3

Tourist Information
Entrance to Zuheros from north (A316)
☎ 957 69 47 75

Zuheros Museum
✉ Plaza de la Paz ☎ 957 69 45 45
🕒 Sat–Sun 12.30–2.30 and 4.30–6.30
💲 Inexpensive

Cueva del Cerro de los Murciélagos
🚹 196 B3 ☎ 957 69 45 45 🕒 Hourly
tours Tue–Thu, Sat–Sun 11–1 and 4–6,
Apr–Sep 💲 Inexpensive

🖪 Jaén

The town of Jaén is worth
visiting for its majestic
cathedral, restored Arab
baths and its old quarter.
The **cathedral**, on Plaza de
Santa María, was erected over
250 years from the mid-16th
century. The huge west facade is a
dramatic display of elegant
Corinthian columns and statuary, the
whole framed by soaring twin towers.
The cavernous interior has clusters of

Santo Rostro (Holy Face) claimed to
be the cloth used by St Veronica to
wipe Christ's brow on the way to his
crucifixion. It is on public display
every Friday.

Jaén's restored Arab baths, the
Baños Árabes, lie beneath the 16th-
century Palacio de Villadompardo
(housing an arts and crafts museum).
The splendid brickwork ceilings are
pierced by star-shaped lights and
supported by typically Moorish
columns and horseshoe arches. A
glass floor reveals Roman remains.
The **Museo Provincial** has
Phoenician, Roman and Moorish artefacts and, in a building adjoining the
main museum, a display of outstanding 5th-century BC stone sculptures.
Moorish character survives in Jaén's
labyrinthine quarters of **La
Magdalena** and **San Juan** on the
northeastern slopes of the scrub-
covered hill of Santa Catalina, itself
crowned by a ruined Moorish castle.

➕ 196 C3

Tourist Information
✉ Calle Arquitecto Bergés 1 ☎ 953 22
27 37

Catedral
✉ Plaza de Santa María ◷ Daily
8.30–1 and 5–8 💶 Free

Baños Árabes
✉ Plaza de Santa Luisa de Marillac
☎ 953 23 62 92 ◷ Tue–Fri 9–8,

**The magnificent facade of Jaén cathedral
towers above the roofs of the city**

Corinthian columns on a monumental scale, and the choir has exquisite
carvings. The cathedral contains the

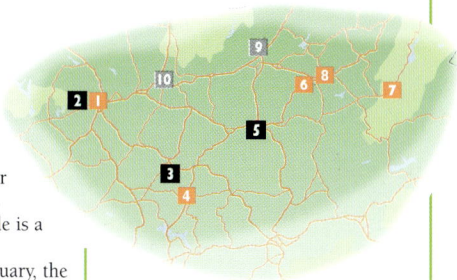

Sat–Sun
9.30–2.30 🛇 Free with EU passport

Museo Provincial
✉ Paseo de la Estación 27 ☎ 953 25
06 00 🕐 Wed–Sat 9–8, Tue 3–8, Sun
9–3 🛇 Free with EU passport

9 Baños de la Encina

Baños de la Encina has one of the
finest hilltop castles in Spain. The
14 towers and massive keep of this
Moorish fortress dominate the tiny
village below. The castle was built
between 967 and 986 by the
Córdoban Emirate as an outlying
defence against belligerent clans in
the nearby Sierra Morena and Sierra
de Cazorla (▶ 124–5). To visit the
castle, ask for the key at the tourist
information office, or at the town hall
in Plaza de la Constitución. The
interior of the castle is now a gaunt
empty space, but you can climb the
great keep, the Tower of Homage,
from which there are sweeping views.
Climb with care: the stairways are
unlit and roosting pigeons tend to fly
suddenly from the gloom. The castle's
narrow, unprotected parapet encircles
the inner walls, but is best avoided.

✠ 196 C4

Tourist Information
✉ Casa de la Juventud, off Plaza de la
Constitución

Previous pages and below: Skyline view of
the village of Baños de la Encina

10 Montoro

Montoro's appeal lies in the
relaxed and friendly atmosphere of its rambling streets
and the charm of its old
buildings. The town stands on
a spur of land within a loop of
the Río Guadalquivir that is
spanned by a handsome 15th-
century bridge. The long main street,
Calle Corredera, leads to the central
square, Plaza de España, and the
three-tiered tower of the church of
San Bartolomé. Opposite the church
is the old ducal palace, now the town
hall. North of the plaza, narrow alleyways lead into an older district,
where you'll find the church of Santa
María de la Mota, now a small
museum of mineralogy and archaeology. If you have time, seek out the
Casa de las Conchas at Calle Grajas
17, which is devoted to seashell decoration inside and out. The owners are
pleased to show visitors around.

✠ 196 B4

Tourist Information
✉ Plaza de España ☎ 957 16 00 89

Santa María de la Mota
✉ Plaza de Santa María 🕐 Sat 6–8,
Sun 11–1

Off the Beaten Track

Just 20km south of Priego de
Córdoba is a large lake, the **Embalse
de Iznájar**, where you can go sailing.
  In the far northeast of Jaén
province is **Segura de la Sierra**.
Approached by a seemingly endless
series of hairpin bends, this wonderful hilltop village has an old Moorish
castle, restored Arab baths, the
smallest bullring in Andalucía, a
Renaissance church and a fountain
with its own shoal of fish.

Where to... Stay

Prices
Expect to pay per person per night
£ up to €36   ££ €36–€96   £££ over €96

CÓRDOBA

Hostal Deanes £

This typical Córdoban private residence-turned-hostal has plenty of old-fashioned charm. A narrow *tapas* bar in front has impressive- (if indigestible-) sounding specials like thistles in almond sauce, while photos of local bullfighters are proudly displayed on the walls. The large central patio with tables and chairs has lived-in appeal; the rooms are simple and far enough from the street to be quiet, despite the location in the centre of town.

✚ 198 B2 ⊠ Calle Deanes 6, Córdoba ☎ 957 29 37 44

Hotel and Hostal Maestro £–££

Aside from price, there is not much difference between the hotel and hostel, tucked down a quiet side street one block back from the river. The hotel rooms look onto a gracious inner courtyard framed by arches, which means plenty of light; the Castilian-style furniture, gleaming marble and quality oil paintings add a touch of class. Rooms in the hostel are smaller, but the entrance patio is pure Córdoba with pots, plants, plates – even a canary in a cage.

✚ 199 D2 ⊠ Calle Romero Barros 4 & 6, Córdoba ☎ 957 47 24 10, fax: 957 47 53 95

Hotel Marisa ££

From the narrow street leading to it, the Marisa presents a traditional whitewashed facade. Located in the centre of the souvenir strip opposite the Mezquita, this 28-room accommodation is 35 years old; its underground parking is a major advantage. Sturdily furnished and comfortable rooms are more spacious than most and overlook an attractive patio. The downstairs bar and sitting area have an appealing, if slightly dowdy air.

✚ 198 B2 ⊠ Calle Cardenal Herrero 6, Córdoba ☎ 957 47 31 42, fax: 957 47 41 44

Mezquita Hotel ££

This was the 16th-century palace of the renowned Córdoban painter Julio Romero de Torres, and the hotel has retained an evocative historical ambience with paintings and antiques. There are original columns and stonework, plus a gracious central patio used for dining during the summer. The rooms have modern facilities and are furnished in a suitably regal fashion with satin drapes and ornate furniture. The location is ideal for sightseeing – right opposite the main entrance to the Mezquita.

✚ 198 C2 ⊠ Plaza Santa Catalina 1, Córdoba ☎ 957 47 55 85, fax: 957 47 62 19

Los Omeyas ££

Superbly located amid the tangle of back streets in Córdoba's former Jewish quarter, Los Omeyas has been refurbished to reflect the city's al-Andaluz heritage, with Mezquita-style arches, white marble and lattice work. A central patio provides access to comfortable, tastefully decorated rooms on two levels with air conditioning. Try for one on the top floor for a panoramic view of the ancient tower of the great Mezquita. Breakfast is a reasonable extra.

✚ 198 C2 ⊠ Calle Encarnación 17, Córdoba ☎ 957 49 22 67, fax: 957 49 16 59

PRIEGO DE CÓRDOBA

Hostal Rafi £

One of very few small hotels in town, the Rafi is right in the centre, with shops and the best-known baroque churches all nearby. Rooms are fairly ordinary but the baths are full-size and modern. A door from the lobby leads to the adjacent bar, which is usually packed with locals who've come to enjoy the good choice of *tapas* and light meals.

➕ **196 B3** ⊠ **Isabel La Católica 4, Priego de Córdoba** ☎ **957 54 07 49**

JAÉN

Parador Castillo de Santa Catalina ££

This is one of the most spectacular *paradores* in Spain, situated on the dramatic Cerro de Santa Catalina mountain amid the towers of a medieval Moorish castle. The rooms have luxurious canopied beds and balconies for marvelling at the view. The décor throughout is magnifi-

cent: a successful interplay of high-vaulted ceilings, baronial spaces and Islamic decorative touches. The restaurant, serving typical Jaén dishes, is also recommended.

➕ **196 C3** ⊠ **El Castillo de Santa Catalina, Jaén** ☎ **953 23 00 00; fax: 953 23 09 30; email: jaén@parador.es**

BAEZA

Hospedería Fuentenueva ££

It's difficult to imagine, but this exquisite, small (12-bedroom) hotel was once a women's prison. The stone walls are still here – as well as the quiet – but the interior has had a sophisticated overhaul with salmon-coloured and stencilled walls, marble floors, modern furnishings and bubbling fountains. The result is a great contemporary look. There are also regular art exhibitions, an excellent restaurant and an outdoor pool.

➕ **196 C3** ⊠ **Paseo Arca del Agua, Baeza** ☎ **953 74 31 00, fax: 953 74 31 00, www.rgo.net/fuentenueva**

Hostal El Patio £

Housed in the 16th-century palace of the Marqués Cuentacilla, on a cobbled side street leading to an old church, this hostel has homey appeal with grandma and children around. The name is appropriate: the central space is vast and filled with overstuffed, heavily brocaded furniture, interspersed with original columns. The rooms are basically furnished but comfortable enough, and the location is wonderfully quiet and central.

➕ **196 C3** ⊠ **Calle Conde Romanones 13, Baeza** ☎ **953 74 02 00**

CAZORLA

Hotel Guadalquivir £

This family-run hotel in the centre of town is a favourite with hikers for its good value and friendliness. The rooms are large and have recently been updated with heating and air conditioning as well as satellite TV. Breakfast is provided

for an extra charge, and owner Pedro is a great source of information ranging from the best *tapas* in town to the most beautiful walks.

➕ **197 D3** ⊠ **Calle Nueva 6, Cazorla** ☎ **953 72 02 68**

ÚBEDA

María de Molina ££

The hotel was newly opened in mid-2000 on the historical central plaza. It's in a 16th-century palace with many of the original elements remaining, such as the columned central patio, wall-hung tapestries and a magnificent stone fountain. Wicker furniture, ochre walls and plenty of palms and plants set the mood in the lobby and restaurant, while the rooms, solidly decorated with dark wood, have walk-in wardrobes and balconies over-looking Úbeda's grandest square.

➕ **196 C3** ⊠ **Plaza del Ayuntamiento s/n, Úbeda** ☎ **953 79 53 56, fax: 953 79 36 94, email: hotelmm@hotel-maria-de-molina.com**

Where to...
Eat and Drink

Prices
Expect to pay per person for a meal, including wine and service
£ up to €12   **££** €12–€30   **£££** over €30

CÓRDOBA

El Burlaero ££–£££

This restaurant is well known among Spaniards, who come from all over to enjoy game dishes of wild boar, pigeon, partridge, rabbit and Iberian pig. The bar is a cosy clutter with a backdrop of guitars, matador capes, hams, barrels and photos. A former Jewish house, the restaurant is spread over several rooms with low, beamed ceilings and typical Cordoban patio. Be bold and start your meal with the delicious local speciality *el salmonerejo*, a thick cold soup of tomato, garlic and egg.

🚹 198 B2 ✉ Calleja de la Hoguera 5, Córdoba ☎ 957 47 27 19, fax: 957 48 15 52 🕐 Daily 11–4.30, 7.30–11

Los Califas ££

Behind a narrow frontage with geranium-filled balconies is the sort of bar where you can happily sip Rioja and sample *tapas* for hours. It has a great atmosphere, with more locals than tourists. The decor consists of warm limestone, brilliant blue tiles and old brick, while the upstairs restaurant *terraza* has a stunning view of the Mezquita tower. The menu includes traditional Córdoban cuisine, as well as several Moroccan-style dishes.

🚹 198 B2 ✉ Calle Deanes 3, Córdoba ☎ 957 47 13 20, fax: 957 48 55 86 🕐 Tue–Sun 1–4.30, 8–midnight

El Rincón de Carmen ££–£££

A romantic-dinner-for-two kind of place, this 18th-century house in the heart of the Jewish quarter has a patio filled with jasmine. The menu is extensive, with an emphasis on rice dishes, including black rice (coloured by squid ink) and several Valencian paella favourites. In the adjacent café you can enjoy drinks and snacks relaxing in the comfort of cushioned cane chairs.

🚹 198 B2 ✉ Calle Romero 4, Córdoba ☎ 957 29 10 55 🕐 Daily noon–4, 8–11.30

Taberna Plateros £

This place dates from the 17th century. A large patio restaurant leads to the upstairs restaurant with more traditional marbled bar where blue collars and businessmen meet. Photographs of late local bullfighter Manolete line the walls, and the patio is decorated with giddily patterned tiles and bricks. The food is solid homestyle cooking, with the starters a meal in themselves.

🚹 199 D2 ✉ San Francisco 6, Córdoba ☎ 957 47 00 42 🕐 Tue–Sat 8–4, 7.30–midnight

Restaurante Vallina ££–£££

Opened in early 2000 as a small hotel-cum-restaurant at the back of the Mezquita, the building dates back an awesome 1,600 years, with Roman columns and an ancient well to prove it. Meat dishes take pride of place, with steaks cooked on a griddle at the table. Vegetarians have a tasty if limited selection, and the vast dessert trolley choice makes a welcome change from the flan and ice-cream norm.

🚹 198 C2 ✉ Corregidor Luis de la Cerda 83, Córdoba ☎ 957 49 87 50, fax: 957 49 87 51 🕐 Daily 8.30 pm–1 am

El Aljibe ££-£££

This is right on the corner of the main plaza. Dark wood, brick and terracotta tile make for cosy informality and the *tapas* choice is good, with some unusual local specialities like dates stuffed with bacon. If you're hungry, head for the restaurant downstairs where a three-course *menú del día* will cost you less than a round of drinks back home.

➕ 196 B3 ✉ Calle Abad Palomino 7, Priego de Córdoba ☎ 957 70 18 56 🕐 Daily 12.30–midnight. Closed Easter week and mid-Sep for the local *feria*

Casa Juanita ££

Owners Juan and Luisa love to introduce ancient local recipes into their menu, so the dishes are tasty and unusual. Extra virgin olive oil is a standard ingredient, made from

their own press. Other specialities include partridge salad, fillet of beef with tomatoes and peppers, and *alcachofas Luisa* (artichoke hearts with tomatoes and garlic). The restaurant is in the hotel of the same name; the décor is nothing special, but the food certainly is.

➕ 196 C3 ✉ Plaza del Arca del Agua s/n, Baeza ☎ 953 74 00 40 🕐 Tue–Sat 1.30–3, 8.30–11.30. Closed 24 and 31 Dec

La Góndola £

Old men in flat caps prop up the bar while noisy families hog the tables. During the winter, there is a roaring fire behind the bar and the low-beamed ceiling and brick-and-tile combo make this a particularly hospitable bar and restaurant. Try the *patatas baezanas* starter, the tasty house speciality of sautéed potatoes topped with fried mushrooms, parsley and garlic.

➕ 196 C3 ✉ Portales Carbonería 13, Baeza ☎ 953 74 29 84 🕐 Daily 8 am–midnight

Juan Carlos £-££

As the row of wild boar heads baring their teeth from the wall might lead you to expect, the menu includes a predominance of game dishes, although there are some surprisingly innovative starters, like cream of melon soup with mint. The home-made fig ice cream makes a refreshing finale to your meal, especially during steamy summer days.

➕ 197 D3 ✉ Plaza Consuelo Mendieta 2, Cazorla ☎ 953 72 12 01 🕐 Daily 11.30–3.30, 7.30–11.30

Deán Ortega ££

A welcome addition to the centre of town, this hotel has an excellent restaurant, elegantly decorated in warm hues of ochre and cream with subtle lighting, modern furnishings and a sophisticated feel. It's a great place to sip an espresso, enjoy a

light lunch or get serious with the three-course *menú del día* dishing up a nouvelle twist to local cuisine.

➕ 196 C4 ✉ María Molina Hotel, Plaza del Ayuntamiento s/n, Úbeda ☎ 953 79 53 56, fax: 953 79 36 94 🕐 Daily 8 am–midnight

Parador Restaurante Nacional del Condestable Dávalos ££-£££

Extensively refurbished for its reopening in 2001, the parador restaurant has an excellent reputation, serving market-fresh produce in recipes which have been handed down for generations, such as partridge with plums and stewed kid with pine nuts. Once those of a 16th-century palace, the surrounds are suitably sumptuous, while the service is formal and attentive. Be sure to have a peek at the wine cellar with its original stone arches, simple wooden tables and giant kegs of wine.

➕ 196 C4 ✉ Plaza de Vázquez de Molina, Úbeda ☎ 953 75 03 45 🕐 Daily noon–4, 7–midnight

Where to... Shop

Córdoba's long-established leather and filigree silver workshops produce exquisite goods. South of the city is the wine- and olive oil-producing area around Priego de Córdoba, with local produce of the finest quality, while some of the best pottery in Andalucía is made by artisans in the town of Úbeda in Jaén province.

CÓRDOBA PROVINCE

For fashion and general shopping in Córdoba city, head for the streets in the area between Plaza de las Tendillas (▶ 118) and the pedestrianised Avenida del Gran Capitán, especially Conde de Gondomar which links the two, and where

you'll find chic dress shops to match any in Seville, among them **Modas Pilar Morales** (Conde de Gondomar 2, tel: 957 41 12 54). Córdoba's **El Corte Inglés** department store is at the junction of Avenida del Gran Capitán and Avenida Ronda de los Tejares. The souvenir scrum round the Mezquita (▶ 115–6) is fine for everyday gifts and postcards, but for some of Córdoba's celebrated leather crafts, a better bet is such leading workshop/outlets as **Meryan** (Calleja de las Flores 2/Encarnación, tel: 957 47 59 02), which sell a good range of pottery, leather goods and other artefacts. **Artesanía La Corredera** (Calle Rodríguez Marín, tel: 957 48 97 16) also sell a good selection of hand-made ceramics, including pots, tiles and ornaments.

In the **Zoco** craft market (▶ 117), there are several shops selling filigree silverware. There is also a highly entertaining **market** in

Plaza de la Corredera trading clothes, craftwork and oddiments every day, but with a big and lively turnout on Saturday mornings. For a marvellous selection of olive oil visit the specialist outlet **La Tienda del Olivo** (Calle San Fernando 124b, tel: 957 47 44 97).

As you head south towards Priego de Córdoba you enter olive oil and Montilla wine country. These sherry-like wines (though with no added alcohol) come under the denomination of Moriles, after the main wine-producing towns in the area. You can sample Montilla just about everywhere and it can be bought, along with olive oil and cheeses of the region, at the **tourist information office in Zuheros** (▶ 128) and in most other villages.

JAÉN PROVINCE

Úbeda (▶ 126–7) is noted for its fine pottery, which is distinguished by its beautiful dark green glaze. Calle de Valencia is the town's

"potters' quarter", where there are several top potter's workshops such as the **Alfarería Paco Tito** (Calle Valencia 22, tel: 953 75 14 96) and nearby **Alfarería Góngora** (Cuesta de la Merced 32, tel: 953 75 46 05). In Calle Real, Úbeda's old main street, there are one or two shops that still sell goods made from esparto grass, a long-established craft in the area. Try **Acuario** (Calle Real 61, tel: 953 75 40 14) which also has good ceramic tiles. **Artificis** (Calle Juan Ruiz González 19, tel: 953 75 81 50), just off Plaza de Vázquez de Molina, is also good for high-quality ceramics and craftwork.

In the **Sierra de Cazorla** browse round **Cazorla's daily market** in Plaza del Mercado and look at the typical village shops in Calle Dr Muñoz, with local goods and food products. For Sierra crafts and gifts, the natural park's information centre, the **Centro de Interpretación** at Torre del Vinagre (tel: 953 72 01 02), has plenty to choose from.

Where to...
Be Entertained

In Córdoba city, ask at the tourist office for a free copy of the monthly listings guide *Qué Hacer en Córdoba?* and the English-language *Córdoba in...* newspaper. There is also a useful guide to *tapas* bars in the city. The daily Spanish-language newspaper is *Córdoba*. A good source of local information on entertainment hot spots is the young tourist guides of Cícerones de Córdoba. You will find them at the Alcázar, Puerta de Almodóvar, Plaza de las Tendillas and Palacio de Viana.

NIGHTLIFE

Though Córdoba is less cosmopolitan than Seville, Granada and Málaga, and nightlife is more tradi-

tional, you'll find lively dance and music bars on Calle Cruz Conde just north of Plaza de las Tendillas.

FLAMENCO

One of the best venues for "classical" flamenco in **Córdoba** city is the **Tablao Cardenal** (Calle Torrijos 10, tel: 957 48 31 12), right opposite the Mezquita. The show is staged in a delightful patio with an authentic ambience. There is a bar and restaurant service, and flamenco sessions start at 10.30 pm. Reservations are advised. Another good Córdoban flamenco venue is **La Bulería** (Calle Pedro López 3, tel: 957 48 38 39) near Plaza de la Corredera.

In Baeza there is a flamenco club, **Peña Flamenco** (Conde Romanones 6), that stages occasional flamenco.

Ask at the tourist information office for details and times. A similar club in Úbeda is **Peña Flamenco El Quejío** (Alfareros 4): again you should enquire at the tourist information centre.

THEATRE

Córdoba has a fine theatre in its **Gran Teatro** (Avenida del Gran Capitán 3, tel: 957 48 02 37) staging excellent music, dance and drama presentations. You can get a monthly programme of events from the theatre or tourist office.

BULLFIGHTING

Córdoba's bullring (Avenida Gran Vía Parque, tel: 957 23 25 07) stages fights throughout the summer. Ask at the tourist office for details and dates. For bullrings and scheduled fights in provincial towns and villages, check with relevant tourist offices or at the relevant bullring.

OUTDOOR ACTION

Get "outdoors" at the heart of Córdoba by hiring a bicycle or by taking a guided cycle tour of the city along the network of dedicated cycle lanes. The friendly bike-hire outfit, **Córdoba en Bici** (Calle Lucano, tel: 639 42 58 84) near Plaza del Potro runs organised trips.

For outdoors enthusiasts, there is plenty of adventure in the mountainous Parque Natural de Cazorla y Segura (▶124–5). The **Quercus** team (Calle Juan Domingo, tel: 953 72 01 15) in Cazorla town organise all sorts of activities, including four-wheel-drive tours, into the remoter areas, as well as horse treks and mountain biking. The **Centro de Interpretación** at Torre del Vinagre (tel: 953 71 30 40) can also arrange four-wheel-drive tours of the park as well as horse treks and mountain biking. Try **Hospedería de Montaña. El Hornico** (Pozo Alcón, tel: 953 12 41 37) for a whole range of outdoor activities.

Seville and Huelva

Getting Your Bearings 138–139
In Four Days 140–141
Don't Miss 142–159
At Your Leisure 160–162
Where to... 163–168

Getting Your Bearings

The city of Seville is the essence of all things Andalucian, a city of enduring excitement and spontaneity, of orange trees and flamenco; a city where the jingle of horse-drawn carriages is still heard in quiet streets and flower-filled parks and where modernistic buildings blend happily with Moorish palaces, majestic churches and medieval streets. It is where you find the best *tapas* bars in Spain and where a hint of pleasurable expectancy is always in the air.

Left: A bird's eye view of Seville's Reales Alcázares, a treasure house of *mudéjar* architecture

Above: Puerta de Sevilla, the old Roman gateway to the city of Carmona

Previous page: The Giralda tower in Seville shows Moorish architecture at its most elegant

Out in the larger province beyond the city are lesser-known but fascinating places to visit such as the old Roman city of Itálica, the walled town of Carmona, with its Moorish streets and Roman necropolis, and historic Écija.

Even further afield is Huelva province, too often neglected by visitors who are entirely seduced by Seville. The city of Huelva, an industrialised port that has no great monuments in its otherwise pleasant old centre, has little to offer the visitor, but the northern part of Huelva province has the peaceful, wooded hills of the Sierra Morena, which it shares with neighbouring Seville province. Here you will find the friendly hill town of Aracena, famous for its limestone caverns, the Gruta de las Maravillas, while a network of winding roads lead to serene villages amid forests of cork oak, where you can stretch your legs and breathe pure mountain air. Huelva's southernmost coastline, the Costa de la Luz, has one of the longest and most remote beaches in Andalucía. Behind the coast lies the huge delta of the Río Guadalquivir and the Parque Nacional de Doñana, a vast area of wetlands, sand dunes and wooded scrubland that is a wildlife site of world importance.

★ **Don't Miss**

1 **Sevilla (Seville)** ➤ 142
2 **Carmona** ➤ 154
5 **Aracena and Gruta de las Maravillas** ➤ 156
7 **Parque Nacional de Doñana** ➤ 158

At Your Leisure

3 Écija ➤ 160
4 Itálica ➤ 160
6 Río Tinto ➤ 161
8 Costa de la Luz (Huelva) ➤ 161
9 El Rocío ➤ 162

Seville's Museo de Artes y Costumbres Populares displays a fascinating mix of architectural styles

Soak up the magic of Seville, then take in the old town of Carmona and the spectacular limestone caverns of Aracena, before unwinding on Huelva's quiet Costa de la Luz and exploring Europe's biggest wildlife reserve, the Parque Nacional de Doñana.

Seville and Huelva in Four Days

Day One

Morning
Visit Seville's **cathedral** and the **Giralda** tower (right, ➤ 143–5) as early as possible, then take a stroll through the streets and plazas of the **Barrio de Santa Cruz** (➤ 148).

Afternoon
See the **Reales Alcázares** (➤ 146–7) and spend a restful hour or two in the shaded grounds of the **Parque de María Luisa** (➤ 151) before

wandering back through the **Plaza de España** (left, ➤ 151). Enjoy a *tapas* tour of **Barrio de Santa Cruz**, followed by a late meal at one of the area's many restaurants (➤ 164–5); or join the locals in the busy shopping streets of **Sierpes** and **Tetuán** (➤ 166–7), sampling *tapas* bars in the adjoining streets and plazas.

Day Two

Morning
Head for the **Museo de Bellas Artes** (➤ 148–50) for a view of some of the finest paintings in Spain; or visit the exquisite **Casa de Pilatos** (➤ 150–1), which reflects the glory of 15th-century *mudéjar* decorative art.

Afternoon

Take the Córdoba road, the NIV, to **Carmona** (right, ➤ 154–5). Visit the atmospheric **Necrópolis Romana** (➤ 154), then explore the narrow streets of the old walled town, including the impressive church of **Santa María la Mayor**. Stay overnight.

Day Three

Morning

Set off towards Seville, then go north onto the N630 and visit the Roman city ruins of **Itálica** (➤ 160). Continue north into the Sierra Morena hills for a night's stay at **Aracena** (➤ 156–7).

Afternoon

Visit Aracena's famous caverns, the **Gruta de las Maravillas** (left, ➤ 156–7), then climb (gently) through cobbled streets to the hilltop Moorish castle and its adjoining church.

Day Four

Morning

Make an early start and drive south to the **Costa de la Luz** (➤ 161) and spend an hour or two on the quiet beaches or go for a walk along the **Playa Cuesta de Maneli** boardwalk (➤ 162) through sand dunes covered with aromatic trees and shrubs. Bring something for a picnic as there are no bars or cafés within miles.

Afternoon

Head for the Centro de Recepción del Acebuche, the main reception centre of the **Parque Nacional de Doñana** (➤ 158–9). If you don't have time for a pre-booked tour of parkland sites (➤ 168), be sure to visit the bird hides near the centre, or visit the centre at **Las Rocinas** (➤ 159), where there is an enjoyable circular walk through a wetland area. Then it's back to Seville for another bout of lively Sevillian nightlife.

Seville

Seville (Sevilla), bestriding the broad Río Guadalquivir, is Andalucía at its most stylish. It is an exciting and theatrical place, scene of Spain's most exuberant festival, the week-long extravaganza of flamenco, horse riding and sherry-drinking that is the Feria de Abril, while the everyday life of the *Sevillanos* is played out with equal verve in the bars, fine restaurants and fashionable shopping streets.

The Seville area came under Moorish control in 712 and their settlement of Ishbiliyya became the basis of the city we see today. Seville prospered under later Christian rule and during the 16th century it was the main port of the Spanish-American trade. Seville's golden days as a port ended during the 17th century with the silting of the Guadalquivir, and for the next 200 years it stagnated, although from the late 18th century the city's faded beauty and romantic reputation attracted travellers. The 20th century saw a revival. Seville staged the Ibero-American Exhibition in 1929, which left it with marvellous public buildings and spaces; 63 years later it hosted Expo 92, when once again the city benefited from development and modernisation to go with its period charms.

You need some degree of physical and emotional stamina to make the best of Seville's fast pace of life. There is enough to satisfy the most devoted cultural tourist (the huge Gothic cathedral and history-laden Reales Alcázares are just the start), but there is much more. The main streets and the bars and cafés are always alive with animated humanity, but away from the most popular areas are leafy plazas, relaxed neighbourhood bars, and church doorways that open into oases of utter peace.

Tourist Information

✚ 202 B3 ✉ Avenida de la Constitución 21 (J de A) ☎ 954 22 14 04/21 81 57; fax 954 22 97 53

✉ Calle Arjona 28 ☎ 954 50 56 00

✉ Paseo de las Delicias 9 ☎ 954 23 44 65

Parking

There is out-of-centre parking near Santa Justa railway station, at Calle Luis de Morales, just off Avenida de Luis Montoro (the approach road from the Costa del Sol, Málaga and Granada). Car parks are signed at various points on Seville's inner ring road.

The Salón de los Embajadores (Room of the Ambassadors), one of the highlights of the Reales Alcázares

La Catedral and La Giralda

Seville's Cathedral of Santa María de la Sede is the largest Gothic church in the world, a treasure house of monumental architecture and great sculptures, paintings and decorative craftwork. The cathedral dominates the heart of the city with all the triumphant certainty that its 15th-century builders aimed for as an indisputable sign of the Christian Reconquest of Islamic Spain.

The upper section of the Giralda soars above the cathedral's pinnacles and flying buttresses

After Seville was wrested from the Moors by Fernando III in 1248, the city's mosque was used for Christian worship until the early 1400s, when plans for a new cathedral were launched. Most of the mosque was demolished and within 100 years the main body of the cathedral was completed. The ambition of its creators was immortalised in their defiant boast: "Let us build a church so great that those who see it may take us for being mad."

The Giralda

The exterior focus of the cathedral is the **Giralda** tower. Originally the minaret of a 12th-century mosque, the Giralda was modelled on the great minaret of the Qutubiya Mosque at Marrakesh and was built by the Moorish Almohad rulers of Seville between 1184 and 1198. The upper belfry was added in the 16th century by the Christian Spanish. It was crowned by a statue representing Faith, in the form of a weathervane, a *giraldillo*, from which the tower's name derives.

It is the Moorish section of the tower that is its great glory, however, a masterpiece of cool and subtle stonework, of geometric tracery that reflects changing patterns as the angle of the light alters. The Christian forces who attacked Seville in 1258 were so enamoured of the minaret that they sent warnings to the besieged Moors that if they destroyed or even damaged the tower they would be executed. The tower was left untouched. The clumsy balconies and the tiered belfry were later Christian additions, but the elegance of the Moorish minaret survives triumphantly.

Horsing Around

Seeing Seville from a horse-drawn carriage is still a popular, though expensive, treat for many visitors. The beautifully maintained carriages wait for custom in Plaza Virgen de los Reyes alongside the cathedral, their shining livery and yellow-rimmed wheels making a colourful sight. It costs about €24 for an hour's tour for up to four passengers.

The entrance to the Giralda is in the northeast corner of the cathedral, immediately to the left as you enter the building through the Puerta de la Concepción. Before you start the climb, be sure you can tackle it; and look out for groups of high-spirited schoolkids racing down the ramps from the top.

The Cathedral

The enormous Gothic cathedral is entered from Calle Alemanes through the **Puerta del Perdón** (Gate of Absolution). A survivor of the original mosque, this gateway retains some Islamic features, including bronze-clad doors. Beyond it lies another survivor of Islamic times, the **Patio de los Naranjos** (Patio of the Orange Trees), where worshippers carried out ritual ablutions before entering the mosque. Towering above the patio is the intricate facade of the **Puerta de la Concepción**, the doorway through which you enter the cathedral proper. Remember that the cathedral is first and foremost a place of worship, and you should dress and behave with due respect. Use of video and still cameras is allowed inside the building, but flash photography and the use of tripods are not permitted.

The dramatic monument to Christopher Columbus in Seville's cathedral

Take some time to appreciate the size of the building's cavernous interior. At the heart of the huge central nave are the **Capilla Mayor**, the main chapel, with the **Coro** (Choir) to its right. The gilded and painted *retablo* (altarpiece) of the Capilla Mayor is one of the cathedral's treasures. The vast screen is composed of 45 carved panels depicting scenes from the life of Christ and featuring over 1,000 biblical figures. The focus of this awesome Gothic masterpiece is a silver-plated cedar statue of the Virgen de la Sede (the Virgin of the Chair). The choir has 117 stalls, each one intricately carved.

Behind the Capilla Mayor, the east wall of the cathedral is lined with chapels, including the centrally placed **Capilla Real** (Royal Chapel), which has an imposing *retablo* in stone. Moving towards the south side of the cathedral takes you to the **Sacristía Mayor**, a beautiful domed chamber with plateresque (16th-century Renaissance) details. It contains many of the cathedral's finest works of art, including a silver monstrance of the 16th century. Among numerous fine paintings here are Zurbarán's *Santa Teresa* and Murillo's *San Leandro* and *San Isidoro*. To the left of the Sacristía Mayor is the oval **Sala**

Opening Times

At almost any time of year, queues can build up for the cathedral from late morning onwards, especially once tour groups begin to assemble. Last entry is one hour before closing. Be prepared to find some areas of the cathedral temporarily out of bounds or with only limited access.

Capitular (Chapter House), which has a superb domed ceiling and a decorated marble floor. Murillo's beautiful *La Immaculada* (The Immaculate Conception) is one of the fine paintings here. To the right of the Sacristía Mayor is the **Sacristía de los Cálices**, with more paintings, including a masterful work by Goya, *Santas Justa y Rufina*, depicting Seville's patron saints.

Adjoining the Sacristía de los Cálices is a striking **monument to Christopher Columbus** depicting the great sailor's coffin held aloft by four crowned figures, bedecked in vestments that bear the symbols of the Spanish kingdoms of Castile, Aragón, León and Navarre. Conventional wisdom claims that the coffin contains the bones of Columbus, his son Diego and grandson Luis, but as the remains have travelled to and fro between Spain and Cuba and Hispaniola, there is doubt about their authenticity.

TAKING A BREAK

Stop for drink at the appropriately named **Cervecería Giralda** at Calle Mateos Gago 1 and enjoy just about the best view of the cathedral at the same time.

Catedral Santa María de la Sede and Giralda
🕀 202 B3 ✉ Plaza Virgen de los Reyes ☎ 954 21 49 71/56 33 21
🕐 Mon–Sat 11–5, Sun and holidays 2–6 🚌 C1, C2, C3, C4
💰 Expensive (free Sun)

The intricately carved altarpiece in the Capilla Mayor is one of the cathedral's highlights. It took 100 years to complete

Reales Alcázares

The Reales Alcázares, a place of serenity and beauty, provides a wonderful respite from the traffic-logged city streets outside. It was the residence of the Christian kings who followed the Moorish rulers of Seville, a triumphant palace in *mudéjar* style displaying artistry as glorious in places as that of Granada's Alhambra.

The layout of the palaces reflects classic Islamic architecture, with central courtyards from which individual halls and chambers lead off to all sides. Great use is made of painted stucco and of tiles known as *azulejos* (► 8), which form a dazzling kaleidoscope of geometric patterns. Not the least of the Alcázar's delights are the beautifully kept gardens.

Seville's original Alcázar was begun in the early 8th century on the ruins of Roman and Visigothic fortifications. The interior of the building dates almost wholly from the later Christian era and owes much to the ambition of the 14th-century king, Pedro I, who hired the finest craftsmen of the day. Later Christian monarchs added their own flourishes.

Visiting the Reales Alcázares

Owing to the number of visitors, a system of controlled admission operates. At the busiest times, usually late morning to late afternoon, groups of several hundred visitors are allowed through the admissions control at 30-minute intervals, so you may have to queue.

Beyond the entrance vestibule is the **Patio del León** (Court of the Lion) and, beyond that, the larger **Patio de la Montería** (Hunting Court). To the right of the latter is the **Salón del Almirante** (Hall of the Admiral), established in 1503 by Isabel I of Castile as a suite of rooms in which to plan voyages to the Americas. The finest room is the **Sala de Audiencias** (Hall of the Audiences) with an *artesonado* ceiling, a fine model of

The palaces' sober exterior (above left) belies the architectural treasures that you'll find within. The Salón de los Embajadores (above right) is among the highlights

Getting Around

Official guidebooks to the Reales Alcázares are on sale at the admissions desk. You can also hire audio guides in your chosen language. These have the advantage of offering one-to-one information as you progress through the buildings.

Below right:
The glorious
gardens of the
Reales
Alcázares

Columbus's vessel the *Santa María*, and a 16th-century *in situ* altarpiece, *The Virgin of the Navigators*, portraying Columbus, Amerigo Vespucci and other voyagers.

You next enter the true Palace of Pedro I. In the central court-yard, the **Patio de las Doncellas** (Court of the Maidens), a space rich with multi-lobed arches and beautiful lattices of stone, a frieze of *azulejos* clads the lower walls and a central fountain sends a slim column of water into the air. The patio is encircled by richly decorated rooms leading one into the other

through narrow doorways. At their heart lies the **Patio de las Muñecas** (Court of the Dolls), so called because of the tiny heads set into its walls. The **Salón de los Embajadores** (Room of the Ambassadors), next to it, is the glory of the Alcázar. Horseshoe arcades punctuate exquisitely tiled walls that rise to a sumptuous dome of interlocking woodwork hanging like clusters of stalactites; the colours are luminous green, red and gold.

A stairway in the corner of the Patio de las Doncellas leads to the gloomy 17th-century **Salones de Carlos V**. From here you burst forth into the gardens, a final joy, although what you see today – tiled walkways, random fountains, shaded seats, orange groves and tall pine and palm trees – bears little resemblance to the intricate gardens of the Moors and of Pedro I. From near the Estanque del Mercurio, a passageway leads you past a cafeteria into a covered coach hall, the Apeadero, and then to the exit.

✚ 202 B3 ✉ Plaza del Triunfo ☎ 954 50 23 23 🕐 Tue–Sat 9.30–8, Sun and holidays 9.30–6, Jun–Oct; Tue–Sat 9.30–6, Sun and public holidays 9.30–2.30, Nov–May 🍴 Café 🚻 C1, C2, C3, C4 💲 Expensive (children under 12 and senior citizens free)

Barrio de Santa Cruz

Alongside the cathedral and
Reales Alcázares are the narrow streets and plazas of
Barrio de Santa Cruz, a welcome antidote to the traffic-
jammed main streets of the
city. Santa Cruz was the
aljama, or Jewish quarter, of
medieval Seville. Much of the
original *barrio* was destroyed
after a vicious pogrom in
1492, and despite rebuilding
work at the beginning of the
20th century some of the style
of the original survives. As
you wander through the
streets, you will catch tantalising glimpses of lovely central
patios through wrought-iron
grilles. A peaceful little
enclave that many visitors seem to miss is **Plaza de Santa
Cruz**; the wrought-iron cross at its centre symbolises the original Iglesia de Santa Cruz, destroyed by Napoleonic troops.
Another pretty square is Plaza Doña Elvira with its central
fountain and dappled shade. The **Hospicio de los Venerables
Sacerdotes**, a one-time hospice for retired priests in Plaza de
los Venerables, now houses a gallery containing paintings and
sculptures by leading Spanish artists. The building has a delectable patio. On the *barrio*'s eastern boundary are the pleasantly
shady **Jardines de Murillo** (Murillo Gardens), and everywhere
you turn there are bars and cafés.

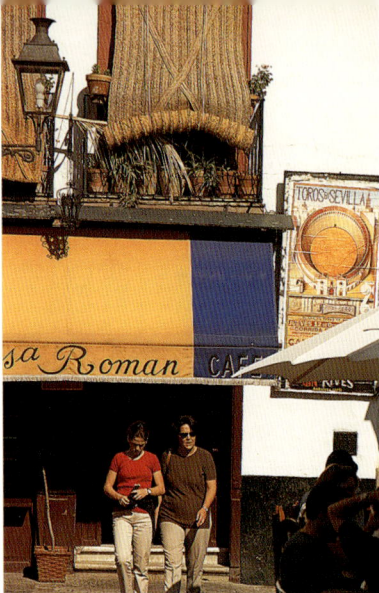

*The streets of
Santa Cruz
provide a
peaceful retreat
at the heart of
the city*

Museo de Bellas Artes

One of Spain's major art galleries, the Museo de Bellas Artes
(Fine Arts Museum) is located in the former Convento de la
Merced Calzada, a short walk north of the cathedral. With its
hushed galleries and peaceful central patio, this lovely building
is a pleasure in itself and an ideal repository for examples of the
finest of Spanish painting from the early medieval period to the
20th century.

The permanent collection is displayed in 14 rooms. The
highlight is **Room V**, the one-time chapel of the convent. As
you enter from the side, you come face to face with the
Apotheosis of St Thomas Aquinas, arguably the finest work of the
17th-century painter Francisco de Zurbarán. Turning to your
right, you'll see the room in its full glory; even the dome of the
chapel is aglow with restored paintings. On the wall of the original apse is a celebration of the work of the Seville-born painter

---

**Hospicio de los Venerables
Sacerdotes**
🔳 202 C3 ✉ Plaza de los Venerables
Sacerdotes 🕐 10–2 and 4–8 (guided tours)
💰 Moderate

Museo de Bellas Artes
🔳 202 A4 ✉ Plaza del Museo ☎ 954 22 07
90 🕐 Wed–Sat 9–8, Tue 3–8, Sun and holidays 9–2 🚇 C1, C2, C3, C4 💰 Inexpensive
(free with EU passport)

Seville by Bus

The Sevirama company (tel: 954 56 06 93) runs open-top bus tours. Buses leave every half hour from the Torre del Oro (► 152) from 10 am onwards, visiting the Plaza de España (► 151), Triana (► 152) and the Isla Mágica (► 152), and pass close to other major sights. Headphone sets offer commentary in your preferred language. You can get on and off at will using the all-day ticket.

The Apotheosis of St Thomas Aquinas by Zurbarán, one of the treasures in the Museo de Bellas Artes

Bartolomé Esteban Murillo (1618–82), including the *Immaculate Conception* and the haunting *Santa Justa and Santa Rufina*. In a small chamber round to the right is Murillo's ravishing *Virgin and Child*, known as *La Virgen de la Servilleta* because it is said to be painted on a dinner napkin. There are more Murillos in **Room VII**, while **Room X** is devoted to Zurbarán. Other artists represented include the painters Goya, Velázquez, El Greco and Murillo's Sevillian contemporary Juan

Seville by Boat

Hour-long river cruises leave every 30 minutes from 11 am to 10 pm from the quayside in front of the Torre del Oro (➤ 152), where there is a booking office (tel: 954 21 55 96).

de Valdés de Leal, and sculptors such as the 15th-century Sevillian Pedro Millán, whose compelling *Entombment of Christ* is in **Room I**.

Rooms XII and XIV show 19th- and 20th-century art. In Room XII look for Gonzalo Bilbao's sentimental but persuasive evocation of the world of *Carmen* and the Seville Tobacco Factory (➤ 12), *Las Cigarreras*, and his clever *Noche de Verano en Sevilla*, in which lanterns glimmer realistically. Other gems here are José García Ramos's dancers in *Bulerías* and his painting of a man drinking in *Hasta Verte Cristo Mío*.

Casa de Pilatos (Pilate's House)

In this 15th-century Renaissance house on the eastern edge of Barrio de Santa Cruz, the *mudéjar* materials of wood, stucco, *azulejos* tiling and brick have been used to produce domestic architecture and decoration of rare beauty. The house was largely built by the son of a governor of Andalucía, whose visit to Jerusalem inspired the Pontius Pilate connection. Much work since the mid-20th century has restored the house to its original splendour. The house is entered through the **Apeadero**, a carriage square with arcaded walls smothered in bougainvillaea. Beyond lies the **Patio Principal**, the central patio, where there is a successful merging of Gothic features and *mudéjar* decoration within the patio's overall Renaissance context, which embraces a central fountain and original

The Patio Principal in the Casa de Pilatos

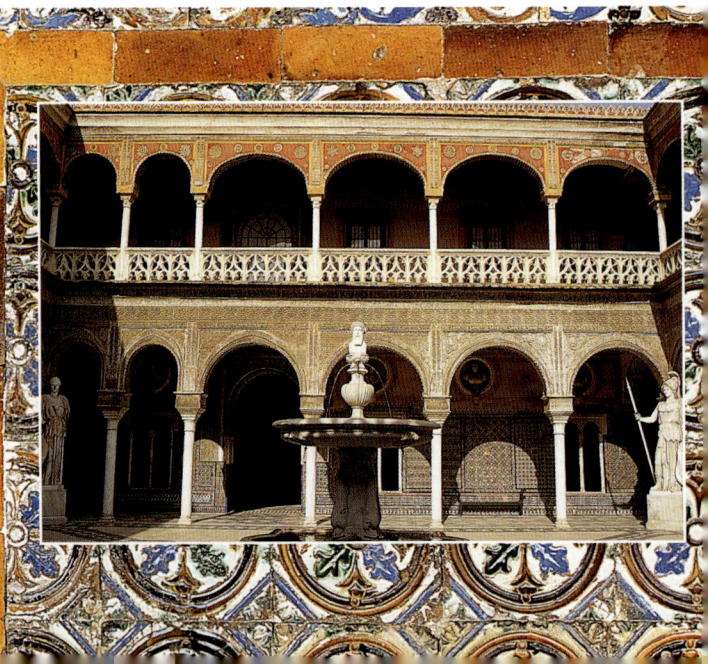

classical sculptures of goddesses Pallas Athene and Minerva. A conducted tour takes you through a succession of chambers and salons exquisitely decorated and furnished. The small interior gardens include Italianate loggias and Roman statuary, amid palm trees and flowers.

Plaza de España and Parque de María Luisa

Of Seville's parks and open spaces, the Plaza de España and Parque de María Luisa are the finest. Both were created as showpieces for Seville's 1929 extravaganza, the Ibero-American Exhibition. Leafy **Parque de María Luisa** is just the place to linger for an hour or two during the heat of mid-afternoon, an oasis of tree-filled gardens, resplendent with colourful ceramics, ornamental bridges and follies, and in summer bright with geraniums and bougainvillaea. At its east end is the handsome Plaza de América, flanked by the **Museo Arqueológico** (Archaeological Museum), whose collections range from prehistory to the Moors, and the **Museo de Artes y Costumbres Populares** (Museum of Folk Art), which displays artefacts and costumes from the 18th and 19th centuries. Both were built as part of the 1929 Exhibition.

Plaza de España lies just north of Parque de María Luisa across the broad Avenida de Isabel la Católica. It is a huge crescent of arcaded redbrick building with curving staircases. At ground level, a series of brightly coloured tile mosaics display the coats of arms of Spain's main provinces. In front of the crescent is a canal-style lake, criss-crossed by ornamental bridges, where people drift sedately in little rowing boats.

Below: Taking a break in the Plaza de España

The crescent-shaped Plaza de España

Plaza de San Francisco and Calle Sierpes

To the north of the cathedral at the end of broad and busy Avenida de la Constitución are two adjoining squares. **Plaza Nueva** has little architectural appeal but buzzes with life in the evenings: car engines rev ceaselessly, horns squeal, and on the central concourse people stream to and fro. Equally busy, **Plaza de San Francisco** has been at the heart of Sevillian life since the 16th century. Political meetings and other major events are staged between the 16th-century Ayuntamiento (city hall) with its Renaissance facade and the 19th-century balconied buildings opposite. From here, stroll along **Calle Sierpes**, Seville's great shopping street, crammed with shops of every kind, its side streets alive with *tapas* bars or sheltering beautiful baroque churches. At the far end of Sierpes you come to the **Campaña** where you can browse through a colourful craft market, then eat pastries at a pavement table of the popular coffee shop and *pastelería*, Confitería La Campaña.

Pedestrianised Calle Sierpes is Seville's principal shopping street

La Maestranza, Seville's 18th-century bull-ring, stages some of the country's most dramatic bull-fights

Torre del Oro, Plaza de Toros de la Maestranza, Triana

Seville is greatly enhanced by its river setting, and both banks repay exploration. On the east side, bordering the older part of the city, is the **Torre del Oro**, a 12th-century Moorish tower that now houses a small maritime museum. Further north along the Paseo de Cristóbal Colón is Seville's huge baroque bull-ring, **La Maestranza** (► 168). Claimed as the finest bullring in the world, it dates from the late 18th century. A little further south, you can cross the Guadalquivir on the Puente de Isabel II to reach the district of **Triana**, once Seville's gypsy quarter, home of flamenco (► 16–18) and of ceramic production. Most of the gypsy families have been rehoused outside the city and the *barrio* has been gentrified, but stroll through its streets will take you to some fine churches, *tapas* bars and cafés, and ceramics outlets.

Expo Island

Isla de La Cartuja, an elongated island formed by two arms of the Río Guadalquivir, was the focus of Seville's Expo 92. The Carthusian monastery which gave the island its name was restored as part of Expo (tel: 955 03 70 70, open Tue–Sat 10 am–9 pm, Sun and holidays 10–3 pm. Free Tue with EU passport). On the eastern side of the island is the lavish entertainment park, **Isla Mágica** (open daily 11 am–midnight, May–Sep).

Casa de Pilatos

✚ 202 C4 ✉ Plaza de Pilatos 1 ☎ 954 22 52 98 ⏰ Daily 9–8, Jul–Sep; 9–6, Oct–Jun 🚍 C1, C2, C3, C4 (for Plaza San Agustín) 💰 Moderate

Plaza de España and Parque de María Luisa

✚ 202 C2 ✉ Avenida de Isabel la Católica 🚍 Bus C1, C2, C3, C4 💰 Free

Museo Arqueológico

✚ 202 C1 ✉ Plaza de América ☎ 954 23 24 01 ⏰ Wed–Sat 9–8, Tue 3–8, Sun and holidays 9–2 💰 Inexpensive (free with EU passport)

Museo de Artes y Costumbres Populares

✚ 202 C2 ✉ Plaza de América ☎ 954 23 25 76 ⏰ Wed–Sat 9–8, Tue 3–8, Sun and holidays 9–2 💰 Inexpensive (free with EU passport)

SEVILLE: INSIDE INFO

Top tips It is often difficult to get detailed **information** from Seville's main tourist office in Avenida de la Constitución, which can become very busy. A better bet might be the municipal tourist office at Calle Arjona 28, several streets to the south of the cathedral, at the start of the Puente de Isabel II (known also as Puente de Triana).

• A good place to escape the afternoon heat is the **Museo de Bellas Artes** (➤ 148), one of the few places to remain open during the mid-afternoon siesta period.

• The most convenient **bus services** for central Seville are Nos C1 and C3, which operate a clockwise route, and C2 and C4, which operate in the reverse direction. Ask for a bus company route map at tourist offices (➤ 142) or at the office of Transportes Urbanos de Seville (TUSSAM) at Calle Diego de Riaña 2.

Hidden gem A few metres down Calle Jovellanos, a narrow street off busy Calle Sierpes (on the left from Plaza San Francisco), is the **Capilla de San José** (St Joseph's Chapel). Its late baroque altar is one of the finest in Andalucía, a gilded extravaganza that is all the more remarkable for being found at the heart of Seville's busiest shopping area.

2

Carmona

The old walled town of Carmona, east of Seville, was important in Roman times (as the Necrópolis Romana, a Roman
cemetery on the town's outskirts, testifies) and again under
the Moors, who fortified it. Both the Roman and Moorish lega-
cies are unmistakable in the town, blended with later
churches and houses within a complex of narrow streets and
attractive squares.

There are over 900 family tombs in
Carmona's **Necrópolis Romana**, mainly in
the form of *columbaria,* deep chambers
carved out of the rock. There are conducted
tours of the site, but you can easily find
your own way around. Highlights include
the **Tumba del Elefante** (Tomb of the
Elephant), so named because of a surviving
stone sculpture of an elephant, possibly a
symbol of longevity. The largest feature of
the necropolis is the **Tumba de Serviliam**, a
huge colonnaded courtyard with covered
galleries and chambers. The site museum
has displays of mosaics, gravestones and
funerary pottery.

The main town of Carmona is entered by
an impressive Roman gateway, the **Puerta
de Sevilla**, which incorporates Moorish features. You can reach the upper walls and
battlements of the gateway through the
tourist office. Across busy Plaza Blas Infante
from the Puerta de Sevilla, outside the walls,
is the 15th-century **Iglesia de San Pedro**,
its tower built in the form of Seville's
Giralda (▶ 143–4). The church's sanctuary
chapel provides a display of decorative
gilded work.

On one corner of Carmona's palm-fringed central square,
Plaza de San Fernando, stands the **Casa de Cabildo**, the old
town hall, with Moorish window arches and red and white
stonework and colourful tiling. East of the plaza, Calle Martín
López de Córdoba takes you to the Gothic **Iglesia de Santa
María la Mayor**, a church built in the 15th century on the site
of Carmona's Moorish mosque. You enter through the mosque's
patio, a peaceful enclave with orange trees and horseshoe
arches; look for a column with a Visigothic calendar inscribed
in the stone. The church has a soaring nave with ribbed arches
and great clustered columns, and a luminous altarpiece. At the
eastern end of the town is the recently refurbished Roman gateway, the **Puerta de Córdoba**, from where a winding road leads
down to the ruins of a Roman bridge.

Carmona's
central square
is the ideal
place to relax

CARMONA: INSIDE INFO

Top tips Protect yourself from the sun at the **Necrópolis Romana**: the heat can be intense and there is not much shade out on the site.
• Visit Carmona's morning **market**, held in the arcaded patio of a 17th-century convent, just south of Plaza de San Fernando.

Hidden gem Carmona's *ayuntamiento* (town hall) is a splendid Renaissance building. A Roman mosaic of the head of Medusa is displayed in its patio (open Mon–Fri 8–2.30; entrance free).

Part of Carmona's charm lies in its attractive squares

TAKING A BREAK

Enjoy a drink, even as a non-resident, at Carmona's exclusive **Parador Nacional** hotel in the renovated Alcázar del Rey Pedro, the remains of a Moorish fortified palace standing high above the town. Many people consider it one of the most magnificent hotels in Spain. If you're feeling flush, stop off for lunch or dinner.

🚗 195 D3

Tourist Information
✉ Arco de la Puerta de Sevilla
☎ 954 19 09 55

✉ Plaza de San Fernando (information point)

Parking
There is limited parking just inside the Puerta de Sevilla and there is random parking in the streets around Plaza de San Fernando (best sought during the mid-afternoon siesta).

Necrópolis Romana
✉ Avenida de Jorge Bonsor 9 ☎ 954 14 08 11 🕐 Tue–Fri 9–5, Sat–Sun 10–2, mid-Sep to mid-Jun; Tue–Sat 9–2, Sun 10–2, mid-Jun to mid-Sep 🎫 Inexpensive (free with EU passport)

Iglesia de San Pedro
✉ Calle San Pedro 🕐 Tue–Sat 9.30–2 🎫 Inexpensive

Iglesia de Santa María la Mayor
✉ Calle Martín López de Córdoba 🕐 Tue–Sat 9.30–2 🎫 Inexpensive

Museo de la Ciudad
✉ Calle Martín López de Córdoba 🕐 Daily 10–2 (also Wed–Mon 6:30–9.30 pm) 🎫 Inexpensive

5

Aracena and Gruta de las Maravillas

The main attraction of the cheerful country town of Aracena is a complex of spectacular limestone caverns that riddle the hillside on which the town stands. Above ground, Aracena's roughly cobbled streets are romantically overlooked by a ruined medieval castle and a 13th-century Gothic church.

Aracena lies at the heart of the Sierra de Aracena, an area of smooth-browed hills covered with cork oak and eucalyptus trees. It is the **Gruta de las Maravillas** (Grotto of Marvels) that brings visitors to the town. The section open to the public extends for about 1.2km through galleries and passageways that bristle with fantastic stalactites and stalagmites. Paved walkways and staircases lead through the complex past a series of small lakes. Lighting and piped music add to the theatrical effect. The guide's commentary is in Spanish, but many of the features speak for themselves, and the guide points out, with a laser pen, figures and "faces" in the rock formations. Highlights include the **Sala de los Culos** (Room of the Backsides), where certain deposits of calcium carbonate resemble well-rounded parts of the human anatomy.

Above: The Gruta de las Maravillas is said to have been discovered by a 19th-century shepherd seeking lost sheep

Heavenly Ham

Aracena is at the heart of the *jamón serrano* (cured ham) country of the Sierra Morena. Several shops in the town sell ham products, including *pata negra*, a delicious *jamón* produced from acorn-eating black pigs. You can sample *jamón* in bars in the lower town. The area's main *jamon*-producing village is nearby Jabugo (see Drive ➤ 182–4).

Back on the surface, it's pleasant to stroll around Aracena's cobbled streets and its busy main square, Plaza Marqués de Aracena. On the hilltop above the town, beyond a 16th-century brick gateway, are the ruins of a Moorish castle along with the adjoining Nuestra Señora de los Dolores, an impressive medieval church with ornamented tower. Although you can take a "road train" of open-sided carriages (a somewhat out-of-character tourist facility) to the castle and church, or go by car, the steep walk through the older part of town, taking in attractive **Plaza Alta**, is the best option. The near-deserted plaza was the central square of old Aracena before the modern town developed round Plaza Marqués de Aracena below. Located in the old town hall in Plaza Alta is the information centre for the surrounding natural park.

✚ 194 B4

Tourist Information
✉ Calle Pozo de la Nieve, Plaza San Pedro (also ticket office for the Gruta de las Maravillas) ☎ 959 12 82 06

Parking
There is a car park in Plaza San Pedro at the entrance to the town from the N433. Pay the fee to the attendant.

Gruta de las Maravillas
✉ off Plaza San Pedro ☎ 959 12 82 06/12 83 55 🕐 Daily 10.30–1.30 and 3–6. Guided tours Mon–Fri every hour, Sat–Sun every half hour. Tickets from tourist centre opposite entrance to caves. Tours limited to 50 people at a time; waits of an hour or two at busy periods.
💷 Expensive

ARACENA: INSIDE INFO

Top tips It can feel very chilly inside the Gruta de las Maravillas, even on the hottest days; take an extra top.
• If you don't understand Spanish, it's best to stay at the back during the guided tour of the caves, and admire the surroundings at leisure. But don't linger too long: the lights in each section switch off automatically soon after the tour group moves on to the next part.
• A flash photography unit may be stationed at the midway point of the Gruta de las Maravillas – you can buy **photographs** of yourself after the tour. If you don't want your picture taken, be ready to raise your hand to your face.

One to miss Attached to the ticket office of the Gruta de las Maravillas is a small **geology museum**. Unless you have a special interest in geology, give the collection a miss.

7

Parque Nacional de Doñana

The wilderness of the Parque Nacional de Doñana (Doñana National Park) forms Spain's largest wildlife reserve. The park is one of the most important wetland sites in the world, a sanctuary for resident and migratory birds and an exciting range of mammals including the Spanish lynx, wild boar and otters.

The park covers over 50,000 hectares of the delta of the Río Guadalquivir and its tributaries, a vast wilderness of pools and marshes known as *marismas*. About half the area is subject to winter flooding, while the rest is made up of shifting sand dunes and great swathes of sand that have become stabilised and vegetated by heath and pine woods. It is this mix of habitats that supports Doñana's huge variety of flora and fauna. The entire area of the Doñana was once a hunting reserve. It gained its present name from "Doña Ana", the wife of a 15th-century Duke of Medina Sidonia. By the mid-20th century, as the area's ecological fragility came under threat from expanding agriculture and other development, the national park was created.

Deer like this red stag wander in Doñana National Park

Over 300,000 birds, representing 120 species, migrate from northern Europe to the Doñana *marismas* in October each year, then head north again in March. Winter is thus the best time for dedicated birdwatchers to visit. In summer you still have a good chance of spotting a variety of birds including flamingos, storks, grebes, hoopoes and large raptors such as eagles, vultures, kites and marsh harriers. Plant life comprises heath species such as heather, juniper, rosemary, thyme and lavender and the yellow-flowered cistus. The commonest trees are the umbrella pine and the tamarisk. Round the edges of the lagoons poplars grow and reeds and rushes thrive. Access to the Doñana is strictly controlled and visits are channeled through a number of information centres (► panel, above).

TAKING A BREAK
Coto de Doñana is a great picnic area, so stop off at a delicatessen and pick up some fresh bread, Manchego cheese, *jamón serrano* and a couple of bottles of Rioja.

The hoopoe is one of the many varieties of bird seen in the park

➕ 194 B2

At Your Leisure

3 Écija

Écija is known as *Ciudad de las Torres* (City of Towers). Its 11 churches, their baroque towers steepled and domed and gleaming with coloured tiles, give the town its dramatic skyline. There is a fine central square, Plaza Mayor or Plaza de España, surrounded by arcades and dotted with palm trees. Écija's remarkable secular buildings include **Palacio de Peñaflor**, the long elegant curve of its balconied facade painted with colourful frescoes, and the interior rich with plasterwork and marble. **Palacio de Benamejí**, with a beautiful central patio, houses the small **Museo Histórico Municipal** providing excellent background to the town's history.

✚ 195 E3

Tourist Information
✉ Palacio de Benamejí, Calle Cánovas del Castillo 4 ☎ 955 90 29 33

Palacio de Peñaflor
✉ Calle Castellar ⏰ Mon–Fri 10.30–1 and 5–8 💰 Free

Museo Histórico Municipal
✉ Palacio de Benamejí, Calle Cánovas del Castillo 4 ⏰ Tue–Fri 9.30–1.30 and 4.30–6.30, Sat–Sun 9–2 💰 Free

4 Itálica

The remains of one of the most important cities of the Roman Empire lie 9km north of Seville. Itálica was established in 205 BC alongside the Río Guadalquivir as a port and an

The evocative ruins of Itálica, the first Roman town in Spain

administrative centre of Roman Spain. It was the birthplace of the emperors Hadrian and Trajan. In time, the river changed course, Itálica lost its trading links, and the city's artefacts, mosaics and magnificent stonework were plundered.

Much of the vast amphitheatre has survived and foundations of villas and streets have been uncovered, along with mosaics, including a beautiful Neptune motif and another that features 33 species of birds.

✚ 194 C3 ✉ Avenida de Extramadura 2, Santiponce ☎ 955 99 65 83 ⏰ Tue–Sat 9–6.30, Sun and holidays 9–3, Apr–Sep; Tue–Sat 9–5.30, Sun and holidays 10–4, Oct–Mar 💰 Inexpensive (free with EU passport)

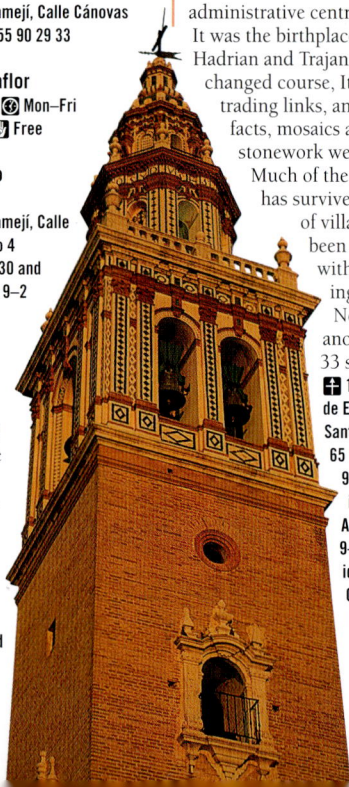

Right: Écija is dubbed the "City of Towers"

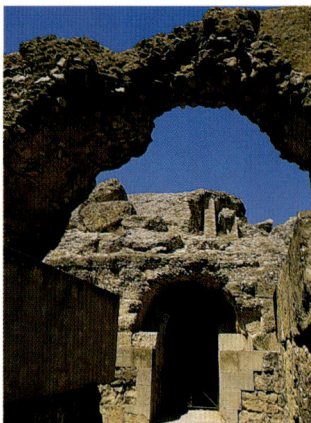

6 Río Tinto

Thousands of years of opencast mining have left huge scars on the Río Tinto landscape. Vivid colours – rust red, emerald green and ochre – stain the ground where iron, copper and silver have been mined since Phoenician and Roman times. In the late 19th century the mines were sold to British and German banks, who formed the Río Tinto Mining Company and began to excavate on a massive scale. Today the mines are again under Spanish control, although production has declined.

The village of Minas de Ríotinto is unattractive, but its **Museo Minero** (Mining Museum) tells a dramatic story through its excellent displays on geology, archaeology and social

Iron oxide and other residues create vivid colours in the opencast mines of Río Tinto

history. You can join a tour taking in underground workings and a huge 330m-deep opencast pit. Or you can ride through dramatic mining country in a train whose restored carriages are 100 years old. You can find out about train trips and special tours at the museum, but phone ahead for up-to-date information about timetables.

➕ 194 B3

Museo Minero

✉ Plaza del Museo ☎ 959 59 00 25/59 10 65 🕐 Daily 10–3, mid-May to mid-Oct; Mon–Sat 10–3, Sat–Sun and holidays 10–6, mid-Oct to mid-May 🎟 Museum: inexpensive. Mining tours: moderate. Train trips: inexpensive

Beaches on Huelva's Costa de la Luz are largely deserted

8 Costa de la Luz (Huelva)

Travel a few kilometres southeast of the estuary of the Río Tinto and Río Odiel, with its factories and refineries, and you reach a largely uninhabited coastline and a beach of golden sand that runs for 25km between the resorts of Mazagón and Matalascañas. The beach, backed by pine-covered sand dunes, is accessible from only a few places on the coast road, behind which lies the Parque Nacional de Doñana (➤ 158–9). The most convenient beach access points are at Mazagón and Matalascañas. Both resorts get very busy in summer, and **Mazagón** may be too close to the estuary mouth for some. A few kilometres southeast of Mazagón is the hotel complex of **Parador Cristóbal Colón** where there is public parking above a popular section of beach. About 8km further down the road there is a roadside car park from where you can take a pleasant stroll

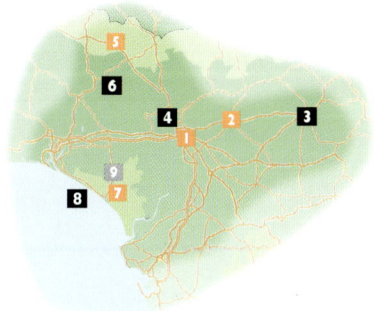

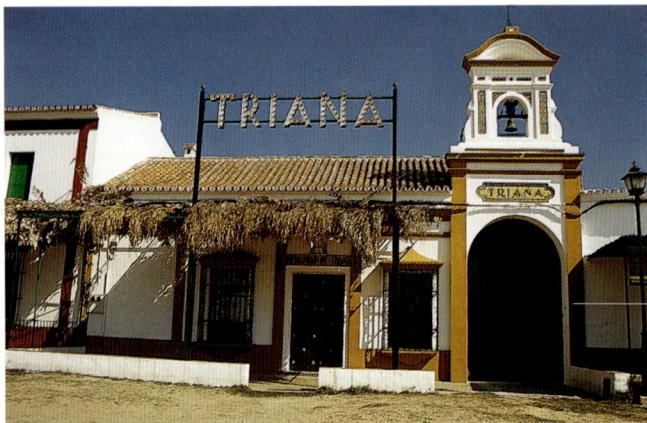

along a 2-km boardwalk, through pine and juniper-covered dunes, to the remote midway point of the Playa Cuesta de Maneli beach. At **Matalascañas** the beach is backed by a soulless, custom-built resort.

✚ 194 B2

9 El Rocío

To the first-time visitor, El Rocío, a village on the western edge of Doñana National Park, resembles a Wild West town. The empty wide streets and broad squares are unsurfaced, and the rows of two-storeyed wooden build-ings with railed verandas add to the impression. The air of desertion is because El Rocío exists chiefly as the centre of an extraordinary pilgrimage, the Romería del Rocío (► 20). The town is the scene of a spectacular climax to the week-long Romería each Whitsun, when up to half a million people from all over Spain pay bois-terous homage to Nuestra Señora del Rocío (Our Lady of the Dew), aka La

A typical *hermandad* house in the pilgrimage centre El Rocío

Blanca Paloma (The White Dove), whose revered image is kept in El Rocío's enormous white-painted church. Most of the buildings in El Rocío are owned by *hermandades*, brotherhoods of devotees, who often stage minor celebrations here on weekends throughout the year.

✚ 194 B3

For Kids

- **Gruta de las Maravillas** caverns at Aracena (► 156–7)
- The train rides at the **Minas de Ríotinto** (► 161)
- **El Castillo de las Guardas Nature Park** (on A476 Río Tinto road from the N433 Seville–Aracena road, tel: 955 95 25 68; open daily 10.30–dusk): you can take an 8-km tour in your own vehicle of a reserve where you can spot elephants, giraffes and zebras and many other exotic species. There is also a popular snake house.

Where to... Stay

Prices
Expect to pay per person per night
£ up to €36   ££ €36–€96
£££ over €96

SEVILLE AND SURROUNDING AREA

Hotel Alfonso XIII £££

Seriously luxurious at prices to match, this five-storey rococo building was built during the 1929 Expo in the *mudéjar*/Andalucian revival style. Even if you can't afford a night, sip a sherry over-looking the plant-filled central patio, surrounded by antique furniture, glittering hand-painted tiles, crystal chandeliers and acres of marble and mahogany. The rooms are predictably sumptuous and the service formal and efficient.
✚ 202 B2 ⊠ San Fernando 2, Seville ☎ 954 22 28 50, fax: 954 21 60 33

La Cartuja de Cazalla ££

Around 80km to the northeast of Seville, the hotel doubles as a Centre for Contemporary Culture; it boasts its own art gallery and displays original artwork in all the rooms. The magnificent stone building is a tastefully restored 15th-century Carthusian monastery set in beautiful grounds, with bird-song in lieu of TV. Just right if you are seeking some out-of-town peace and repose.
✚ 195 D4 ⊠ Carretera Cazalla–Constantina A455 Km 55.2, Cazalla de la Sierra, Seville ☎ 954 88 35 15 ☎ 954 88 45 16, fax: 954 88 35 15 🛇 Closed 24–26 Dec

Las Casas de la Judería £££

This is one of the prettiest hotels in Seville, tucked down an alleyway on the edge of the Barrio de Santa Cruz, but close to the shops and commercial centre. The rooms are around three classic courtyards, once incorporated into three palaces. The bedrooms are individually decorated and appropriately palatial, painted in subdued pastel colours and with high ceilings and plush furniture.
✚ 202 C3 ⊠ Callejón de Dos Hermanas 7, Seville ☎ 954 41 51 50, fax: 954 42 21 70

Hostal Goya £

The *hostal* is in a traditional old building in the atmospheric Barrio de Santa Cruz. The rooms are simple (there are no TVs or phones) but they are comfortable, and the water pressure is excellent – not always the case in budget places! Downstairs, light streams in via a skylight to a marble-floored salon furnished with sofas and chairs, where guests can congregate or write postcards.
✚ 202 B3 ⊠ Mateus Gagos 31, Seville ☎ 954 21 11 70, fax: 954 56 29 88 🛇 Closed Jan

Hostería del Laurel ££

This 21-room hotel is in an unbeat-able position, on a small tree-lined square in the heart of the Barrio de Santa Cruz. It is better known for its *bodega*, which is mentioned in Zorilla's popular 19th-century play *Don Juan Tenorio*, as well as for the adjoining restaurant. The rooms are a relatively recent addition, spread between two floors. They are spot-lessly clean and simply furnished.
✚ 202 C3 ⊠ Plaza de los Venerables 5, Seville ☎ 954 22 02 95, fax: 954 21 04 50

CARMONA

El Comercio £

This *pension* is incorporated into the ancient city walls at the Puerta de Sevilla, the magnificent western

Where to...
Eat and Drink

Prices
Expect to pay per person for a meal, including wine and service
£ up to €12   ££ €12–€30   £££ over €30

ARACENA

Los Castaños ££

The elegant Los Castaños is just a few minutes' walk from the caves, and has plenty of shops, restaurants and bars on the doorstep. The rooms are modern and spacious with balconies. The best view is from the dining room, which looks out to the surrounding Sierra de Aracena.

☐ 194 B4 ☒ Avenida Huelva 5
☎ 959 12 63 00, fax: 959 12 62 87

Finca Valbono ££

In a nature reserve surrounded by rolling hills, and with a choice of self-contained cabins or hotel rooms, Finca Valbono is the perfect place for a family to stay. There are horse-riding facilities, as well as a large pool and wonderful walks. The restaurant specialises in *cordon bleu* cuisine with a few down-to-earth choices for children.

☐ 194 B4 ☒ Carretera de Carboneras, Km 1, Aracena ☎ 959 12 77 11, fax: 959 12 76 79

gateway to the town. There are no mod cons, but the pretty central patio is the perfect place to relax away from the noise of the street. The rooms are simple with high ceilings and comfortable beds, and guests always get a good welcome.

☐ 195 D3 ☒ Calle Torre del Oro 56, Carmona ☎ 954 14 00 18

Parador de Carmona £££

One of Spain's top paradors is a subtly transformed Moorish fortress and Christian palace in a stunning clifftop location, with sweeping views across the flat plain of the River Corbones to the east. The public rooms surround a central Moorish-style patio, and the bedrooms are large and luxuriously furnished; all look out either onto the inner courtyard or the valley. If you can't afford a room, have a drink at the bar or check out the excellent restaurant (▶ 165).

☐ 195 D3 ☒ Alcázar s/n, Carmona ☎ 954 14 10 10, fax: 954 14 17 12, email: carmona@parador.es

SEVILLE

La Albahaca £££

La Albahaca, one of Seville's best-known restaurants, stands on one of the city's prettiest squares. There is an attractive outdoor patio, as well as four intimate dining rooms, decorated with dazzling *azulejos*, antique oil paintings, chandeliers and plants galore. The menu is well rounded and the food delicious, including several truly delicious desserts.

☐ 202 C3 ☒ Plaza de Santa Cruz 12, Seville ☎ 954 22 07 14, fax: 954 56 12 04 ❿ Mon–Sat 12.30–4, 8.30–midnight. Closed 24 and 31 Dec

Restaurant La Cueva £–££

This is a picture-postcard sort of place, with a cool green patio for dining al fresco. Ochre walls, cobbles and columns complete the look, while the indoor dining room is hung with all the matador paraphernalia – including the bull (his stuffed head, that is). The food is surprisingly reasonable, including the 3-course *menu del día*, and the dishes are solidly Andaluz with some good fish choices and an above-average paella.

☐ 202 B3 ☒ Rodrigo Caro 18, Seville ☎ 954 21 31 43 ❿ Tue–Sat 12.30–3.30, 7.30–11.30

Habanita £–££

One of Seville's few vegetarian restaurants is tucked down a side street in the buzzing Alfalfa *barrio*, within easy walking distance north of the city centre. The reasonable prices attract students and travellers and the menu is vast, with an emphasis on Cuban and Mediterranean dishes. There are some real one-offs like yucca with garlic, plus black beans, tamales and strict vegan fare. They are not too pious to serve alcohol and sugar-laden desserts though!

➕ 202 B4 ✉ Calle Golfo 3, Seville ☎ 606 71 64 56 (mobile) 🕐 Mon–Sat 12–4.30, 8.30–late

Jamón Real £–££

This tiny restaurant and bar, with typical Andaluz decor of hams over the bar and coloured tiles on the walls, is popular with locals. As the name suggests, the speciality is ham, and you can order a selection with sausages. Vegetarians may prefer the cheese plate with around

eight different choices. This is genuine country cuisine with most of the main dishes hailing from the Extremadura region of Spain.

➕ 202 A3 ✉ Calle López de Arenas 5, Seville ☎ 954 56 39 98 🕐 Tue–Sun 11–4.30, 7.30–midnight. Closed 25 Dec–7 Jan

El Patio £

In this famous bar there's enough tilework for a mini *alcázar*, with *azulejo* steps providing additional seating. Popular with students, shoppers and business people, the *tapas* menu includes a vast range of multi-tiered sandwiches with interesting fillings plus the usual *tortilla* (omelette), *jamón* and olives, best washed down with an ice-cold *fino* direct from the barrel.

➕ 202 B4 ✉ San Eloy 9, Seville ☎ 954 22 11 48 🕐 Daily 11.30–11.30

Casa Robles ££

On a pretty cobbled street near Calle Sierpes, this popular

traditional restaurant specialises in seafood with more than a dozen types of shellfish served daily. It has been family-run since 1954, and owner Juan Robles is a dab hand in the kitchen. There are three small dining rooms and a bustling *tapas* bar serving all the usual favourites, plus a selection of dainty small sandwiches called *emparedados* and some interesting *revuelto* (scrambled egg) combinations.

➕ 202 B3 ✉ Calle Álvarez Quintero 58, Seville ☎ 954 56 32 72, fax: 954 56 44 79 🕐 Daily 1–4.30, 8–1. Closed 24 Dec for dinner

Pizzería San Marco ££

Not your usual fast-food Italian, this one is housed in an authentic Muslim bath house, giving it a great atmosphere – rather like sitting inside your own private mosque. The menu has a good range of typical pizza and pasta dishes, and the place is usually packed. Enjoy a glass of house Rioja while you wait at San Marco's very own Harry's Bar,

not quite as grand as the prototype in Venice, but fun.

➕ 202 C3 ✉ Calle Mesón del Moro 6, Seville ☎ 954 21 43 90 🕐 Tue–Sun 1.30–4.30, 8.30–12.30

CARMONA

Restaurante Alcázar de la Reina, Parador of Carmona £££

A former Moorish fortress provides a superb setting, and the dining room with its vaulted ceiling, chandeliers and clifftop views makes this restaurant a winner for special occasions. The menu is select with an emphasis on game, particularly partridge and venison; the house wine is excellent and a reasonable price.

➕ 195 D3 ✉ Calle Alcázar s/n, Carmona ☎ 954 14 10 10, fax: 954 14 17 12 🕐 Daily 1.30–4, 8.30–11. Closed Jul and 24 Dec

Molino de la Romera ££–£££

This 15th-century mill has retained much of its original character with ancient cobbled floors, arches and patio. The bar does a brisk trade in drinks and *tapas* for a predominantly student crowd, while the restaurant has a typical Andalucian menu with *gazpacho*, salads and soups, *tortilla*, fried fish, grilled meat and various seafood dishes. There is also a fabulous *mesón* (period-décor restaurant), open at weekends only, located in an evocative church-like space with its own bar and fireplace.

🔁 195 D3 ☒ Calle Pedro I, Carmona ☎ 954 14 20 00, fax: 954 14 01 025 🕐 Bar: Mon–Fri 1–11. Restaurant: Mon–Fri 7.30–11 pm. Closed 24 and 31 Dec

ARACENA

Restaurante Casas ££

There's not much wall space left at this typical Sierra Morena restaurant specialising in the region's famous ham and pork. Mirrors, plates, religious pictures, and pots and pans are the backdrop to the cosy beamed dining room. The food represents honest, home-style cooking at its best, although the choice is rather limited, with dishes prepared according to what is in season.

🔁 194 B4 ☒ Colmenetas 41, Aracena ☎ 959 12 80 44, fax: 959 12 82 12 🕐 Daily noon–5

Montecruz ££

Hams hang above the bar in this colourful, bright bar/restaurant. There's a stunning view of the castle from the formal dining room upstairs, which is packed out with Spanish families at weekends. The décor is upbeat with colourful tiles, blue and yellow paintwork and pine furnishings; you can eat on an outdoor terrace in summer. Starters include such local specialities as *migas* (fried breadcrumbs) with sardines, and spinach and chickpeas, available in either *tapa* or *ración* size.

🔁 194 B4 ☒ Plaza de San Pedro, Aracena ☎ 959 12 60 13 🕐 Daily 11–4.30, 9–midnight

Where to... Shop

The city of Seville encourages chic fashion, and there are numerous clothes and shoe shops with leading brand names well represented. Souvenir outlets crowd the main tourist venues of the city, but there are top-quality gift and jewellery shops too, as well as shops specialising in ceramics and traditional crafts.

Huelva city and province cannot match Seville for general shopping, but in the Sierra Morena hill towns of Aracena and Jabugo you can buy some of the finest *jamón serrano* (mountain-style cured ham) and other food products that you'll ever taste.

Seville's main shopping area lies between the bustling Plaza Nueva (▶ 152) and adjacent Plaza de San Francisco (▶ 152) and, to their north, the Plaza del Duque de la Victoria. Central to it all is the pedestrianised **Calle Sierpes** (▶ 152) which, together with its neighbouring streets of Velázquez, Tetuán, Méndez Nuñez and their interconnecting alleyways, has a vast range of shops selling clothes, shoes, leatherwear, children's wear and ceramics. For the ultimate in style, **Max Mara** (Plaza Nueva 3, tel: 954 21 48 25) has up-to-the-minute fashions, as does top Spanish style house **Zara** (Plaza del Duque de la Victoria, tel: 954 21 48 75). For American fashion try **Nicole Miller** (Albareda 16, tel: 954 56 36 14), and for Spanish with a touch of Italian couture there's **Vittoria & Lucchino** (Calle Sierpes, tel: 954 22 71 51).

For something quintessentially

Spanish, Sierpes has a number of splendid shops selling flamenco scarves and veils, shawls and shoes, including **Molina** (Sierpes 11, tel: 954 22 92 54) and **Modas Muñoz** (Cerrajería 5, tel: 954 22 85 96). At **Artesanía Textil** (Calle Sierpes 70, tel: 954 56 28 40), you can buy gifts such as place mats, wall hangings and tablecloths in the finest Andalucian styles. And check out **Sombrería Maquedano** (Sierpes 40, tel: 954 56 47 71) for truly stylish hats and impeccable service.

For jewellery of the highest quality, try **Joyería Abrines** (Calle Sierpes 47, tel: 954 22 84 55) and **Casa Ruiz** (O'Donnell 14, tel: 954 22 21 37 and Sierpes 68, tel: 954 22 77 80). Near the north end of Sierpes is a branch of the department store **El Corte Inglés** (Plaza del Duque de la Victoria, tel: 954 22 29 91). For something less mainstream, have a look round the **jewellery and clothes market**, staged every Thursday, Friday and Saturday in Plaza del Duque de la Victoria itself. And to see what gets Sevillanos really excited as the Feria de Abril (▶ 21) approaches, look into **Arcab** (Paseo de Cristóbal Colón 8, tel: 954 56 14 11) for all things equestrian.

At **La Campaña** (tel: 954 22 35 70), at the north end of Sierpes, you find a superb selection of cakes and pastries. **Horno San Buenaventura** (Avenida de la Constitución/Calle G Vinuesa, tel: 954 92 32 64), directly opposite the cathedral, has a café-restaurant with a mouthwatering selection of sweets, chocolates and ice cream, as well as cakes and pastries.

Other good shopping areas include the narrow Calle Hernando Colón that leads from Alemanes, opposite the main entrance to the cathedral, to Plaza de San Francisco, and is packed with gift, clothes and souvenir shops. In Barrio de Santa Cruz (▶ 148), mixed in with the souvenir shops are some classy shops. One such is **Agua de Sevilla** (Rodrigo Caro 16, tel: 954 21 06 54), a very stylish perfumery and accessories shop near the Reales Alcázares (▶ 146–7), where you can buy exquisite jasmine-scented cologne. For ceramics and other crafts try **El Azulejo** (Mateos Gago 10, tel: 954 21 80 88), **El Postigo** (Arfe, tel: 954 21 39 76), **Sevilleart** (Calle Sierpes 66, tel: 954 21 28 36), or across the river in the Triana district, **Azulejos Santa Isabel** (Alfarería 12, tel: 954 34 46 08) and a number of other outlets.

CARMONA

For excellent pottery, including hand-painted tiles and nameplates to order, look in **Cerámica San Blas** (Domínguez de la Haza 18, tel: 954 14 40 49). For typical rural goods, visit Carmona's morning **market** just off Calle Domínguez de Aposanto.

HUELVA PROVINCE

The Sierra Morena hills to the north of Seville are *jamón* country, where delicious cured ham known as *pata negra* is produced. Aracena's **Jamones y Embutidos Ibéricos, La Trastienda** (Plaza San Pedro 2, tel: 959 12 71 58) sells all manner of cured and cooked meats, but the widest (though priciest) choice is in the village of **Jabugo** (▶ 184). Enticing selections of *jamón, chorizo* (spicy sausage) and *salchichón* (salami) are all on sale at top outlets such as **La Cañada de Jabugo** (Carretera San Juan del Puerto-Cáceres 2, tel: 959 12 12 07).

For traditional Sierra Morena crafts, you won't do better than a visit to **Artesanía Pascual** (Plaza de San Pedro 47, tel: 959 12 80 07), a colourful craft shop, located alongside the car park in Aracena.

Down on Huelva's Costa de la Luz there are few out-of-the-ordinary shopping options, but the main information centre of the Parque Nacional de Doñana, the **Centro de Recepción del Acebuche** (▶ 159), has a useful gift shop that sells some craftwork of the area.

Where to...
Be Entertained

Seville's monthly listings magazine *El Giraldillo* can be bought at kiosks, or is sometimes available free at tourist offices, as is the glossy magazine *Sevilla Welcome & Olé*.

NIGHTLIFE

Seville does not have big clubbing venues, but there are plenty of music bars in the Plaza de la Alfalfa area, a few streets east of Calle Sierpes. On the west bank of the Río Guadalquivir is Calle del Betis where there are a number of lively music bars fronting the Triana district.

FLAMENCO

Seville is big on flamenco and there are any number of "spontaneous"

venues that are difficult for the visitor to track down. There are also some fairly phoney shows, but a good compromise is **El Arenal** (Calle Rodo 7, tel: 954 21 64 92), a long-established venue with twice-nightly *tablaos* (▶ 17) and optional dinner. At the heart of the Barrio de Santa Cruz (▶ 148) are **Los Gallos** (Plaza de Santa Cruz 11, tel: 954 21 69 81) and **El Tamboril** (Plaza de Santa Cruz), both worthwhile venues. For a bit more atmosphere, the popular **La Carbonería** (Calle Levíes 18, tel: 954 21 44 60) often has flamenco on Thursday and Monday nights, and at other times, but rarely before 10 pm. Calle Levíes is reached off Calle San José, which is a few streets northeast of Calle Mateos Gago in Barrio de Santa Cruz.

THEATRE

Seville's **Teatro de La Maestranza** (Paseo de Cristóbal Colón 22, tel: 954 22 65 73), about 100m from the bullring, stages outstanding productions of opera, classical music and jazz. **Teatro Lope de Vega** (Avenida María Luisa, tel: 954 59 08 46) also puts on a programme of theatre, music and dance.

BULLFIGHTING

At Seville's magnificent 18th-century bullring, **La Maestranza** (Paseo de Cristóbal Colón, tel: 954 22 45 77), top *corridas* are always packed out, and to get a ticket, even for the sunny side, you need to book well ahead – not always easy as there is great demand. The season runs from Easter Sunday to October, with big names fighting during June and July and novices taking up the rest of the calendar. Fights are on Sunday evenings and on every evening during the Feria de Abril (▶ 19). It

is always best to try to buy tickets direct from the box office at the ring.

OUTDOOR ACTIVITIES

The Aracena area of the **Sierra Morena** has numerous opportunities for walking and, although there is not a great deal of organised activity, it's worth checking at Aracena's tourist office for current information on guided walks and cycle trips.

On Huelva's Costa de la Luz (▶ 161–2) there are opportunities within **Doñana National Park** (▶ 158–9) for more intensive bird-watching trips than are possible on the standard motorised tours of the park. These tend to be on a group basis (contact the Centro de Recepción del Acebuche, tel: 959 44 87 11). You can even birdwatch from horseback on day-long rides through the Doñana marshland that surrounds the village of El Rocío (contact **Doñana Ecuestre**, El Rocío, tel: 959 44 24 74).

Walks and Tours

1 Granada's Albaicín 170–172
2 Hidden Corners of Córdoba 173–175
3 Sierra de Grazalema 176–178
4 Pottery Villages and Cowboy Country 179–181
5 Sierra de Aracena 182–184

1 GRANADA'S ALBAICÍN

Walk

Granada's picturesque old Moorish quarter, the Albaicín (➤ 87), is explored on this circular walk that offers stunning views of the Alhambra and the Sierra Nevada on the way. The route climbs the Albaicín hill along narrow alleyways, past historic churches and through the bustling heart of the quarter to the magnificent viewpoint of the Mirador de San Nicolás.

DISTANCE 3km
TIME 2–3 hours
START/END POINT Plaza Nueva ✚ 200 C2

1–2

From Plaza Nueva walk through Plaza Santa Ana past a church, the Iglesia de Santa Ana y San Gil, and along the narrow Carrera del Darro, keeping a close lookout for traffic. Down on your right the minuscule Río Darro filters its way through water weed. As you walk along the street you pass first the old Moorish bridge, the Puente de Cabrera, and then the Puente de Espinosa, both rising at an angle as they span the river. From here you can see the walls of the Alhambra looming high above. On the opposite bank of the stream, just beyond the second bridge, are the ruins of an 11th-century gateway, the Puerta de los Tableros, and of an old bridge, the Puente del Cadí. Look left for the alleyway called Bañuelo with, just left of the entrance, the 11th-century **Baños Árabes** (➤ 87).

2–3

Continue along Carrera del Darro, passing the **Convento de Santa Catalina de Zafra** (open daily, closed throughout August) where you can buy delicious almond cakes from the nuns, and the **Museo Arqueológico** (➤ 87) on your left. Keep on past the wide terrace of Paseo del Padre Manjón, known also as Paseo de los Tristes because priests once publicly prayed here; today it is crammed with café tables served from the long line of bars along the street front. The Alhambra towers above.

The classic view of the Alhambra, with the snow-capped Sierra Nevada in the distance

3–4

Just past the Café Bar La Fuente, turn left up narrow, pebbled Calle Horno del Oro. Go up steps at the top of the alley, then turn right up some more steps. Cross a lane and continue up roughly pebbled Calle Valenzuela. At its top go up more steps, bear left, then turn right at a junction. In 20m go sharply left, then uphill and round to the right. At a junction with Carril de San Agustín, go sharply left and up the pebbled lane. There are fine views of the Alhambra to your left.

Bibalbonud, a brick-built Moorish well, and Convento Santo Tomasas de Villanueva. Continue through the tree-lined Placeta del Abad and go alongside the wall of the church of **San Salvador**. Turn left to reach the entrance to the church. The church was built on the site of a 13th-century mosque, and the original patio, complete with arcades and pointed horseshoe

arches, still survives.

Steps lead down to Caldereria Nueva, near the end of the walk

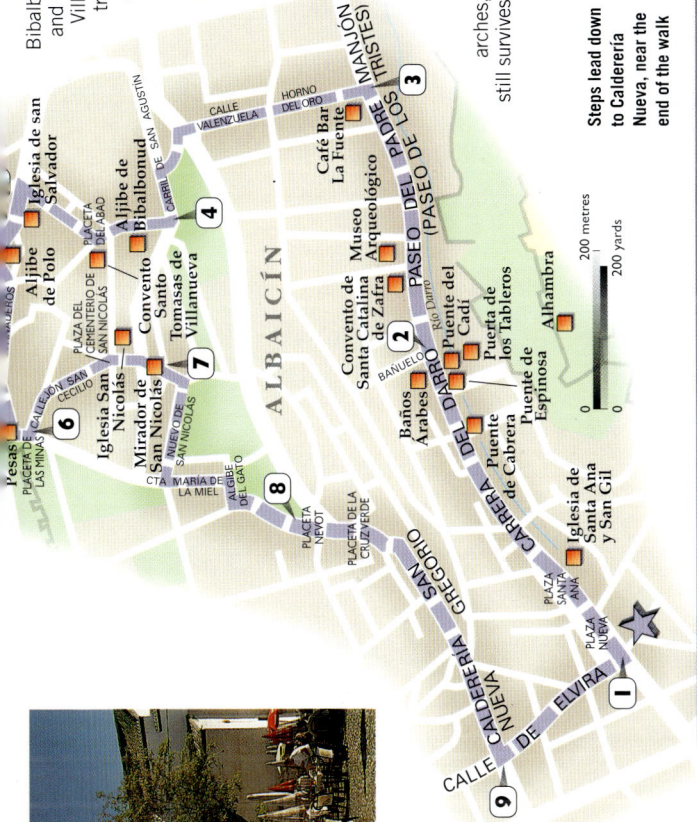

The cafés in Plaza del Cementerio de San Nicolás are a good place to take a half-way break

4–5

Follow the lane round to the right and keep on, past a junction on the left. Pass the Aljibe de

5–6

Leave the church and turn left, and then left again into Calle Panaderos. Pass another old well, the Aljibe de Polo, and continue past small local shops and characterful bars to reach pleasant, tree-shaded Plaza Larga, lined with more bars and shops and filled with fruit and flower stalls in the mornings. Cross the plaza to its opposite corner and go under the **Puerta de la Pesas** (Gate of the Weights), an arched gateway in the old walls of the Albaicín's original Moorish castle, its Alcazaba.

6–7

Beyond the arch, climb some steps into Placeta de las Minas, turn left along Callejón San Cecilio and follow the lane round right to reach Plaza del Cementerio de San Nicolás and the 16th-century church, Iglesia San Nicolás. To the right of the church is a Moorish cistern, its faucets still spouting water. Immediately in front of the church is the **Mirador de San Nicolás**, Granada's most famous viewpoint. Keep a strong grip on your belongings here.

7–8

Go down the right hand-side of the Mirador, keep downhill, then go right along Nuevo de San Nicolás. At a crossing, turn left onto narrow Cuesta María de la Miel, then at a T-junction turn right along Algibe del Gato. In a few metres, go down left and into **Placeta Nevot**. On the right-hand side of the square is an Arabic-style building with a fine arched doorway.

Street sellers congregate at the Mirador de San Nicolás, from where there are spectacular views of the Alhambra

8–9

Keep going downhill and on through **Placeta de la Cruz Verde** (from where you'll get a fleeting glimpse of the Alhambra). Continue down San Gregorio, then along Caldería Nueva passing Granada's fast-growing modern "Arab quarter", with its Islamic food shops, tea houses and craft galleries. Reach a T-junction with Calle de Elvira, and turn left to return to Plaza Nueva.

Taking a Break

In Plaza del Cementerio de San Nicolás just before the Mirador de San Nicolás are two bar-restaurants with outside seating, **Café-Bar El Mirador** and **Café-Bar Kiki San Nicolás**.

When?

Mid-morning is a good time for this walk. The area is full of the morning sun and the plazas and busier streets are full of life.

Places to Visit

Iglesia de San Salvador
🕑 Mon–Sat 10–1 and 4–6.30
💰 Inexpensive

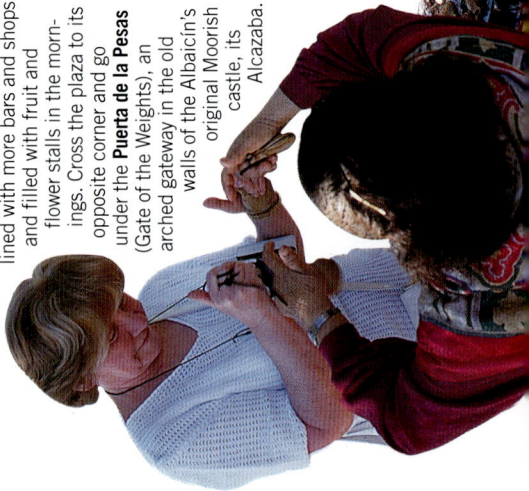

2 HIDDEN CORNERS OF CÓRDOBA

Walk

Escape from the crowds round the Mezquita by heading off to explore a Córdoba where there are no souvenir shops but instead fascinating old buildings, hidden corners, and engaging local bars and cafés.

DISTANCE 4km
TIME 2–3 hours
START/END POINT The Mezquita ✚ 198 C2

1–2

Start outside the north corner of the Mezquita where Magistral González Francés meets the narrow Calle Encarnación. Go up Encarnación passing the patio entrance to **Meryan**, one of Córdoba's finest leathercraft shops. At a T-junction alongside the Iglesia de la Encarnación turn right down Calle del Rey Heredia. Embedded in the corner of the church is a Roman column, one of numerous relics of pre-Muslim Córdoba found all over the city. In 20m, turn left along Horno del Cristo, then bear left into Plaza Jerónimo Paez. Beyond the square's screens of palm trees, cypresses and orange trees stands the ornate Renaissance facade of the **Museo Arqueológico** (➤ 118).

2–3

Follow narrow Marqués del Villar to the right of the museum. The street twists to left and right, and leads past a splendid baroque entranceway with spiral columns and a studded door. At a T-junction, turn right down Ambrosio de Morales to reach **Plaza Seneca** with its broken statue and Roman capitals, reminders of one of Córdoba's famous sons, the philosopher Seneca, born there in 55 BC. Here too is the **Taberna Sociedad Plateros** bar, one of several bars owned by the city's venerable Society of Silverworkers. The bar's beamed ceiling is supported by old stone columns.

3–4

Carry on in the same direction along San Eulogio and Calle Cabezas past Hostal Portillo, named after the **Arco de Portillo**, a Moorish gateway seen down to the left. Just beyond yet another Roman column incorporated into a wall is the imposing, though decaying facade of a Renaissance palace, **Casa de los Marqueses del Carpio**. A few metres further on is a narrow gated alleyway called **De los Arquillos**. On the wall to its left a plaque relates the harsh story of how a 10th-century knight took revenge for insults made to his bride by seven noble brothers. He had the seven killed, imprisoned their father in the house adjoining los Arquillos, and displayed the brothers' severed heads above the archway. Continue to a junction and turn left down Caldereros. Keep ahead through

Iglesia de la Trinidad is one of Córdoba's finest churches

(being slowly restored) has been the scene of *autos da fé* during the Inquisition, bullfights, festivals, and latterly rock concerts.

5–6
Leave the square by its far left-hand corner and go up Rodríguez Marín. At its top cross the busy junction of Tundidores and Capitulares and keep ahead along Claudio Marcelo. On the right side of the road stands a cluster of reconstructed columns of a 1st-century Roman temple. Continue into **Plaza de las Tendillas** with its flamenco-chiming clock (▶ 118).

6–7
Cross Plaza de las Tendillas and go down the shopping street of Conde de Gondomar to

Plaza de la Pescadería past its central palm tree, then continue to a T-junction with Calle de San Fernando.

4–5
Turn left up Calle de San Fernando. Cross over and in a few metres go right and along Calle San Francisco past a junction (**Plaza del Potro**, ▶ 118, is down to the right) and bear round left along Calle Armas. At a junction keep along S Peña and through Plaza Canas to reach the arcaded Plaza Corredera. This 17th-century creation

the right of the flamenco clock tower. Reach the top of the broad Avenida del Gran Capitán and the **Iglesia de San Nicolás de la Villa**. This is one of Córdoba's finest churches, notable for its handsome bell tower. Turn left down San Felipe, to the left of the church. Pass through Plaza de San Nicolás to reach Plaza de Ramón y Cajal.

Bear round right into Tesoro and reach Plaza Trinidad and the **Iglesia de la Trinidad**, which has magnificent gilded altarpieces set off by pristine white walls and roof. In front of the church is a statue of the 16th-century Cordoban poet Luis de Góngora. Cross in front of the church and continue down Sánchez de Feria, passing the little Plaza Profesor López-Neyra. Turn right at a junction and go along Calle Fernández Ruano, with a great collection of tapas bars, to reach **Puerta de Almodóvar** (▶ 117).

7–8

Return through Puerta de Almodóvar, then go right down Calle Judíos. On the left, a short way down the street, is the splendid bar Bodega Guzmán, a local favourite. Just past here is **Casa No 12**, an unusual museum in which the patios and rooms are furnished as they would have been in the 12th century; in the cellar are Visigothic reliefs and a fine Roman mosaic. Further down the street you pass the **Zoco** craft market, the **synagogue** and the **Maimonides statue** (all ▶ 117). Reach Plaza Maimónides and turn left past the **Museo Taurino** (▶ 117). Keep ahead along the narrow alleyway of Cardenal

Salazar to reach Plaza del Cardenal Salazar, which is overlooked by the monumental doorway of the Facultado de Filosofía y Letras. Turn right out of the plaza and into crowded Calle Romero. Turn right at the next junction into Calle Deanes, then bear left, past a traffic barrier of little posts, to go along Judería to the Mezquita.

Taking a Break

There are numerous bars and cafés along the way. The **Taberna Sociedad Plateros** (Calle San Francisco 6) is popular and has a splendid covered patio. On the corner where Sánchez Peña enters Plaza Corredera is the down-to-earth but excellent bar, **Taberna Corredera**.

When?

Mid-morning, or early evening if you want to tie in the walk with visits to the Museo Arqueológico and to the other attractions in the Calle Judíos area.

Places to Visit

Casa No 12
✉ Casa No 12 Calle Judíos
🕐 Tue–Sat 10–2 and 6–8

Casa No 12 re-creates a 12th-century Moorish interior

3 SIERRA DE GRAZALEMA

Tour

The *pueblos blancos*, the "white towns" of Málaga and Cádiz provinces, are in reality small mountain villages of whitewashed houses set amid the spectacular mountains of the Parque Natural Sierra de Grazalema. This tour takes you to some of the finest.

DISTANCE 80km
TIME 4–5 hours
START/END POINT Grazalema ✚ 195 D2

1–2

Leave **Grazalema**, sheltering beneath the rocky peak of Peñón Grande, by the Ronda road and keep ahead at a junction, following signs for Ronda and Ubrique. The road winds uphill beneath huge overhanging cliffs. At a junction, keep ahead along the A374, signed Ubrique. Follow the road beneath the impressive rocky crags of the Sierra del Caillo and pass **Villaluenga del Rosario**, the highest village in Cádiz province.

2–3

Continue through a flat-bottomed valley where rocky slopes rise to either side and stone walls wriggle along the base of the cliffs. The valley is known as La Manga (The Sleeve). Soon, the road bends sharply to the right just after a picnic spot and viewpoint. In about 1km turn off right at a junction, signed **Benaocaz**, and enter the village. There is parking for a few cars in Plaza de Vista Hermosa on the outskirts. The village, an 8th-century Moorish settlement, is a typical *pueblo blanco*, with whitewashed houses clustered on the hillside against a background of limestone crags and wooded slopes. Encircling the main square, Plaza de las Libertades, are pillars with small ceramic tiles picturing local landmarks.

3–4

From Plaza de Vista Hermosa, keep left down Calle Lavadero and on through Plaza de las Libertades. Turn left down Calle San Blas, then at the main road turn right, signed A373 Villamartin. In about 3km turn right at a junction. The quite large town of Ubrique lies down to the left below the dramatic cliffs of Cruz

Right: The village of Benaocaz is a good starting point for a number of walks

numbers of pinsapo pines, a conifer that has had a tenuous continuity since the last European Ice Age but which now flourishes in the Parque Natural Sierra de Grazalema. The road climbs steadily through a spectacular series of S-bends to reach the Puerto de Palomas (Pass of the Doves) at 1,357m, from where it descends through more S-bends. About 4km below the pass, there is a car park on the left from where a path leads for several kilometres to the spectacular Garganta Verde ravine (see panel). Continue towards Zahara de la Sierra and soon pass an olive oil production centre, **El Vínculo Molino de Aceite Alojamiento Rural**, which is open for visits during normal working hours (▶ 74). You may be offered a taster glass of olive oil; too big a sip is not recommended for the unaccustomed palate. In a further 4km, reach the village of Zahara de la Sierra.

6–7

Enter **Zahara de la Sierra** by a winding uphill road. There are parking spaces just before you reach the narrow entrance to the village and it is advisable to park here, or further downhill. Zahara, one of the loveliest of the *pueblos blancos*, was declared a national monument in

4–5

Watch for signposts for El Bosque and for a junction on the right, signed Benamahoma and Grazalema. Bear right here, then keep right at the next junction on to the A372, signed Benamahoma, Ronda and Grazalema. The road now climbs towards the Sierra del Pinar, passing above **Benamahoma**, another attractive *pueblo blanco*. It celebrates its Moorish heritage with a colourful festival that includes mock battles between "Moors and Christians" on the first Sunday of August. Continue along the A372 with stupendous views of limestone crags on your right. In about 8km turn left, signed Zahara de la Sierra.

5–6

You now enter a beautiful area of mountains swathed in cork oak and holm oak and large

de Tajo. Continue along the wider and faster A373 for about 8km.

The Garganta Verde

If you have 2–3 hours to spare, a walk into this magnificent area of the Sierra is immensely rewarding. However, to visit you must obtain a permit from the information offices at El Bosque or Grazalema (▶ 66–7). The path to and from the roadside car park is well signposted and takes you high above the deep gorge of the Garganta Verde. Just before the path begins its descent into the bed of the gorge, divert up a steep, signposted path to the spectacular **Las Buitreras de Garganta Verde**, a viewpoint into the upper gorge and to the huge cliffs that are the roosting and nesting site of dozens of griffon vultures. Be patient and quiet and you should be rewarded by the sight of these magnificent birds with a 3m wingspan cruising past, their wings creating a sound like the wind. The main path takes you down into the stony bed of the gorge which leads to the great cavern of the **Garganta la Ermita** with its multicoloured rock formations.

the 1980s. The village clings to a rocky hill crowned by a 12th-century castle. Its narrow main street leads to a central plaza overlooked by the baroque church of Santa María de Mesa

The restored 12th-century Moorish castle dominates the village of Zahara de la Sierra

and with a *mirador* giving fine views of the reservoir, the Embalse de Zahara, below. The castle is reached from the square by a rocky path; the views from its battlements are worth the effort.

Leave Zahara along the main street. At the central plaza keep right, and then left, round a tiny roundabout, before following exit signs down very steep and narrow streets. On reaching the one-way approach road that you came up earlier, go sharply right and down a short side road to a T-junction with the main road. Turn right, signed Grazalema, and at the next junction turn left onto a road signed Arroyo Molinos. At the next T-junction turn right, signed Arroyo Molinos, and follow the road above the reservoir.

7–8

Just past where the reservoir ends, turn right, signed Grazalema, and continue through wooded mountains to reach a T-junction. Turn right to return to Grazalema.

Taking a Break

At Benaocaz, the **Restaurante Las Vegas**, in Plaza de las Libertades, has great views from its windows. At Zahara de la Sierra, the restaurant at the **Marqués de Zahara Hotel** in the main street may be able to supply lunch (tel: 956 12 30 61). The simple **Bar Nuevo** just across the road also does food.

4 POTTERY VILLAGES AND COWBOY COUNTRY

Tour

First stop on this tour is the village of Níjar, one of Andalucía's most important pottery-making centres. From here the route continues through remote mountains and into Almería's astonishing desert canyons. This is where filmmakers produced a string of "spaghetti westerns", including *A Fistful of Dollars*, and where the "Wild West" lives on in the theme parks.

DISTANCE 100km
TIME 3 hours (longer if time is spent at Níjar and Mini Hollywood)
START/END POINT Almería ✚ 197 E2

1–2

Drive east out of Almería from the big roundabout at the bottom of the Rambla de Belén, following signs for Murcia and Mojácar. In 17km

join the E15. Once clear of Almería's outskirts and beyond its airport, you approach the bizarre world of *plasticultura*, the intensive production of fruit and vegetables inside *invernaderos*, plastic greenhouses (▶ panel, page 181). Behind the plastic-wrapped plains of the Campo de Níjar rise the mountains of the Sierra de Alhamilla. In about 30km turn off left, signed Níjar, and, in a few kilometres, enter **Níjar** (▶ 100) by its long main street, Avenida García Lorca,

where there are numerous parking bays. Níjar's ceramics industry has flourished since Moorish times and there are numerous craft shops along Avenida García Lorca and the adjoining Barrio Alfarero. While in Níjar stop off in Plaza la Glorieta, the main square of the upper town, reached by continuing uphill from the top of Avenida García Lorca. The 16th-century church of Santa María de la Anunciación, which overlooks the square, has a fine *mudéjar* coffered ceiling in the central nave.

2–3

Leave Níjar by returning down Avenida García Lorca, and then turning left at the T-junction, signed Campohermosa and Murcia. At the next T-junction turn left, signed Lucainena, AL 103, and drive uphill. Stop at the next junction before turning right, signed Lucainena.

Níjar has a long-established ceramics industry and is noted for its pottery

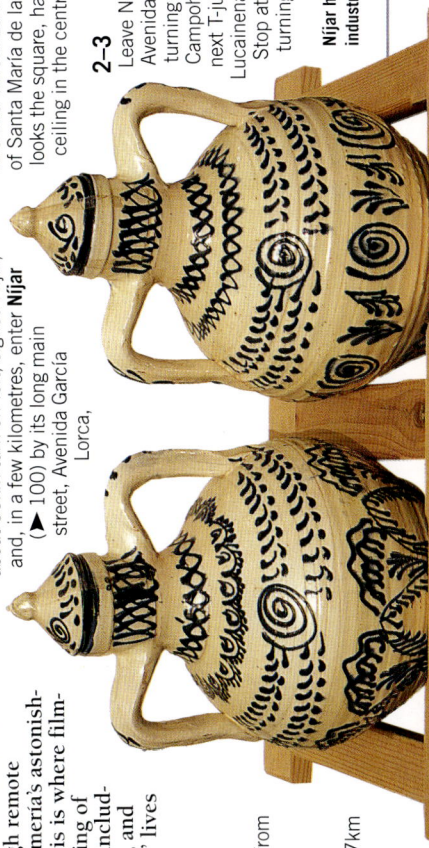

Sorbas
Cuevas de Sorbas
A370

Murcia

Níjar de

Campohermosa

5 km

3 miles

A370

③

Lucainena de las Torres

AL102

Níjar

②

E15

1092m
Peñón
de Turrillas

Sierra   de   Alhamilla

Campo   de

Cuevas de los Ube

El Alquián

Los Yesos

A370

Tabernas

Texas Hollywood

Mini Hollywood

Pechina

Western Leone

④

Viator

Granada - Almería Autovía

The arid landscapes around Tabernas

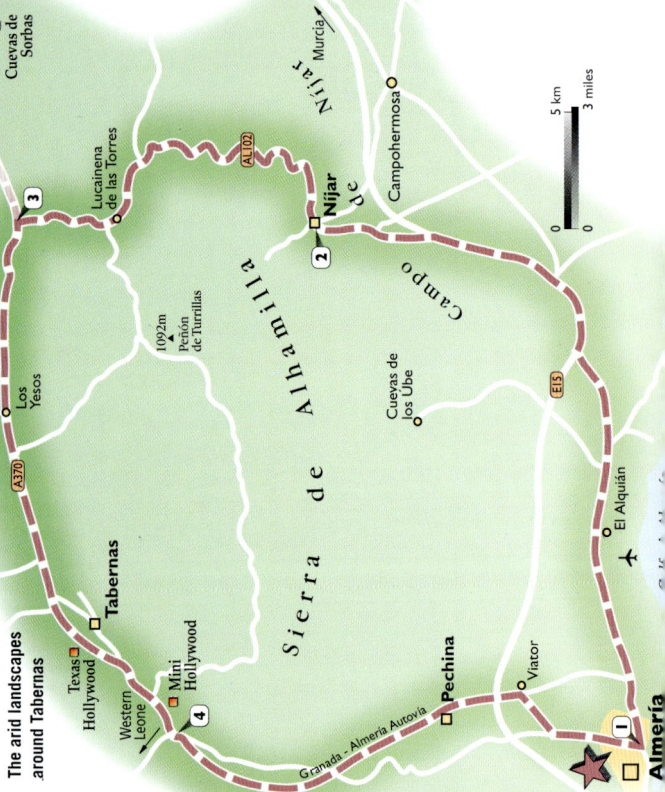

Almería

①

(The signpost indicating Lucainena is on the corner opposite, but it may be obscured by a tree). Continue into the heart of the hills of the **Sierra de Alhamilla** where you soon reach uninhabited country, a dry mountain landscape made appealing by its numerous oak trees and low scrub. From high above Níjar you can see the sprawling expanse of the plastic *invernaderos* that cover the plain of the Campo de Níjar below. Watch out for potholes in the road ahead. About 16km from Níjar, the road descends from the hills to the village of **Lucainena de las Torres,** where whitewashed houses surround a pretty church beneath the soaring crags of the Peñón de Turrillas. Continue for 9km, finally descending a long, straight stretch of road lined with eucalyptus trees to a junction with the A370.

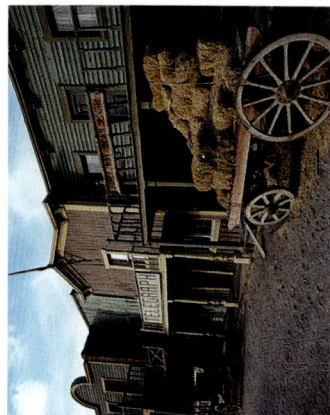

Mini Hollywood, west of Tabernas, is the best known of the Wild West theme parks

The Plastic Sea

In western Almería province, around the town of El Ejido, the once empty flatlands are covered with over 25,000 hectares of flat-roofed polythene greenhouses in which vegetables, fruit and flowers are grown using drip-feed irrigation. This agricultural industry has transformed a poverty-stricken area and earned fortunes for some, but it has also brought serious social and physical problems to many of those who work within it, while the environmental cost and the depletion of scarce water resources pose potential problems for the future.

3–4

You have the option of turning right here to reach the village of Sorbas in 8km. **Sorbas** (▶ 101) is perched dramatically on the cliff edges of a rugged gorge. Its tradition of ceramics is similar to that of Níjar, but Sorbas pottery is more functional and less decorative. The limestone cave complex **Cuevas de Sorbas** (tours available, ▶ 101) is about 2km southeast of the village. On the main route, turn left at the junction with the A370, signed Almería. Continue for 17km through country that becomes increasingly arid

and desert-like, its grey-brown sandstone hills barren of vegetation and sculpted into fantastic shapes by the wind.

The road bypasses **Tabernas**, overlooked by a Moorish castle which may look impressive, but is disappointingly ruinous. You are now in the land of Wild West theme parks, the legacy of decades of film-making during the mid-20th century when the surrounding landscapes were used to replicate the cowboy country of North America. The first of three Wild West attractions is **Texas Hollywood**, reached down a dirt track. There's a dusty cowboy town, complete with a cavalry fort and Native American wigwam village. As with the other Western attractions, mock gunfights are staged at set times and you can hire horses and dress up in cowboy gear. The best organised (and most expensive) of the three is **Mini Hollywood** (▶ 102), about 6km west of Tabernas. About 1km further on, the A370 joins the recently constructed Granada–Almería Autovía. By turning right you can reach the approach track to a third cowboy "town", named **Western Leone** after Sergio Leone, the maker of *A Fistful of Dollars* and *The Good, the Bad and the Ugly*. The cheapest of the Western attractions, this has the most authentic setting, above a dry gulch. To return to Almería, head south on the *autovía* to reach the city.

Taking a Break

In the main square of the old part of Níjar are the **Café Bar La Glorieta** and the **Bar Restaurant El Pipa**. There are no refreshment points elsewhere on the route, but there is a café, bar and restaurant at Mini Hollywood.

DISTANCE 60km
TIME 2–3 hours (longer if stops are made at villages and points of interest along the way)
START/END POINT Aracena ✚ 194 B4

5 SIERRA DE ARACENA

Tour

The Sierra de Aracena is a world of wooded hills traversed by roads that wind lazily between delightful villages where cobbled streets spill down to a central plaza, its fountain brimming with crystal-clear water even in high summer.

1–2

Leave Aracena by Plaza San Pedro, just beyond the car park, and take the road leading south-west, signed Alájar. Drive down an avenue lined with plane trees. Keep ahead at the next junction, signed Alájar, and immediately enter the beautiful hill country of the **Sierra de la Virgen**. You need old-fashioned driving skills here: there are lots of gear changes as the road, the A470, twists and turns through woods of chestnut, ash and oak. Soon you catch glimpses of the tiny village of **Linares de la Sierra**, in the valley below. The village is worth a short

Alájar is typical of the hidden villages in the Sierra de la Virgen

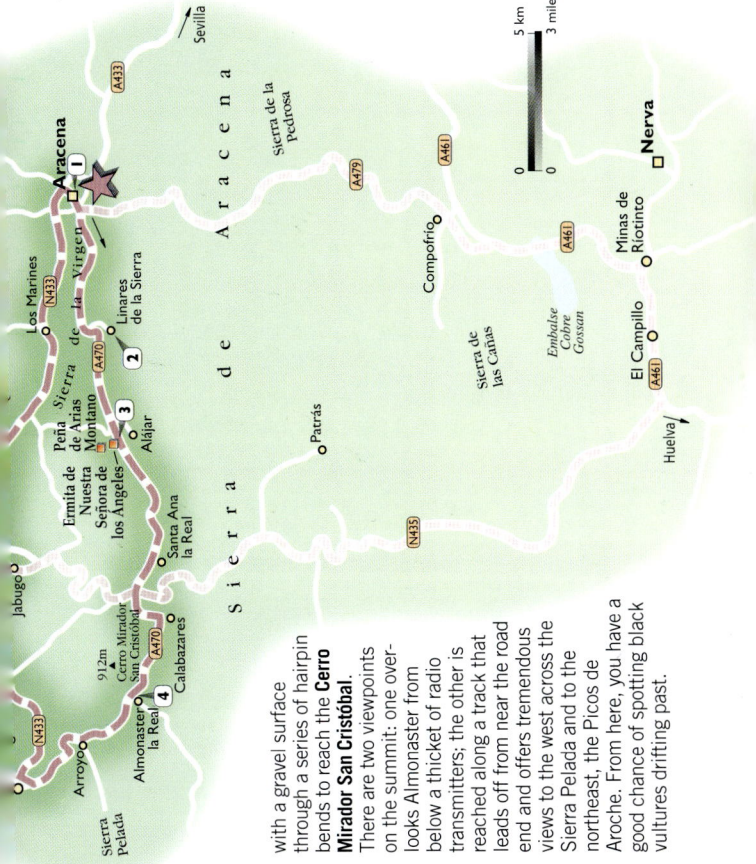

diversion. Park on the road above Linares and stroll downhill to the main square; every household has an individual mosaic of pebbles, like a stone doormat, outside its door.

2–3

Continue along the A470 to reach a turn-off on the left that descends to the larger village of **Alájar**. Above is the rocky outcrop of **Peña de Arias Montano**, with caverns said to have served as human shelters from prehistoric times. A side road leads off right from the main route to the **Ermita de Nuestra Señora de los Ángeles**. This was the retreat of 16th-century cleric and scholar Benito Arias Montano. He was confessor to Philip II, who visited the hermitage and meditated in a nearby cave (below the modern car park). A large rock beside the cave has been known ever since as the King's Chair.

3–4

Back on the A470, carry on to a junction with the Huelva road, the N435. Opposite is the Hostal el Cruce, which has a good *tapas* bar. Go straight across, and take the road opposite, the continuation of the A470, signed Almonaster la Real and Cortegana. Continue through wooded country towards Almonaster. A detour just before the village takes you up to the right along a side road

with a gravel surface through a series of hairpin bends to reach the **Cerro Mirador San Cristóbal**. There are two viewpoints on the summit: one overlooks Almonaster from below a thicket of radio transmitters; the other is reached along a track that leads off from near the road end and offers tremendous views to the west across the Sierra Pelada and to the northeast, the Picos de Aroche. From here, you have a good chance of spotting black vultures drifting past.

To continue direct to **Almonaster**, keep to the main road for a short distance, then turn left. There is parking at the entrance to the village, just where you turn off. Almonaster has a lovely 10th-century **mosque**, built partly into a rock face and left virtually intact after it was converted to Christian worship in the 13th century. It has little horseshoe arches in brick, supported by what are probably Roman and Visigothic columns, recalling, in miniature, the arches of Córdoba's Mezquita. From the adjoining minaret tower you can look down into the bull-ring (take care at the top: the window vents are unguarded). To view the inside of the mosque you need to ask for the key at the town hall in the village square.

4–5

Continue from Almonaster on the A470 and in about 3km, at a

There is always a feast of nuts and fruit in the Sierra de Aracena

Diversion to Minas de Ríotinto

The drive can be extended to take in a visit to dramatic landscapes of the Río Tinto mining area (▶ 161). To do so, leave Jabugo by its southern exit, signed Huelva, and join the southbound N435.

In 25km, turn off left onto the A461, signed Río Tinto and Nerva. Follow signs into the village of **Minas de Ríotinto** (▶ 161). To leave the village take the exit road signed Sevilla and continue on the A461 through wooded hills. Cross an embankment over a reservoir, the Embalse Cobre Gossan. Soon go left onto the A479, signed Campofrío and Aracena, in 18km reach Aracena. This extension adds 60km to the main drive.

junction, turn right down a side road, signed Estación FFCC. Keep left at the next junction, then ignore a turning, signed Canaleja. Reach a junction with the main N433, the Portugal–Seville road, and turn right, signed Aracena and Sevilla. In about 2km turn off for Jabugo.

5–6

The otherwise quiet little village of **Jabugo** is the centre of the *jamón* (ham) curing industry. On reaching the first buildings of the town, turn right, signed Centro Urbano, into a quiet, cobbled street where you have a fair chance of parking. Walk up the street and keep left at a junction, then go immediately left and up Calle Silencio to meet a road lined with bars and shops selling an astonishing variety of *jamón* and other meats. From Jabugo return to the N433 and turn right to reach Aracena.

Taking a Break

Stop for a relaxed lunch in the friendly little **Bar Buenos Aires** in Almonaster la Real's main square. The bars and cafés in Jabugo offer snacks and meals featuring local *jamón*. But, be warned: the often high prices may spoil your appetite.

Practicalities

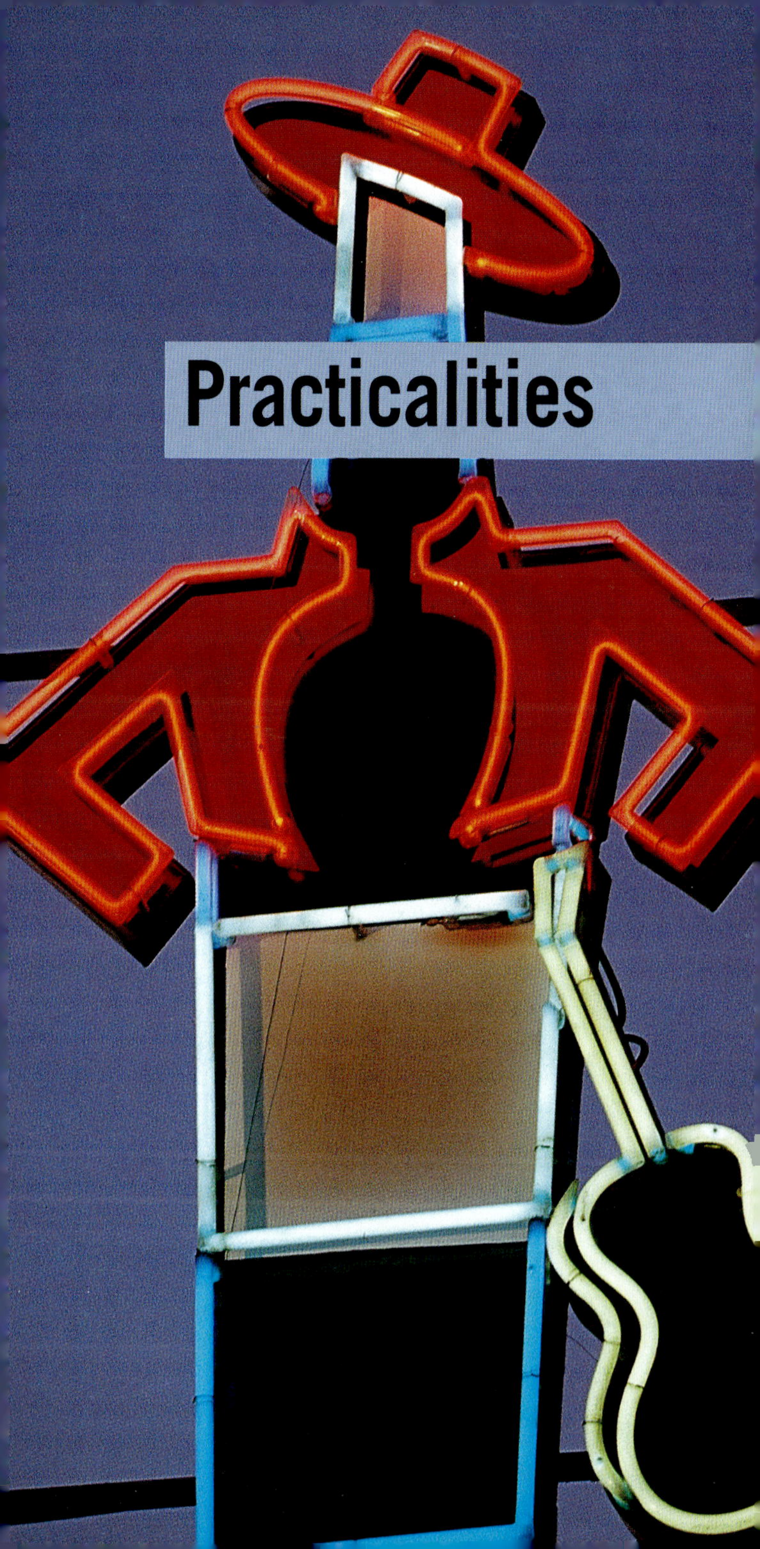

Websites
• Tourism office of Spain: www.spaintour.com

•Links to other Andalucían sites: www.andalucia.org

• General information about Andalucía: www.andalucia.com

In the UK
Spanish Tourist Office
22/23 Manchester Square
London W1M 5AP
☎ (020) 7486 8077

BEFORE YOU GO

WHAT YOU NEED

		UK	Germany	USA	Canada	Australia	Ireland	Netherlands	Spain
●	Required								
○	Suggested								
▲	Not required								
△	Not applicable								
Passport/National Identity Card		●	●	●	●	●	●	●	●
Visa		▲	▲	▲	▲	▲	▲	▲	▲
Onward or Return Ticket		▲	▲	▲	▲	▲	▲	▲	▲
Health Inoculations (tetanus and polio)		▲	▲	▲	▲	▲	▲	▲	▲
Health Documentation (▶ 190 Health)		●	●	●	●	●	●	●	●
Travel Insurance		○	○	○	○	○	○	○	○
Driving Licence (national)		●	●	●	●	●	●	●	●
Car Insurance Certificate (if own car)		●	●	△	△	△	●	●	●
Car Registration Document (if own car)		●	●	△	△	△	●	●	●

WHEN TO GO

Andalucía

High season   Low season

JAN	FEB	MAR	APR	MAY	JUN	JUL	AUG	SEP	OCT	NOV	DEC
16°C	17°C	18°C	21°C	23°C	27°C	29°C	29°C	27°C	23°C	19°C	17°C

☀ Sun   ☁ Cloud   🌧 Wet   ⛅ Sun/Showers

Temperatures are the **average daily maximum** for each month. Easter is usually bright and sunny without being too hot; however, accommodation in cities is heavily booked. The best time to visit is in May and early June when there is plenty of sunshine, and the average daytime temperature is 23 to 25°C. Visitor levels are not too high and there is a choice of accommodation. Peak tourist times are in July and August, when the weather is hottest. Andalucíans holiday in August, and there is a huge exodus to the coast. September and October can be delightful, with the sunny weather lingering well into autumn. Winter temperatures on the coast and in low-lying regions are pleasant, but in the mountains expect chilly to very cold weather. Winter can also bring heavy rain and high winds.

Spanish Tourist Office
35th Floor
666 Fifth Avenue
New York, NY 10103
☎ (212) 265 8822

Tourist Office of Spain
34th Floor
2 Bloor Street West
Toronto M4W 3E2
☎ (416) 961-3131

Tourist Office of Spain
Myliusstrasse, 14
60325 Frankfurt Main
Frankfurt
☎ (49) 69 72 50 53

GETTING THERE

By Air From the UK Cheap flights to Málaga Airport are possible with Easyjet from Luton and Liverpool, GO from Stanstead, and Monarch Airlines from Luton and Manchester. Monarch also flies to Gibraltar from Luton. Scheduled flights to Málaga, Seville and Gibraltar are available with BA from Heathrow and Gatwick, and to Málaga and Seville with Iberia from Heathrow. Iberia has a regular service from Heathrow to Madrid from where connections fly to Almería, Granada and Jerez de la Frontera. Charter flights from the UK to Málaga and Almería are worth investigating as they often have spare seats.

From Dublin and Belfast There are no direct flights to Andalucía, but summer charter flights to Málaga and scheduled services to Madrid and Barcelona operate from both.

From Australia, New Zealand, America and Canada There are no direct flights, but national carriers from all four countries fly to Madrid and Barcelona where connections can be made.

Approximate flying times to Málaga: UK airports (2½ hours–3 hours), Dublin and Belfast (3½–4 hours), West Coast USA (12 hours), Vancouver (10 hours), Montreal (8 hours), Sydney (24 hours + connections), Auckland (22 hours + connections).

By Rail Travelling by train from the UK to Andalucía is time-consuming and will take anything up to 30 hours with several changes of train. You need to first travel to Paris, then change trains, changing once more at the Spanish border for connections to Madrid. There are further connections from Madrid to Córdoba, Seville and other main Andalucían cities.

By Bus Travel by bus from the UK to Andalucía is also time-consuming; at least 24 hours to Madrid, over 30 hours to Málaga. The cost can be more expensive than the cheaper flights.

TIME

Spain is one hour ahead of Greenwich Mean Time (GMT +1), but from late March until the last Sunday in September, summer time (GMT+2) operates.

CURRENCY AND FOREIGN EXCHANGE

Currency Spain is one of the 12 European Union countries to use a single currency, the **Euro**. Euro notes and coins, issued on 1 January, 2002, replace the peseta (pta), formerly the unit of currency. Coins are issued in denominations of 1, 2, 5, 10, 20 and 50 Euro cents and 1 and 2 Euros. Notes are issued in denominations of 5, 10, 20, 50, 100, 200 and 500 Euros. The peseta is due to be phased out by the end of June 2002. 100 pesetas is 0.6 Euros. Travellers' cheques are accepted by most hotels, shops and restaurants in lieu of cash.

Exchange The best places to exchange **travellers' cheques** are banks, bureaux de change at airports, main railway stations or in some department stores, and exchange booths. All transactions are subject to a commission charge. Travellers' cheques can also be changed at main city post offices.

Credit cards are widely accepted in shops, restaurants and hotels. VISA, MasterCard and Diners Club cards with four-digit PINs can be used in most ATM cash dispensers.

GMT	Spain	New York	West Coast USA	France	Sydney
12 noon	1 pm	7 am	4 am	1pm	10 pm

WHEN YOU ARE THERE

CLOTHING SIZES

UK	Spain	USA	
36	46	36	**Suits**
38	48	38	
40	50	40	
42	52	42	
44	54	44	
46	56	46	
7	41	8	**Shoes**
7.5	42	8.5	
8.5	43	9.5	
9.5	44	10.5	
10.5	45	11.5	
11	46	12	
14.5	37	14.5	**Shirts**
15	38	15	
15.5	39/40	15.5	
16	41	16	
16.5	42	16.5	
17	43	17	
8	34	6	**Dresses**
10	36	8	
12	38	10	
14	40	12	
16	42	14	
18	44	16	
4.5	38	6	**Shoes**
5	38	6.5	
5.5	39	7	
6	39	7.5	
6.5	40	8	
7	41	8.5	

NATIONAL HOLIDAYS

1 Jan	New Year's Day
6 Jan	Epiphany
28 Feb	Andalucían Day (regional)
Mar/Apr	Easter Monday
1 May	Labour Day
24 Jun	St John the Baptist (regional)
25 Jul	St James (regional)
15 Aug	Assumption of the Virgin
12 Oct	National Day
1 Nov	All Saints' Day
6 Dec	Constitution Day
8 Dec	Feast of the Immaculate Conception
25 Dec	Christmas Day

OPENING HOURS

○ Shops ● Churches
● Offices ● Museums/Monuments
● Banks ● Pharmacies

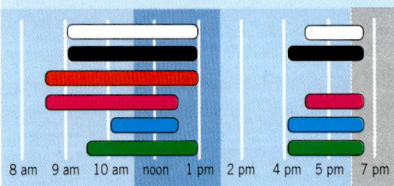

□ Day   ■ Midday   □ Evening

Department stores, large supermarkets and shops in tourist resorts open from 10 am to 8, 9 or even 10 pm. The vast majority of shops close Sun and some close in Aug. Some banks open Sat (Oct–May only) 8:30 am to 1 pm. The opening times of museums is just a rough guide; some open longer in summer, while hours may be reduced in winter. Many museums close Sun afternoon, some also on Sat afternoon, as well as Mon or another day in the week. Some museums offer free entry to EU citizens (take your passport). **Remember – all opening times are subject to change.**

PERSONAL SAFETY

Snatching of handbags and cameras, pickpocketing, theft of unattended baggage and car break-ins are the principal crimes against visitors.

Any crime or loss should be reported to the national police (Policía Nacional), who wear blue uniforms.

Some precautions to take are:

- Do not leave valuables on the beach or poolside.
- Place valuables in a hotel safety-deposit box.
- Wear handbags and cameras across your chest.
- Avoid lonely, seedy and dark areas at night.

Police assistance:
☎ **091**
from any payphone

TELEPHONES

All telephone numbers throughout Spain now consist of nine digits (incorporating the former area code, preceded by 9), and no matter where you call from, you must always dial all nine digits. Many public telephones (*teléfono*) take phonecards (*credifone*), which are available from post offices and some shops for €6 or €12.

International Dialling Codes
Dial 00 followed by:
UK: 44
USA/Canada: 1
Ireland: 353
Australia: 61
New Zealand: 64
Germany: 49
Spain: 34

POST

Post offices (*correos*) are generally open 9–2 (1 pm Sat); closed Sun (tel: 952 35 90 08 Málaga). In main centres they may open extended hours. Málaga's main post office is at Avenida de Andalucía 1. Stamps (*sellos*) can also be bought at tobacconists (*estancos*).

ELECTRICITY

The power supply is: 220/230 volts (in some bathrooms and older buildings: 110/120 volts). Type of socket: round two-hole sockets taking round plugs of two round pins. British visitors will need an adaptor and US vistors a voltage transformer.

TIPS/GRATUITIES

Tipping is not expected for all services and rates are lower than those elsewhere. As a general guide:

Restaurants (if service not included)	5–10%
Cafés/bars	Change
Tour guides	Change
Taxis	2–3%
Chambermaids	Change
Porters	Change
Cloakroom attendants	Change
Toilets	Change

UK	USA	New Zealand	Australia	Canada
☎ 952 21 75 71 (Málaga)	☎ 952 47 48 91 (Fuengirola)	☎ 915 23 02 26 (Madrid)	☎ 954 22 09 71 (Seville)	☎ 914 23 32 50 (Madrid)

HEALTH

Insurance Nationals of EU and certain other countries can get free medical treatment in Spain with the relevant documentation (Form E111 for Britons), although private medical insurance is still advised and is essential for all other visitors.

Dental Services Dental treatment normally has to be paid for in full as dentists operate privately. A list of *dentistas* can be found in the yellow pages of the telephone directory. Dental treatment should be covered by private medical insurance.

Sun advice The sunniest (and hottest) months are July and August, when daytime temperatures are often into the 30s. Try to avoid the midday sun, use a high-factor sun cream to start with, and allow yourself to become used to the sun gradually.

Drugs Prescription and non-prescription drugs and medicines are available from pharmacies (*farmacias*) distinguished by a large green cross. They are able to dispense over the counter many drugs which would be available only on prescription in other countries.

Safe Water Tap water is chlorinated and generally safe to drink; however, unfamiliar water may cause mild abdominal upsets. Mineral water (*agua mineral*) is cheap and widely available. It is sold *sin gas* (still) and *con gas* (carbonated).

CONCESSIONS

Students/Youths Holders of an International Student Identity Card (ISIC) can get some concessions on travel, entrance fees etc, but the Costa del Sol is not really geared up for students. However, low-cost package deals are available for students and young people.

Senior Citizens The Costa del Sol is an excellent destination for older travellers. Travel agents offer tailored package holidays, and in winter there are special low-cost, long-stay holidays. The best deals are through tour operators who specialise in holidays for senior citizens.

TRAVELLING WITH A DISABILITY

Facilities in Andalucía for travellers with disabilities are slowly improving as more hotels install ramps and special lifts etc. For information contact Las Gerencias Provinciales del Instituto Andaluz de Servicios Sociales (The Provincial Management of the Andalucían Institute of Social Services), Avenida Manuel Augustin 26, Málaga (tel: 952 21 04 12/13/14).

CHILDREN

Children are revered in Spain, and are welcome in most cafés, bars and restaurants. Many attractions have cut-price or free entry for children; museum entry is free to under-18s.

TOILETS

There are few public toilets. Bars and cafés do not mind you using their toilets even if you are not buying anything. Carry a supply of toilet paper. Signs are *Aseos*, *Servicios*, and *Señoras* (Ladies) and *Caballeros* or *Señores* (Men).

CUSTOMS

The import of wildlife souvenirs from rare and endangered species may be either illegal or require a special permit. Before purchase you should check customs regulations.

SURVIVAL PHRASES

Yes/no **Sí/no**
Please **Por favor**
Thank you **Gracias**
You're welcome **De nada**
Hello **Hola**
Goodbye **Adiós**
Good morning **Buenos días**
Good afternoon **Buenas tardes**
Good night **Buenas noches**
How are you? **¿Qué tal?**
How much is this? **¿Cuánto vale?**
I'm sorry **Lo siento**
Excuse me **Perdone**
I'd like **Me gustaría…**
Open **Abierto**
Closed **Cerrado**

Today **Hoy**
Tomorrow **Mañana**
Yesterday **Ayer**
Monday **Lunes**
Tuesday **Martes**
Wednesday **Miércoles**
Thursday **Jueves**
Friday **Viernes**
Saturday **Sábado**
Sunday **Domingo**

DIRECTIONS

I'm lost **Me he perdido**
Where is…? **¿Dónde está?**
How do I get to…?
¿Cómo se va…?
the bank **al banco**
the post office
a la oficina de correos
the train station
a la estación de trenes

Where are the toilets?
¿Dónde están los servicios?
Left **a la izquierda**
Right **a la derecha**
Straight on **todo recto**
At the corner **en la esquina**
At the traffic-light **en el semáforo**
At the crossroads **en la intersección**

IF YOU NEED HELP

Help! **¡Socorro! / ¡Ayuda!**
Could you help me, please
¿Podría ayudarme, por favor?
Do you speak English? **¿Habla inglés?**
I don´t understand **No comprendo**
I don't speak Spanish
No hablo español
Could you call a doctor?
**¿Podría llamar a un médico,
por favor?**

ACCOMMODATION

Do you have a single/double room?
**¿Le queda alguna habitación
individual/doble?**
with/without bath/toilet/shower
**con/sin baño propio/
lavabo propio/ducha propia**
Does that include breakfast?
¿Incluye desayuno?
Could I see the room?
¿Puedo ver la habitación?
I'll take this room
Me quedo con esta habitación
The key to room…, please
**La llave de la habitación…,
por favor**
Thanks for your hospitality
Muchas gracias por la hospitalidad

NUMBERS

1	**uno**	11	**once**	21	**veintiuno**	200	**doscientos**
2	**dos**	12	**doce**	22	**veintidós**	300	**trescientos**
3	**tres**	13	**trece**	30	**treinta**	400	**cuatrocientos**
4	**cuatro**	14	**catorce**	40	**cuarenta**	500	**quinientos**
5	**cinco**	15	**quince**	50	**cincuenta**	600	**seiscientos**
6	**seis**	16	**dieciséis**	60	**sesenta**	700	**setecientos**
7	**siete**	17	**diecisiete**	70	**setenta**	800	**ochocientos**
8	**ocho**	18	**dieciocho**	80	**ochenta**	900	**novecientos**
9	**nueve**	19	**diecinueve**	90	**noventa**	1000	**mil**
10	**diez**	20	**veinte**	100	**cien**		

RESTAURANT

I'd like to book a table
¿Me gustaría reservar una mesa?
Have you got a table for two, please
¿Tienen una mesa para dos personas, por favor?
Could we see the menu, please?
¿Nos podría traer la carta, por favor?
Could I have the bill, please?
¿La cuenta, por favor?
service charge included
servicio incluido

breakfast **el desayuno**
lunch **el almuerzo**
dinner **la cena**
table **una mesa**
waiter/waitress **camarero/camarera**
starters **los entremeses**
main course **el plato principal**
dessert **postres**
dish of the day **plato del día**
bill **la cuenta**

MENU READER

aceituna olive
ajo garlic
alcachofa artichoke
almejas clams
almendras almonds
anguila eel
arroz rice
atún/bonito tuna

bacalao cod
berenjena aubergine
biftec steak
bocadillo sandwich
boquerones anchovies

calamares squid
caldo broth
callos tripe
cangrejo crab
cebolla onion
cerdo pork
cerezas cherries
cerveza beer
champiñones mushrooms
chorizo spicy sausage
chuleta chop
churros fritters
ciruela plum
cochinillo asado roast suckling pig
codorniz quail
conejo rabbit
cordero lamb

crema cream
criadillas sweetbreads
crudo raw

endibia chicory
ensalada (mixta) mixed salad
ensaladilla rusa Russian salad
espárragos asparagus
espinaca spinach

fideos noodles
filete fillet
flan crème caramel
frambuesa raspberry
fresa strawberry
fruta (de temporade) seasonal fruit

galleta biscuit
gambas prawns
garbanzos chick peas
gazpacho andaluz gazpacho (cold soup)
grosellas red/black currants
guisantes peas

habas broad beans
helado ice cream
hígado de oca goose liver

huevos fritos/ revueltos fried/scrambled eggs

jamón ham
judías verdes French beans
jugo fruit juice

langosta lobster
langostino crayfish
leche milk
lechuga lettuce
legumbres vegetables
lengua tongue
lenguado sole
liebre hare
lomo de cerdo pork tenerloin

manzana apple
mariscos seafood
mejillones mussels
melocotón peach
melón melon
merluza hake
mero sea bass
morcilla black pudding

pan bread
pato duck
pepino cucumber
pepinillos gherkins
pera pear

perdiz partridge
perejil parsely
pez espada swordfish
pescado fish
pimientos red/ green peppers
piña pineapple
plátano banana
pollo chicken
puerro leek
pulpo octopus

queso cheese

rape monkfish
riñones kidneys
rodaballo turbot

salchicha sausage
salchichón salami
salmón salmon
salmonete red mullet
solomillo de buey fillet of beef
sopa soup

tocino bacon
tortilla española Spanish omelette
tortilla francesa plain omelette
trucha trout

verduras green vegetables

zanahorias carrots

Atlas

194/195

Huelva

■ **SEVILLA**
202

Cádiz

CÓRDOBA
198/199

Málaga

196/197

■ **GRANADA**
200/201

Almería

To identify the regions, see the map
on the inside of the front cover

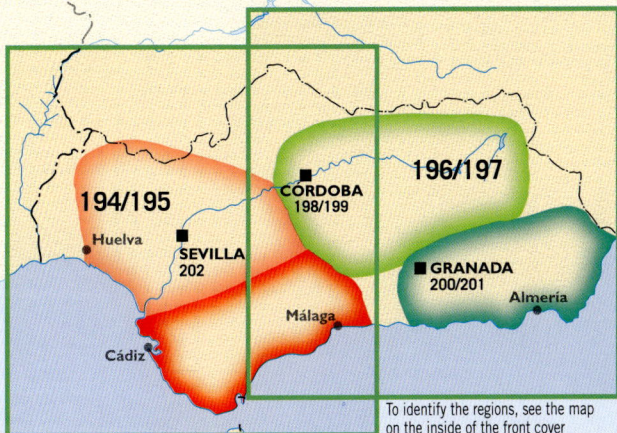

Regional Maps

— · · — International boundary
— · — · — Regional boundary
══════ Major route
══════ Motorway
────── Main road
────── Other road
▢ City
▫ Major town
○ Town
∘ Village
National Park

🔲 Featured place of interest
▪ Place of interest
Built up area

Streetplans

─────── Main roads
─────── Other roads
Park
Important building
Featured place of interest
ℹ Information

Estremoz
A6
N4
Elvas
Badajoz
Mérida
Guareña
C

Vila Viçosa
N373
N432
Alange
Embalse de Alange
Alandroal
NV
E90
422
N381

N254
Olivenza
423
La Albuera
Almendralejo
Palomas
Puebla de la Reina
Redondo
436
Almendral
Santa Marta
N423
Villafranca de los Barros
Hornachos
N255
Táliga
N435
Salvatierra de los Barros
N432

N256
N381
E803

N256-I
Feria
Zafra
N630
Matachel

Reguengos de Monsaraz
Mourão
Villanueva del Fresno
Zahinos
Jerez de los Caballeros
C311
Usagre
Valencia de las Torres

SERRA MENDRO
N385
4311
N435
Ardila
Ríodón
Bienvenida
437

N385
Amareleja
Barrancos
439
Fuente de Cantos
Fregenal de la Sierra
Llerena
413

N258
Moura
N255
Ardila
Martigas
Encinasola
434
Segura de León
Monesterio
Puebla del Maestre

Pias
N392
P
Huelva
1110m
SIERRA DE TUDI
A434

Serpa
N260
Rosal de la Frontera
N433
Aroche
Cortegana
Jabugo
PARQUE NATURAL SIERRA DE ANDÚJAR
Embalse de Aracena
A461
Santa Olalla del Cala

N258
Vila Verde de Ficalho
Almonaster la Real
959m
Aracena & Gruta de las Maravillas
N433
Cala

N265
Chanca
Santa Bárbara de Casa
SIERRA DE ATACENA
San Telmo
A470
Alajar
Compofrio
A461
El Ronquillo

Espíritu Santo
Embalse del Chanza
Puebla de Guzmán
Cabezas Rubias
Cañalas
N476
Zalamea la Real
Minas de Riotinto
A476
Embalse de la Minilla
Embalse de Cala
N432

N122
Alcoutim
A499
Alosno
A495
San Bartolomé de la Torre
Río Tinto
Venta El Alto
E803
Viar

Pereiro
Villanueva de los Castillejos
A490
N435
Valverde del Camino
A493
Aznacóllar
N630
Alcalá del Río
A431
Guado

Odeleite
S Silvestre de Guzmán
A495
Trigueros
La Palma del Condado
A472
Itálica
Sanlúcar la Mayor
SEVILLA

Castro Marim
A499
Lepe
A492
Gibraleón
Niebla
E01 (A49)
Almonte
Alcalá de Guadaira

Ayamonte
N431
Huelva
A472
San Juan del Puerto
A484
A483
Dos Hermanas
NIV
A376

Monte Gordo
Isla
La Antilla
A497
A494
Moguer
El Rocío
El Acebrón
Los Palacios y Villafranca
A362

Vila Real Cristina de Santo António
El Portil
Punta Umbría
N442
Mazagón
A494
El Rocina
Las Rocinas
A483
Marismas del Guadalquivir
A364

Golfo de Cádiz
Costa
PARQUE NACIONAL DE DOÑANA
A471

Torre de la Higuera
Matalascañas
Las Cabezas de San Juan
A371

Lebrija
Trebujena
A471
NIV
A4
E05

Punta de Maladar
Sanlúcar de Barrameda
A443
Arcos de la Frontera

de
A480
Chipiona
Jerez de la Frontera
A382
Embalse de Guadalcacín

Luz
A491
CA603
Rota
El Puerto de Santa María
Guadalete
A393

Bahía de Cádiz
Puerto Real
A381
Paterna de Rivera

Cádiz
San Fernando
Medina-Sidonia

NIV
E05
A390

Chiclana de la Frontera
La Barrosa
Conil de la Frontera
N340
Vejer de la Frontera

Cabo Roche
Los Caños de Meca
Cabo de Trafalgar
Barbate

Zahara de los Atunes

Punta Camarinal

0 10 20 30 40 50 km
0 10 20 30 miles

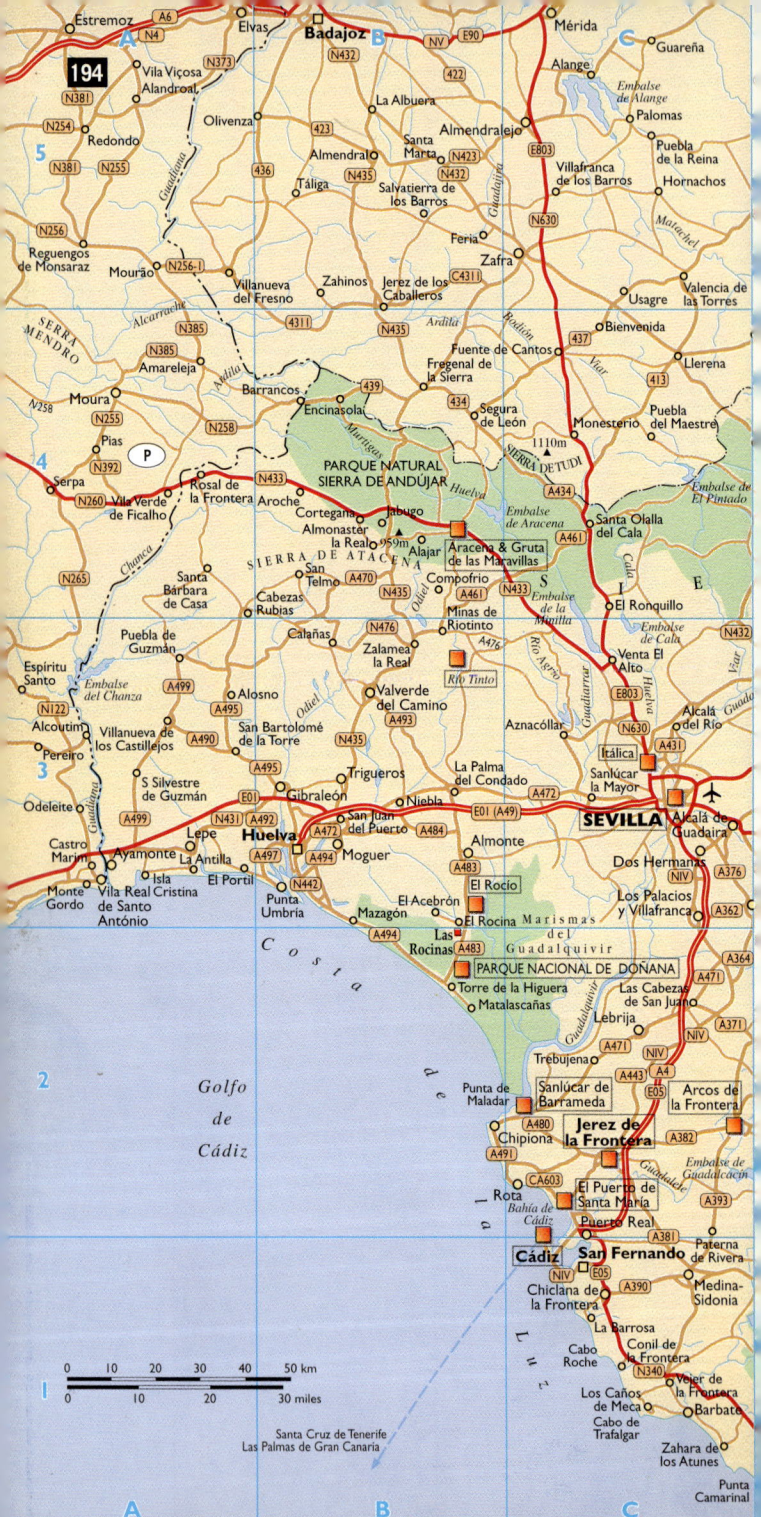

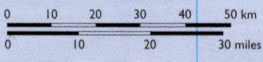

Santa Cruz de Tenerife
Las Palmas de Gran Canaria

A   B   C

D | E | F

Campanario
Quintana de la Serena
413
420
Embalse de Zújar
Castuera
Cabeza del Buey
Embalse de la Serena
Esteras
415
Abeñojar
Cabezarados
4110
195
Almadén
Almadenojos
Almodóvar del Campo
Argamasilla de Calatra
4
Zalamea de la Serena
413
420
Helechal
Puertollano
N420
SIERRA
Santa Eufemia
NS02
Brazatortas
Mestanza
Embalse de Montoro
5
Campillo de Llerena
Belalcázar
420
1106m
Judío
Fuencaliente
1323m
Berlanga
N432
Peraleda del Zaucejo
A420
Hinojosa del Duque
El Guijo
SIERRA
DE
ALCUDIA
Guadalmez
SIERRA MADRONA
Parque Natural
SIERRA DE ANDÚJAR
A449
Alcaracejos
A437
Conquista
Azuel
Venta de Cardeña
A420
Embalse de Jandúla
Granja de Torrehermosa
Azuaga
Peñarroya-Pueblonuevo
La Granjuela
A449
A430
Pozoblanco
A420
Villanueva de Córdoba
Fuente-Obejuna
A435
A421
N432
Virgen de la Cabeza
SIERRA DE LOS SANTOS
Espiel
Obejo
N420
Andújar
A447
896m
Guadalcanal
Alanis
Villaviciosa
Embalse de Puente Nuevo
M
O
R
E
NIV E05
4
Guadalquivir
S Nicolás del Puerto
PARQUE NATURAL DE LA SIERRA NORTE
Cerro Muriano
Montoro
Lopera
Cazalla de la Sierra
El Pedroso
Constantina
PARQUE NATURAL SIERRA DE HORNACHUELOS
Medina Azahara
Embalse de la Breña
Córdoba
El Carpio
Bujalance
Porcuna
A306
Embalse del Hornachuelo
Hornachuelos
Almodóvar del Río
N432
Torredonjimeno
Villanueva del Río y Minas
A431
Posadas
A445
E05
La Carlota
N331
Espejo
Castro del Río
Martos
Lora del Río
Palma del Río
A453
NIV
La Rambla
Baena
A316
Alcaudete
Carmona
E05
NIV
La Luisiana
Écija
Montilla
Doña Mencía
Luque
N432
Corbones
Fuentes de Andalucía
A388
Aguilar de la Frontera
A340
Zuheros
Cabra
Cueva del Cerro de los Murciélagos
A380
A364
A351
A342
A340
A340
Priego de Córdoba
3
Marchena
La Lantejuela
Herrera
A340
Lucena
A331
Tiñosa 1570m
A360
Arahal
La Puebla de Cazalla
Osuna
A92
Estepa
Embalse de Cordobilla
Rute
A333
Iznájar
Montefrío
A335
A364
A361
A441
SIERRA
DE
YEGUAS
La Roda de Andalucía
El Tejar
Embalse de Iznájar
Loja
Utrera
196
A365
Campillos
N331
A341
El Coronil
A376
Morón de la Frontera
A360
El Saucejo
A441
A382
Antequera
Archidona
Alhama de Granada
Montellano
Almargen
A367
Embalse del Guadalteba-Guadalhorce
PARQUE NATURAL DEL TORCAL
A359
Periana
2065m los Ber
Embalse de la Torre de Águila
A371
Algodonales
A382
Olvera
Cuevas del Becerro
A343
A356
A355
Colmenar
A356
SIERRA
2
Villamartín
Bornos
Garganta
Verde
Zahara de la Sierra
PARQUE NATURAL SIERRA DE GRAZALEMA
Embalse de Zahara
El Burgo
Embalse del Conde de Guadalhorce
Álora
N331
A335
Vélez-Málaga
Torrox Cos
Embalse de Bornos
A373
El Bosque
A372
Grazalema
Benaocaz
Ronda
Casarabonela
A366
Pizarra
A357
Málaga
Rincón de la Victoria
Torre del Mar
Ubrique
Prado del Rey
Embalse de Los Hurones
1918m
SIERRA BERMEJA
Coín
Alhaurín el Grande
A366
Bahía de Málaga
Embalse del Guadarranque
SIERRA DE RONDA
Embalse de la Concepción
A355
Benalmádena
Torremolinos
Benalmádena Costa
S
o
l
PARQUE NATURAL DE LOS ALCORNOCALES
Gaucín
San Pedro de Alcántara
Marbella
Ojén
Mijas
Fuengirola
d
e
l
I
Alcalá de los Gazules
Cosares
E15
Puerto Banús
Calahonda
Cala Moral
Embalse de Barbate
Jimena de la Frontera
Guadalmina
Bahía de Marbella
A381
Castellar de la Frontera
Estepona
C
o
s
t
a
A369
N340
Punta de Chullera
Sotogrande
Punta Mala
196
Embalse del Guadarranque
Los Barrios
San Roque
La Línea de la Concepción
Algeciras
Gibraltar (GB)
SIERRA DEL CABRITO
Bahía de Algeciras
Punta de Europa
Tarifa
Tánger
Ceuta
Estrecho de Gibraltar
D | E | F

195

196

N401
N420
E05
N IV
CM4124

Herrera del Duque
A
Puebla de Don Rodrigo
B
Porzuna
Embalse de Gasset
Zoncaya
C
Daimiel
N430
403
Piedrabuena
Ciudad Real
Carrión de Calatrava
Retama
Luciana
N430
Manzanares
Agudo
Saceruela
Guadiana
Almagro
Bolaños de Calatrava
412
Embalse de la Serena
Estercia
415
Abenójar
Cabezarados
4110
Aldea del Roy
Valdepeñas
Almadén
Almadenojos
Almodóvar del Campo
Argamasilla de Calatrava
413
Puertollano
Jabalón
Valdeazogues
Brazatortas
N420
La Calzada de Calatrava
Santa Cruz de Mudela
Santa Eufemia
SIERRA
1106m
Mestanza
Embalse de Montoro
Montoro
SIERRA MESTANZA
Fresneda
Viso del Marqués
Amuradiel
Belalcázar
A420
DE
Guadalmez
El Guijo
Fuencaliente
1323m
SIERRA MADRONA
PARQUE NATURAL SIERRA DE ANDÚJAR
Colonia Selladores
Santa Elena
Hinojosa del Duque
A449
A430
Alcaracejos
Pozoblanco
A420
Villanueva de Córdoba
Azuel
Venta de Cardeña
N
Virgen de la Cabeza
Embalse de Jándula
La Carolina
A301
Vilches
Arquillos
A449
A435
Conquista
A421
Guadalén
Guarrizas
Baños de la Encina
Guarromán
Embalse de Guadalén
Espiel
Guadalbarbo
Cuzna
A420
A437
Embalse de Puente Nuevo
Andújar
N IV E05
Bailén
Linares
A312
Úbeda
Villaviciosa
N432
Montoro
Cerro Muriano
Lopera
Guadalquivir
Mengíbar
N322
Baeza
Medina Azahara
El Carpio
Bujalance
N323
Mancha Real
A320
Jimena
Jódar
Córdoba
Porcuna
A306
Jaén
A316
Almodóvar del Río
N432
Castro del Río
Torredonjimeno
195
Martos
Campillo de Arenas
Guadahortuna
Posadas
A445
E05
N331
Espejo
Baena
A316
Alcaudete
N432
SIERRA MÁGINA
2167m
Huelma
A324
La Carlota
La Rambla
Doña Mencía
Luque
Ecija
A453
N IV
Montilla
Zuheros
Cabra
Cueva del Cerro de los Murciélagos
Alcalá la Real
A340
Iznalloz
SIERRA ARANA
A388
Aguilar de la Frontera
A342
A340
Priego de Córdoba
A340
1931m
A351
A340
Lucena
N432
N323
Herrera
Puente-Genil
A331
Rute
A333
Tíñosa 1570m
Montefrío
N432
Osuna
A92
Estepa
Embalse de Cordobilla
Iznájar
Embalse de Iznájar
A335
Pinos Puente
Granada
A441
La Roda de Andalucía
A365
El Tejar
Loja
Santa Fe
Monachil
El Saucejo
Campillos
A382
Antequera
A341
A385
Sierra Nevada
Pico de Veleta
A441
Embalse del Guadalteba-Guadalhorce
N331
Archidona
A359
Alhama de Granada
A338
Padul
Dúrcal
Capileira
Bubión
Almargen
A367
PARQUE NATURAL DEL TORCAL
A356
Periana
2065m
Embalse de los Bermejales
Jayena
Pampaneira
Béznar
Lanjarón
N323
NATURAL
Embalse del Conde de Guadalhorce
A343
A355
Colmenar
A356
A335
SIERRA
Órgiva
El Burgo
N331
Alora
Vélez-Málaga
Cuevas de Nerja
DE
ALMIJARA
Motril
Casarabonela
Pizarra
A357
Torrox Costa
Nerja
Almuñécar
Salobreña
Coín
A366
Alhaurín el Grande
Málaga
Rincón de la Victoria
Torre del Mar
Balcón de Europa
Torrenueva
Cabo Sacratif
1918m
A376
A355
Benalmádena
A366
Torremolinos
Bahía de Málaga
Punta de Torrox
San Pedro de Alcántara
Ojén
Embalse de la Concepción
Benalmádena Costa
Fuengirola
Costa
Marbella
Puerto Banús
Calahonda
Cala Moral
d
e
l
S
o
l
Guadalmina
Bahía de Marbella
Estepona
Melilla
Costa
A
B
C

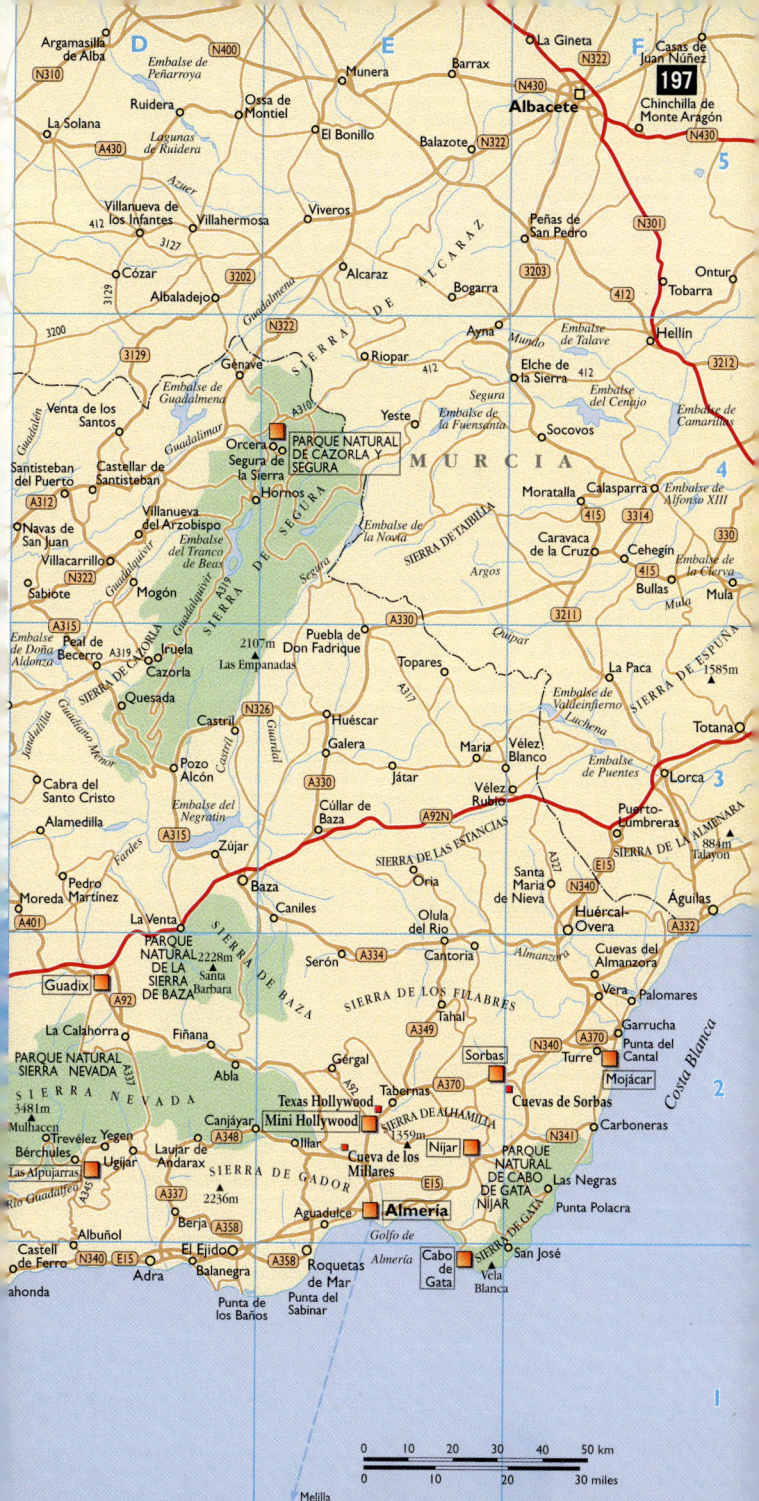

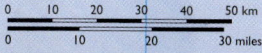

Argamasilla de Alba
D
E
F
Casas de Juan Núñez
N310
Embalse de Peñarroya
N400
Munera
Barrax
La Gineta
N322
Chinchilla de Monte Aragón
Albacete
5
Ruidera
Ossa de Montiel
El Bonillo
Balazote
N430
N301
N370
La Solana
A430
Lagunas de Ruidera
El Bonillo
N322
Peñas de San Pedro
412
Ontur
Villanueva de los Infantes
412
Villahermosa
Viveros
Alcaraz
Bogarra
3203
412
Tobarra
3127
Cózar
3202
Guadalmena
N322
Ayna
Mundo
Embalse de Talave
Hellín
3129
Albaladejo
SIERRA DE
ALCARAZ
Riopar
412
Elche de la Sierra
3212
3200
Génave
Embalse de Camarillas
3129
Venta de los Santos
Embalse de Guadalmena
Guadalimar
A310
Yeste
Segura
Embalse de la Fuensanta
Socovos
Embalse del Cenajo
Santisteban del Puerto
Castellar de Santisteban
Orcera
Segura de la Sierra
PARQUE NATURAL DE CAZORLA Y SEGURA
M U R C I A
4
A312
Hornos
SIERRA DE TAIBILLA
Moratalla
Calasparra
Embalse de Alfonso XIII
Navas de San Juan
Villanueva del Arzobispo
SIERRA DE SEGURA
Embalse de la Novia
415
3314
330
Villacarrillo
Embalse del Tranco de Beas
Segura
Argos
Caravaca de la Cruz
Cehegín
Embalse de la Cierva
N322
A319
Mula
Sabiote
Guadalquivir
Mogón
SIERRA DE CAZORLA
Bullas
415
Mula
A315
Embalse de Doña Aldonza
Peal de Becerro
A319
Iruela
2107m
Las Empanadas
Puebla de Don Fadrique
A330
Topares
3211
La Paca
SIERRA DE ESPUÑA
1585m
Guadiana Menor
Cazorla
A317
Embalse de Valdeinfierno
Luchena
Totana
3
Cabra del Santo Cristo
Quesada
Castril
N326
Huéscar
Galera
María
Vélez Blanco
Embalse de Puentes
Lorca
Alamedilla
SIERRA DE CAZORLA
Guardal
Pozo Alcón
A330
Játar
Vélez Rubio
Puerto-Lumbreras
A315
Embalse del Negratín
Cúllar de Baza
A92N
E15
SIERRA DE LA ALMENARA
884m Talayón
Fardes
Zújar
SIERRA DE LAS ESTÁNCIAS
Oria
A337
Águilas
Moreda Pedro Martínez
Baza
Caniles
Olula del Rio
Santa Maria de Nieva
N340
A332
A401
La Venta
PARQUE NATURAL DE LA SIERRA DE BAZA
SIERRA DE BAZA
Cantoria
Almanzora
Huércal-Overa
Cuevas del Almanzora
Guadix
A92
2228m
Santa Bárbara
Serón
A334
Tahal
Vera
Palomares
Costa Blanca
2
La Calahorra
Fiñana
SIERRA DE LOS FILABRES
A349
Garrucha
Punta del Cantal
PARQUE NATURAL SIERRA NEVADA
A337
Abla
Gérgal
A370
Sorbas
N340
A370
Turre
Mojácar
SIERRA NEVADA
3481m
A92
Tabernas
SIERRA DE ALHAMILLA
Cuevas de Sorbas
Mulhacén
Canjáyar
Texas Hollywood
1359m
Carboneras
Trevélez
Yegen
A348
Mini Hollywood
Níjar
N341
Bérchules
Ugíjar
Laujar de Andarax
Illar
Cueva de los Millares
PARQUE NATURAL DE CABO DE GATA
Las Alpujarras
SIERRA DE GADOR
E15
NIJAR
Rio Guadalfeo
A345
2236m
Aguadulce
Almería
Las Negras
Albuñol
Berja
A358
Golfo de Almería
SIERRA DE GATA
Punta Polacra
Castell de Ferro
N340
E15
El Ejido
A358
Cabo de Gata
San José
ahonda
Adra
Balanegra
Roquetas de Mar
Vela Blanca
Punta de los Baños
Punta del Sabinar
Melilla
I

0   10   20   30   40   50 km
0   10   20   30 miles

D
E
F

Córdoba

A — B — C

MOLINOS ALTA

Torre de la Malmuerta

BERENGUELA

Estación

ACERA GUERRITA

Palacio de la Diputación

DOCE

RTE

CATÓLICOS

PLAZA DE COLÓN

MARROQUIES

AVENIDA DE AMÉRICA

ALAKEN II

AVENIDA

REYES

OCTUBRE

AVENIDA DE CERVANTES

LA BODEGA

AVENIDA RONDA DE LOS TEJARES

DEL

GRAN

JOSÉ

CRUZ

CONDE

MM

ARJONA

C. DEL CANO

LINDO

DEL OSARIO

TTE ALBÁNOZ

CABRERA

C. DE TORRES

CASAS DEZA

CONDE DE R

PZA CAPUCHINOS

Iglesia de Capuchinos

Casa de los Fernández de Córdoba

CUESTA BAILIO

C. CARBONELL Y MORAND

CALLE ALFAROS

Jardines Diego de Rivas

AVENIDA DE LOS MOZÁRABES

CÓRDOBA

VERACRUZ

LA ZAHIRA

SANDOVAL

PLAZA CHITINOS

RTE

C. ROBLEDO

CABRERA

RAMÍREZ ARELLANO

PLAZA CARRILLOS

DOMINGO MUÑOZ

OBISPO

HITERO

PLAZA CARDENAL TOLEDO

S. ZOILO

PLAZA CAPUCHINAS

DON ALONSO AGUILAR

San Hipólito

PELAYO

CAPITÁN

GÓNGORA

LA PORTILLA

HIGH DIAZ

CONDE

S. ÁLVARO

San Miguel

PLAZA CARDENAL TOLEDO

MENÉNDEZ

JOSÉ ZORRILLA

TTE

C. MORERIA

J. RIVERA

C. DE ALFONSO XIII

Ayuntamiento

AV MEDINA AZAHARA

AVENIDA DE LA REPÚBLICA ARGENTINA

Jardines de la Victoria

PASEO DE LA VICTORIA

CONCEPCIÓN

Iglesia de San Nicolás de la Villa

Casa de los Hoces

EDUARDO DATO

PÉREZ

SAN FELIPE

PL DE SAN NICOLAS

CONDE DE GONDOMAR

CALLE DE SEVILLA

MÁLAGA

JESÚS MARÍA

PLAZA DE LAS TENDILLAS

DUQUE DE HORNACHUELOS

CONDE DE CÁRDENAS

REID

MUNDA

MORALES

CLAUDIO MARCELO

DIARIO CÓRDOBA

CALLE DE

CASTRO

PL DE RAMÓN Y CAJAL

CALLE

R SÁNCHEZ

JUAN DE MENA

POMPEYOS

Santa Victoria

PLAZA SENECA

LÓPEZ DE HOCES

TESORO

VALLADARES

CALLE BARROSO

JUAN VALERA SANTE VICTORIA

Museo Arqueológico

MARQUÉS DEL VILLAR

Arco del Portillo

Iglesia de la Trinidad

PLAZA TRINIDAD

DE FERIA

SÁNCHEZ

PL PROFESOR LÓPEZ-NEYRA

RUANO

C. SARAVIA

LEIVA

SAAVEDRA

CALLE DEL

HORNO

PL JERÓNIMO PÁEZ

De los Arquillos

TEJÓN Y MARTÍN

FERNÁNDEZ

JUDERÍA

Casa del Indiano

BUEN

PASTOR

BLANCO BELMONTE

Iglesia de la Encarnación

ENCARNACIÓN

CRISTO

HEREDIA

CALDEREROS

Puerta de Almodóvar

CALLE ALMANZOR

PLAZA DEL CARDENAL SALAZAR

PLAZA BENAVENTE

CALLE JON DE LA FLORES

V. BÁSCO

PL SANTA CATALINA

Zoco

San Bartolomé

CALLE

ROMERO

C DE LA HOGUERA

CÉSPEDES

CARDENAL HERRERO

Puerto del Perdón

MAESTRAL GLEZ

RONDA DE ISASA

Sinagoga

Museo Taurino

JUDÍOS

SALAZAR

CAIRUÁN

TOMÁS CONDE

PL JUDÁ LEVI

PLAZA MAIMÓNIDES

MANRIQUES

JUDERÍA

MEDINA Y CORELIA

CUE TORRIJOS

Mezquita-Catedral

CORREGIDOR LUIS DE LA CERDA

AVENIDA DOCTOR FLEMING

AV DEL AEROPUETO

AVENIDA VALLELLANO

AVENIDA CONDE VALLELLANO

DOCTOR BARRAQUER

SAN BASILIO

ENMEDIO

POSTRERA

CABALLERIZAS REALES

CAMPO SANTO DE LOS MÁRTIRES

Alcázar de los Reyes Cristianos

AMADOR DE LOS RÍOS

AVENIDA DEL ALCÁZAR

Puerta del Puente

Triunfo

PUENTE ROMANO

Torre de la Calahorra

PLAZA RASTRO

AVENIDA GRAN VÍA PARQUE

5 — 4 — 3 — 2 — I

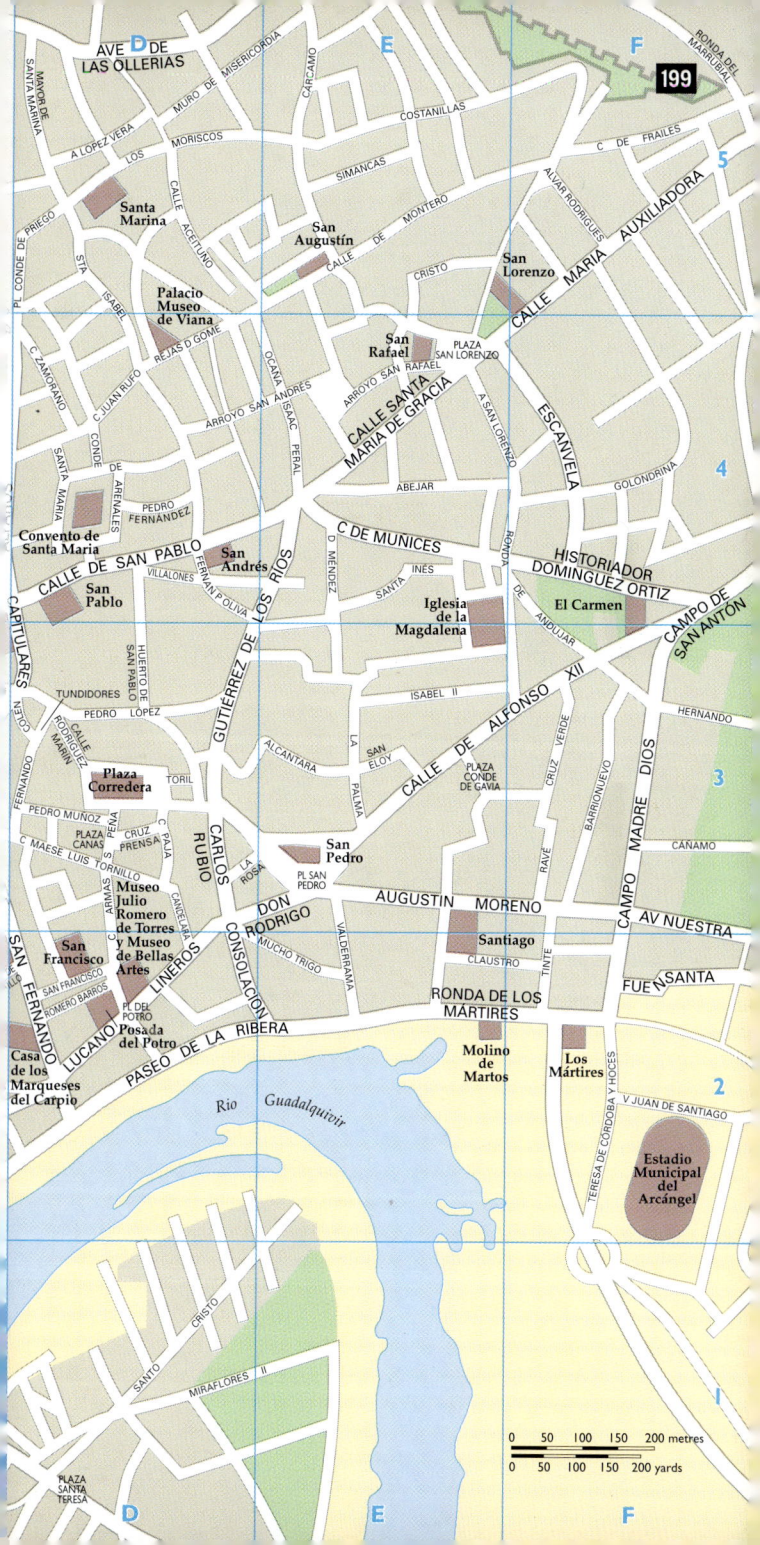

AVE DE LAS OLLERIAS

D
E
F

RONDA DE MARRUBIAL

MAYOR DE SANTA MARINA

A LOPEZ VERA
LOS
MORISCOS

MURO DE MISERICORDIA

CARCAMO

COSTANILLAS

C DE FRAILES

5

PL CONDE DE PRIEGO
STA ISABEL

Santa Marina

CALLE ACEITUNO

SIMANCAS

MONTERO

ALVAR RODRIGUEZ

CALLE MARIA AUXILIADORA

C ZAMORANO

Palacio Museo de Viana

San Augustín

CALLE

CALLE DE

CRISTO

San Lorenzo

C JUAN RUFO
CONDE DE ARENALES

REJAS D GOME

OCAÑA

San Rafael

PLAZA SAN LORENZO

A SAN LORENZO

ESCAÑUELA

SANTA MARIA

ARROYO SAN ISAAC

PERAL

ARROYO SAN ANDRES

CALLE SANTA MARIA DE GRACIA

ARROYO SAN RAFAEL

ABEJAR

GOLONDRINA

4

PEDRO FERNANDEZ

Convento de Santa Maria

CALLE DE SAN PABLO

San Andrés

GUTIÉRREZ DE LOS RIOS

FERNAN P OLIVA

C DE MUÑICES

D. MENDEZ

SANTA INES

RONDA

HISTORIADOR DOMÍNGUEZ ORTIZ

CAPITULARES

San Pablo

VILLALONES

Iglesia de la Magdalena

El Carmen

DE ANDUJAR

CAMPO DE SAN ANTÓN

HUERTO DE SAN PABLO

TUNDIDORES

ISABEL II

ALFONSO XII

HERNANDO

3

NEZON
FERNANDO

CALLE RODRIGUEZ MARIN

PEDRO LOPEZ

ALCANTARA

LA PALMA

SAN ELOY

CALLE DE ALFONSO XII

CRUZ VERDE

BARRIONUEVO

CAMPO MADRE DIOS

CAÑAMO

Plaza Corredera

TORIL

PLAZA CONDE DE GAVIA

RAVÉ

PEDRO MUÑOZ

PLAZA CAÑAS

CRUZ C PAJA

CARLOS RUBIO

LA ROSA

San Pedro

PL SAN PEDRO

AUGUSTIN MORENO

TINTE

AV NUESTRA

C MAESE LUIS TORNILLO
PRENSA

Museo Julio Romero de Torres y Museo de Bellas Artes

DON RODRIGO

VALDERRAMA

Santiago

FUENSANTA

SAN FERNANDO

San Francisco

SAN FRANCISCO

CARRERA

CONSOLACIÓN

LINEROS

MUCHO TRIGO

CLAUSTRO

RONDA DE LOS MÁRTIRES

ROMERO BARROS

LUCANO

PL DEL POTRO

Posada del Potro

PASEO DE LA RIBERA

Molino de Martos

Los Mártires

V JUAN DE SANTIAGO

2

Casa de los Marqueses del Carpio

Río Guadalquivir

TERESA DE CORDOBA Y HOCES

Estadio Municipal del Arcángel

CRISTO

SANTO

MIRAFLORES II

1

PLAZA SANTA TERESA

D
E
F

0 50 100 150 200 metres

0 50 100 150 200 yards

Granada

A   B   C

5

4

3

2

1

Monasterio de la Cartuja

ANCHA DE CAPUCHINOS

Hospital Real

HORNILLO DE CARTUJA

REAL DE CARTUJA

CARRETERA

SAN ANTONIO

CAMINO DE

CARTUJA DEL HOSPICIO

CAMPO MORENO

ACERA DE SAN ILDEFONSO

DE MURCIA

PASTORA

D

AVENIDA

San Ildefonso

Iglesia de San Cristóbal

AVENIDA DE LA CONSTITUCIÓN

DEL TRIUNFO

C. ACERA

FUENTO

NUEVA

NATALIA

RIVAS

NUEVA SANTISIMO

Gobierno Militar

La Merced

PL DEL TRIUNFO

Puerta de Elvira

CUESTA

DE

ALHACABA

Muralla de Picazaba

LARGA

CALLE

BAJO ARQUEROS

CTE'S

CRISTOBAL

CITES

CALLE

CTA ABARQUEROS

SERRANO

San Andrés

CALLE

CALLE DE SAN JUAN DE DIOS

GRAN VIA DE

NUEVA SANTISIMO

SANTISIMO

LAVADERO DE

MANO

HIERRO

ARRIOLA

CALLE

ARANDAS

CRUZ

V/D CAPILLA SAN ANDRÉS

CEDRÁN

CALLE

LUCIA

DE COLON

H. S. ANDRÉS

CORTEZA DE S. ANDRÉS

ZENETE

LA LONA

Hospital de San Juan de Dios

RECTOR LOPEZ ARQUETA

Monasterio de San Jerónimo

GRAN CAPITAN

CALLE DE LA DUQUESA

CALLE DE SAN GERÓNIMO

Universidad

MISERICORDIA

HAZA

DE

PLAZA DE LA TRINIDAD

CALLE MALAGA

Santa Paula

AZACAYAS

MOLINO

STA PAULA

MARQUÉS DE FLACES

Santiago

TENDILLAS

BDE ELVIRA

GRAN VIA DE COLON

ELVIRA

BAZÁN

ALVARO

SAN AGUSTIN

VALENTIN BARRECH EGUREN

CARCEL

BAJA

CALDERERIA NUEVA

CALDERERIA VIEJA

Palacio de Dar Alhorra

Monasterio Santa Isabel la Real

LAS MONJAS

PLTA CRISTO AZUCENAS

GALLO

PL SAN MIGUEL EL BAJO

CHINCHES

SANTA ISABEL

REAL

CASCA LLÁU

PL SAN MIGUEL

BOCANEGRA

CLAVEL

O'DORES

SAN JOSÉ

QUIROS

ALAMO MARQUES

CORREO VIEJO

San Jose

BRAVO OLIJADA

PLTA DE LA CRUZ VERDE

CTA DE SAN GREGORO

HUERTO

CONVALECEN

JUAN

CARCEL ALTA

PLAZA SANTA ANA

Audiencia

Iglesia de Santa Ana y San Gil

San Matias

Corpus Cristi

PLAZA NUEVA

JOAQUIN COSTA

Catedral

Capilla Real

Pal Madraza

CALLE DE LOS MESONES

PLAZA ROMANILLA

CALLE

TERESA

PAZ

ALHONDIGA

GRACIA

LA

PLAZA BIB-RAMBLA

ALCAICERIA

C.

PESCADERIA

ZACATIN

REYES

CATOLICOS

PLAZA DE ISABEL LA CATÓLICA

SANTI

SANTI

CUCHILLEROS

RODRIGUEZ

PAVANERAS

Capitania

Casa de los Tiros

OBISPO DE LAS TABLAS

CALLE DE LOS

SANTA

VERONICA

CALLE

CALLE

SAN MIGUEL

MAGDALENA

MORAL

SOLARILLO DE GRACIA

PUENTEZUELAS

La Magdalena

ALHONDIGA

PARRAGA

CRUZ

ANGEL

RECOGIDAS

LAS

DR LAGOS

CALLE NUEVA SAN ANTÓN

LOS FRAILES

PADRE ALCOVER

SAN JOSE

BAJU

PINO

ESPADERO

HORNO

Puerta Real de Espana

San António Abad

ANGEL GANIVET

Correos

SARABIA

CERVANTES

NAVAS

SAN RAFAEL

JESUS Y MARIA

ACERA DEL CASINO

CALLE PIEDRE SANTA

PLAZA MARIANA PINEDA

Corral del Carbon

Ayuntamiento

PL DEL CARMEN

CARMEN

MARIANA PINEDA

CALLE DE VARELAO

SANTA

PL CAMPOS SANTO

ENRIQUETA LOZANO PORCEL

CONCEPCION

ACERA DEL CASINO

CAMPILLO BAJO

Diputacion

ACERA DEL DARRO

Parque de las Ciencias

CALLE

A   B   C

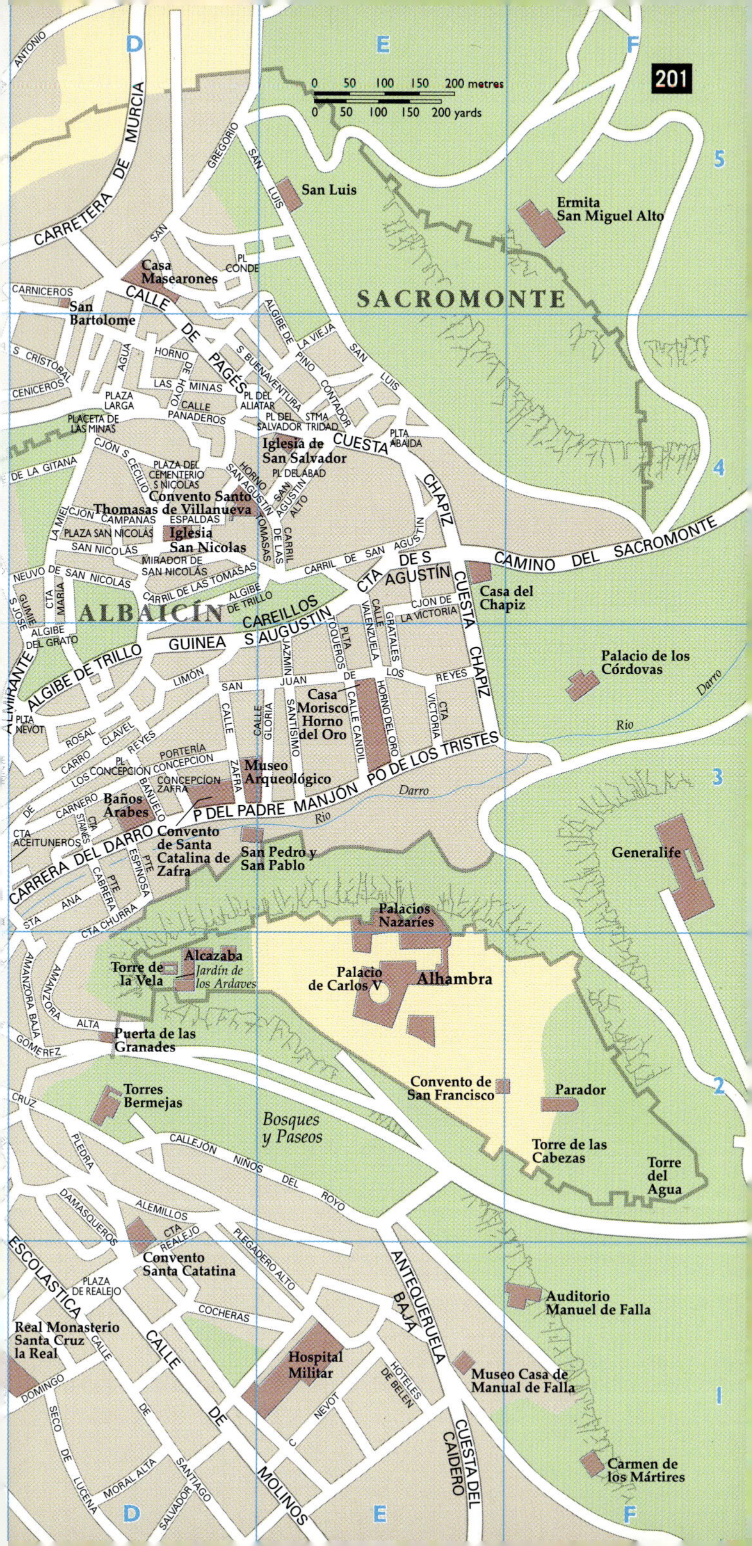
D
E
F
0 50 100 150 200 metres
0 50 100 150 200 yards
5
4
3
2
1
SACROMONTE
ALBAICÍN
San Luis
Ermita San Miguel Alto
Casa Masearones
San Bartolome
Iglesia de San Salvador
Convento Santo Thomasas de Villanueva
Iglesia San Nicolas
Casa del Chapiz
Palacio de los Córdovas
Casa Morisco Horno del Oro
Museo Arqueológico
Baños Árabes
Convento de Santa Catalina de Zafra
San Pedro y San Pablo
Generalife
Palacios Nazaríes
Alcazaba
Torre de la Vela
Jardín de los Ardaves
Palacio de Carlos V
Alhambra
Puerta de las Granades
Torres Bermejas
Bosques y Paseos
Convento de San Francisco
Parador
Torre de las Cabezas
Torre del Agua
Convento Santa Catatina
Auditorio Manuel de Falla
Real Monasterio Santa Cruz la Real
Hospital Militar
Museo Casa de Manual de Falla
Carmen de los Mártires
Rio Darro
CARRETERA DE MURCIA
ANTONIO
GREGORIO
SAN LUIS
CALLE DE PAGÉS
CAMINO DEL SACROMONTE
CUESTA CHAPIZ
CTA DE S AGUSTÍN
CARRIL DE SAN AGUSTÍN
GUINEA
CAREILLOS
S AUGUSTIN
ALGIBE DE TRILLO
ALMIRANTE
P DEL PADRE MANJÓN
PO DE LOS TRISTES
CARRERA DEL DARRO
CTA CHURRA
AMANZORA BAJA
AMANZORA ALTA
GOMEREZ
CRUZ
PIEDRA
CALLEJÓN NIÑOS DEL ROYO
ALEMILLOS
DAMASQUEROS
ESCOLASTICA
PLAZA DE REALEJO
CTA REALEJO
PLEGADERO ALTO
COCHERAS
ANTEQUERUELA BAJA
CUESTA DEL CAIDERO
CALLE DE MOLINOS
HOTELES DE BELÉN
NEVOT
SANTIAGO
SALVADOR
MORAL ALTA
SECO DE LUCENA
DOMINGO
CARNICEROS
S CRISTÓBAL
CENICEROS
PLAZA LARGA
PLACETA DE LAS MINAS
LAS MINAS
HORNO DE HOYO
CALLE PANADEROS
PL DEL ALIATAR
PL DEL SALVADOR
STMA TRIDAD
PLTA ABAIDA
PL DEL ABAD
PL CONDE
ALGIBE DE PINO
LA VIEJA
CONTADOR
S BUENAVENTURA
DE LA GITANA
CJÓN S CECILIO
PLAZA DEL CEMENTERIO S NICOLÁS
CAMPANAS
ESPALDAS
PLAZA SAN NICOLÁS
SAN NICOLÁS
MIRADOR DE SAN NICOLÁS
NEUVO DE SAN NICOLÁS
CARRIL DE LAS TOMASAS
CJÓN DE LA VICTORIA
VALENZUELA
GRATALES
DE LOS REYES
JAZMÍN
SAN JUAN
LIMÓN
GLORIA
SANTÍSIMO
CALLE CANDIL
HORNO DEL ORO
CTA VICTORIA
PLTA NEVOT
ROSAL
CLAVEL
CARRO
REYES
PORTERÍA CONCEPCIÓN
PL LOS CONCEPCIÓN
CONCEPCIÓN ZAFRA
ZAFRA
BAÑUELO
CARNERO
CTA ACEITUNEROS
STA ANA
PTE ESPINOSA
PTE CABRERA

Sevilla

Isla de
La Cartuja
(EXPO '92)

Río Guadalquivir

CALLE DE RESOLANA ANDUEZA

CALLE DE LA FERIA

C PERAL

C DE BECQUER

Basilica
de la
Macarena

Convento de
Capuchinos

C MUÑOZ LEON

Monasterio
de San
Clemente

C DE RELATOR

Convento
de Santa
Clara

LA MACARENA

C ARRAYAN

CALLE DE SAN LUIS

Santa
Marina

Hospital
Santa
Cruz

RONDA DE CAPUCHINOS

CALLE DEL TORNEO

CALLE SANTA LUMBRERAS

San
Lorenzo

Iglesia de
San Luis

CALLE DE JESUS DEL GRAN TRAJANO

ALAMEDA

AMOR DE DIOS DE HERCULES

Convento
Santa Isabel

CALLE DEL SOL

CALLE MARIA AUXILIADORA

SAN VICENTE

JUAN RABADAN

CONDE
DE BARAJAS

Convento
de Santa Paula

Cuartel del
Carmen

CALLE

CASTELLAR

PLAZA DE
LA GAVIDIA

Palacio de
las Dueñas

BUSTOS TAVERA

CALLE GERONA

CALLE MARIA AUXILIADORA

Policia

CALLE JESUS DEL GRAN PODER

CENTRO

San
Andrés

San
Pedro

PLAZA
PONCE DE
LEON

ALFONSO XII

PLAZA DEL
DUQUE DE LA
VICTORIA

C DE
LARAÑA

IMAGEN

C DE SAN ELOY

CALLE O'DONNELL

Casa de la
Condesa de
Lebrija

C MEJIAS

Convento de
San Leandro

CALLE DEL RECAREDO

C DE AMADOR DE LOS RIO

Museo de
Bellas Artes

La
Magdalena

CALLE

CALLE SIERPES

Campana

Cappilla de San José

6

Casa de
Pilatos

San Salvador

C AGUILAS SAN ESTEBAN

AV DEL
CRISTO DE LA
EXPIRACION

CALLE MARQUES DE PARADAS

SAN PABLO

CALLE MADRID ZARAGOZA

PLAZA
NUEVA

PLAZA DE
SAN FRANCISCO

VIRGENES

17

16

Mercado
de Pescado

R CATOLICIS

Mercado de
Entradores

Ayuntamiento

ARGOTE DE MOLINA

SAN JOSE

PELAYO

Santa
Maria la
Blanca

PASEO DE CRISTOBAL COLON

SANTA
CRUZ

Giralda

PLAZA
VIRGEN DE
LOS REYES

Palacio
Arzobispal

Santa
Cruz

PL DE VIRGEN
LOS REYES

18

DEMETRIO
DE LOS RIOS

CALLE DE ADRIANO

Plaza
de
Toros de
la
Maestranza

AVENIDA DE LA CONSTITUCION

Catedral Santa
Maria de la Sede

13

14

Casa de
Murillo

19

PLAZA DE
SANTA CRUZ

PUENTE DE ISABEL II

CALLE DEL BETIS

TRIANA

PAGES DEL CORRO

Santa
Ana

Hospital
de la
Caridad

Torre
del
Oro

PUERTA DE
JEREZ

Archivo
de
Indias

i

Reales
Alcázares

PLAZA DEL
TRIUNFO

PLAZA DOÑA
ELVIRA

20

Hospicio de los
Venerables
Sacerdotes

CALLE DE MENENDEZ

Jardines de Murillo

CAPITAN VIGERAS

Jardines del
Alcázar

Palacio de Justicia

PUENTE DE SAN TELMO

PLAZA
DE
CUBA

CALLE SAN
FERNANDO

AV DE ROMA

Hotel
Alfonso XIII

Universidad

Palacio de
San Telmo

Teatro
Lope de
Vega

Pab de
Uruguay

PLAZA
D JUAN
DE
AUSTRIA

Prado
San Sebastián

AVENIDA DE CARLOS V

Estación de
Autobuses

AVENIDA DE PORTUGAL

Canal de Alfonso XIII

PASEO

PTE DEL
GENERALISIMO

AV DE MARIA LUISA

AV DE ISABEL LA CATOLICA

Parque
de
María
Luisa

PLAZA
DE
ESPAÑA

Capitania
General

C BRASIL

C PORVENIR

Museo de Artes
y Costumbres
Populares

AVENIDA DE BORBOLLA

CALLE DE
FELIPE II

PRES CARRERO BLANCO

AV SANTIAGO MONTOTO

LAS DELICIAS

AVENIDA DE PIZARRO

PLAZA
DE
AMERICA

Museo
Arqueológico

C COLUMBIA

Club
Naútico

PUENTE DE
ALFONSO XIII

AV DE
MOLINI

AV DE
ERITANA

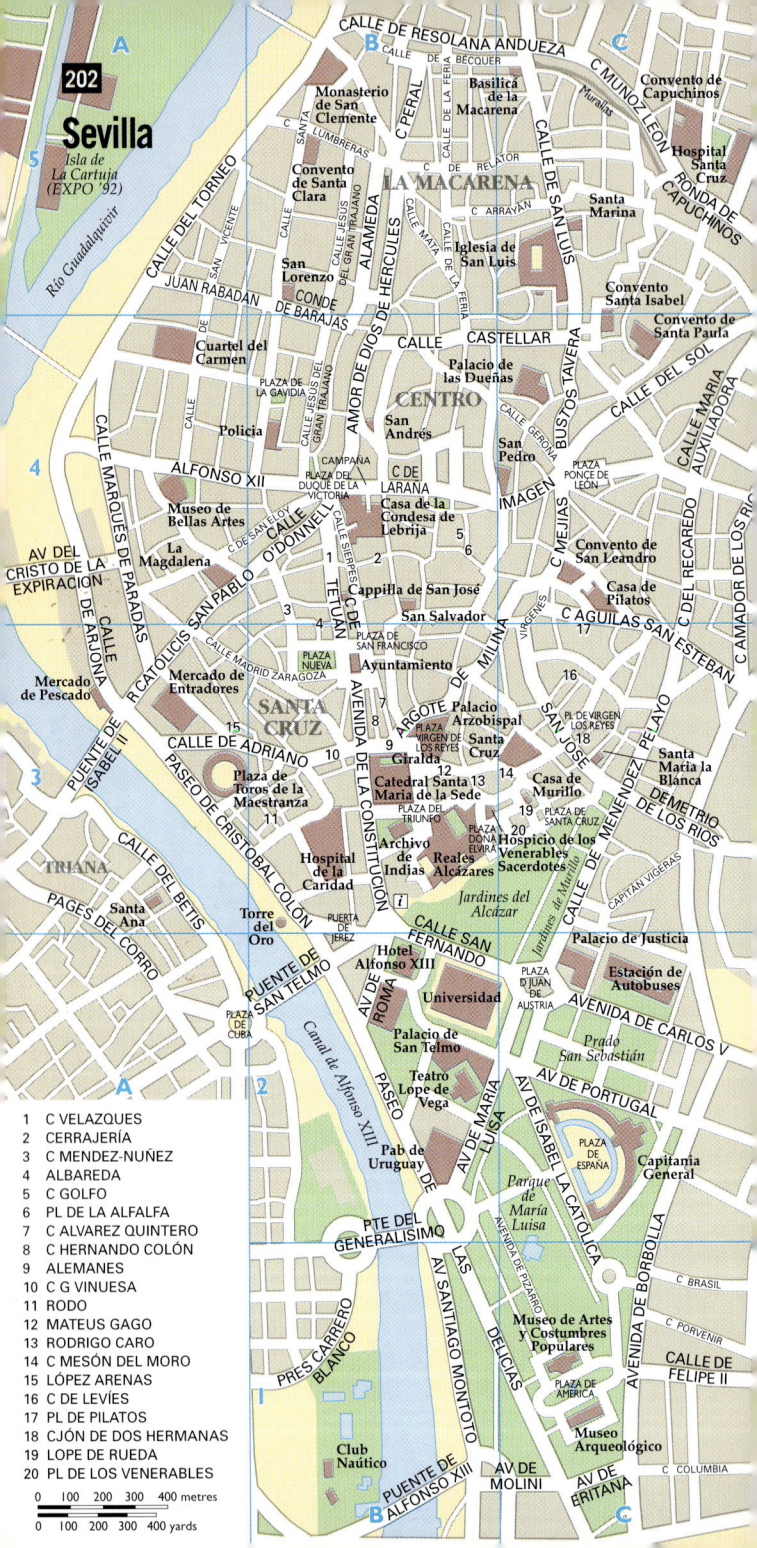

1 C VELAZQUES
2 CERRAJERÍA
3 C MENDEZ-NUÑEZ
4 ALBAREDA
5 C GOLFO
6 PL DE LA ALFALFA
7 C ALVAREZ QUINTERO
8 C HERNANDO COLÓN
9 ALEMANES
10 C G VINUESA
11 RODO
12 MATEUS GAGO
13 RODRIGO CARO
14 C MESÓN DEL MORO
15 LÓPEZ ARENAS
16 C DE LEVÍES
17 PL DE PILATOS
18 CJÓN DE DOS HERMANAS
19 LOPE DE RUEDA
20 PL DE LOS VENERABLES

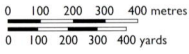

0 100 200 300 400 metres
0 100 200 300 400 yards

Accommodation 38–9
see also individual areas
admission charges 37
air travel 187
airports 34, 35
Alájar 182, 183
Alcalá de los Gazules 66
Alhambra 78, 79, 83–6
Alcazaba 83
Generalife 83, 86
Jardín de los Ardaves 83
Museo de Bellas Artes 86, 91
Museo Hispano–Musulmán 86
Palacio de Carlos V 83, 85–6
Palacio Nazaríes 26, 83, 84–5
Almería 79, 96–8, 179
airport 34
Alcazaba 96–7, 98
Barrio de la Chanca 97, 98
cathedral 97, 98
Centro de Artes 98
Museo Arqueológico 97–8
Almería (province) see Granada and Almería
Almonaster 184
Alpujarras see Las Alpujarras
Antequera 65–6
Alcazaba 66
Arco de Los Gigantes 66
Church of Santa María 66
Menga and Viera dolmens 66
Nuestra Señora del Carmen 66
Parque Natural del Torcal 27, 66
Aquapark Torremolinos 62
Aracena 138, 156–7, 182
Gruta de las Maravillas 156, 157
architecture 8
Arcos de la Frontera 67

Baeza 111, 122–3
Catedral de Santa María 122, 123
Iglesia de Santa Cruz 122, 123
Palacio de Jabalquinto 122, 123
sculpture studio 123
bandoleros 10, 11
banks 188
Baños Arabes 55, 87, 129
Baños de la Encina 130
Barbary apes 69
beaches 26
bed and breakfast 39
Benalmádena Costa 63
Benamahoma 177
Benaocaz 66, 176–7
Bérchules 95
Bubión 93
bullfighting 13–15, 44
Córdoba 136
Málaga and Cádiz 55, 76
Seville 168
Burriana 65
buses 36
buses, long-distance 187
Busquístar 94

Cabo de Gata 26, 99
Cádiz 59–60
Catedral Nueva 60
Hospital de Mujeres 60
Museo de Cádiz 59, 60
Oratorio de San Felipe Neri 59–60
Torre Tavira 59
Cádiz (province) see Málaga and Cádiz
camping 39
Capileira 94
car hire 37
Carmen 12
Carmona 154–5
Iglesia de San Pedro 154, 155
Iglesia de Santa María la Mayor 154, 155
Necrópolis Romana 154, 155
Casa Natal de Picasso 52
Casa de Pilatos 150–1, 153

Casares 63
cave dwellings 102–3
Cazorla 124, 125
Balcón del Pintor Zabaletato 124
La Yedra 124, 125
Cerro Mirador San Cristóbal 183
Cervantes 24
children 26, 62, 162, 190
church and museum opening hours 188
climate and seasons 186
clothing sizes 188
Columbus, Christopher 145
concessions 190
consulates and embassies 190
Córdoba 8–9, 110, 114–19
Alcázar de los Reyes Cristianos 117, 119
Casa de los Marqueses del Carpio 173
Casa No 12 Museum 175
Fiesta de los Patios 119
Iglesia de San Nicolás de la Villa 175
Iglesia de la Trinidad 175
Judería 117
map 174
Mezquita 115–16
Museo Arqueológico 118, 119
Museo de Bellas Artes 118, 119
Museo Julio Romero de Torres 118, 119
Museo Taurino 117, 119
Palacio Museo de Viana 119
Plaza de las Tendillas 118, 174
Plaza del Potro 118, 174
Puente Romano 119
synagogue 117
walk 173–5
Córdoba and Jaén (provinces) 109–36

accommodation 131–2
Baeza 111, 122–3
Baños de la Encina 130
Córdoba 8–9, 110, 114–19
eating out 133–4
Embalse de Iznájar 130
entertainment 136
five–day itinerary 112–13
Jaén 111, 129
map 110–11
Medina Azahara 128
Montoro 130
Parque Natural de Cazorla y Segura 124–5
Priego de Córdoba 110–11, 120–1
Segura de la Sierra 130
shopping 135
Sierra Cazorla 27, 111
Úbeda 111, 126–7
Zuheros 128
Costa de la Luz 68–9, 138, 161–2
Los Caños de Meca 26, 68
Matalascañas 162
Mazagón 161
Tarifa 68
Vejer de la Frontera 68
Zahara de los Atunes 68
Costa del Sol 61–4
Benalmádena Costa 63
Casares 63
Estepona 26, 61
Fuengirola 62–3, 64
fun parks 62
Marbella 27, 61–2, 64
Mijas 63
Puerto Banús 27, 62, 64
Torremolinos 63, 64
Costa Natura 61
Costa Tropical 100
crafts 42
credit cards 187
crime 189
Cueva de los Millares 103
Cueva del Cerro de los Murciélagos 128

Cuevas de Nerja 65
Cuevas de Sorbas
    101, 181
currency and cur-
    rency exchange
    187
cycling 136

dental services 190
disabilities, travel-
    ling with 190
dolphin watching
    26, 68, 69
Doñana National
    Park 158–9, 168
drinking water 190
driving 37, 186
drugs and
    medicines 190

eating out 27,
    30–2, 40–1
see also individual
    areas
Écija 160
    Museo Histórico
        Municipal 160
    Palacio de
        Benameji 160
    Palacio de
        Peñaflor 160
El Castillo de las
    Guardas Nature
    Park 162
El Puerto de Santa
    María 68
    bodegas 68
    Castillo de San
        Marcos 68
    Iglesia Mayor
        Prioral 68
El Rocío 162
El Vinculo Molino
    de Aceite
    Alojamiento
    Rural 74, 177
electricity 189
Embalse de Iznájar
    130
emergency phone
    numbers 189
entertainment 44
see also individual
    areas
Ermita de Nuestra
    Señora de los
    Angeles 183
Estepona 26, 61

Fernando and
    Isabel 9, 23, 82,
    88
festivals 19–21, 26
flamenco 16–18, 26
    Córdoba and
        Jaén 136
    Granada 108
    Málaga and Cádiz
        57–8, 76

Seville 168
food and drink
    40–1, 43
see also eating out;
    sherry
Ford, Richard 11,
    12, 20
Fuengirola 62–3,
    64
fun parks 26, 62,
    102

Garganta Verde 67,
    178
Gibraltar 69
    Apes' Den 69
    North Town 69
    St Michael's Cave
        69
    Upper Galleries
        69
golf 44, 76
Granada 9, 78,
    82–91
    airport 35
    Albaicín 87,
        170–2
    Alcaicería 89
    Alhambra Palace
        78, 79, 83–6
    Baños Árabes 87
    Capilla Real 88,
        89
    cathedral 88–9
    Convento de
        Santa Catalina
        de Zafra 170
    map 171
    Mirador de Cruz
        de Quirós 89
    Mirador de San
        Nicolás 172
    Monasterio de la
        Cartuja 27, 90
    Monasterio de
        San Jerónimo 91
    Museo
        Arqueológico 87
    Parque de las
        Ciencias 26, 90
    San Salvador 171
    tourist offices 91
    university district
        91
    walk 170–2
Granada and
    Almería
    (provinces) 77–
    108
    accommodation
        104
    Almería 79,
        96–8,   179
    Cabo de Gata 26,
        99
    Costa Tropical
        100
    Cueva de los
        Millares 103

Cuevas de Sorbas
    101, 181
    eating out 105–6
    entertainment
        108
    four–day
        itinerary 80–1
    Granada 9, 82–
        91, 78
    Guadix 102–3
    Las Alpujarras
        27, 92–5
    map 78–9
    Mini Hollywood
        26, 102, 181
    Mojácar 100–1
    Níjar 100
    shopping 107
    Sorbas 101, 181
Grazalema 66, 176
Gruta de las
    Maravillas 156,
    157
Guadix 102–3

health 186, 190
Hemingway, Ernest
    13–14
history 6–9, 22–3
horse riding 76,
    108, 136
hostales 39
hotels 38–9
see also individual
    areas
Huelva (province)
    see Seville and
    Huelva

inoculations 186
insurance 186, 190
Iruela 124
Irving, Washington
    11, 12, 85
Isla de La Cartuja
    152
Isla Mágica 26, 152
Itálica 160

Jabugo 184
Jaén 111, 129
    Baños Árabes 129
    cathedral 129
    Museo Provincial
        129, 130
Jaén (province) see
    Córdoba and
    Jaén
Jerez de la Frontera
    56–8
    Alcázar 57
    Centro Andaluz
        de Flamenco
        57–8
    Museo
        Arqueológico 58
    Real Escuela
        Andaluza del
        Arte Ecuestre 57

bodegas 56–7
Jimena de la
    Frontera 66

La Maestranza 152,
    168
Lanjarón 92
Las Alpujarras 27,
    92–5
    Bérchules 95
    Bubión 93
    Capileira 94
    Casa Tradicional
        Alpujarreña
        93–4
    Lanjarón 92
    Pampaneira 93
    Poqueira Gorge
        92–4
    Solynieve (Sun
        and Snow) 95
    Trevélez 94–5
    walking routes
        93
    Yegen 94, 95
Las Salinas 99
Linares de la Sierra
    182–3
Lorca, Federico
    García 24–5,
    83
Los Caños de Meca
    26, 68
lost property 190
Lucainena de las
    Torres 180

Málaga 50–2
    airport 34
    Alcazaba 50–1,
        52
    Casa Natal de
        Picasso 52
    Castillo de
        Gibralfaro 51
    cathedral 51, 52
    Iglesia del
        Sagrario 52
    Museo de Artes y
        Costumbres
        Populares 52
    Museo Provincial
        de Arqueología
        51, 52
Málaga and Cádiz
    (provinces) 45–
    76
    accommodation
        70–1
    Antequera 65–6
    Arcos de la
        Frontera 67
    Cádiz 59–60
    Costa de la Luz
        68–9, 138,
        161–2
    Costa del Sol
        61–4
    eating out 71–3

El Puerto de Santa María 68
entertainment 75–6
four–day itinerary 48–9
Gibraltar 69
Jerez de la Frontera 56–8
Málaga 50–2
map 46–7
Nerja 26, 65
Parque Natural de los Alcornocales 66
Parque Natural Sierra de Grazalema 66–7, 176–8
Ronda 53–5
Sanlúcar de Barrameda 67
shopping 74–5
Marbella 27, 61–2
markets 43
Museo del Grabado Contemporáneo 64
Matalascañas 162
Mazagón 161
medical treatment 190
Medina Azahara 128
Medina-Sidonia 66
Menga and Viera dolmens 65
Mezquita 115–16
Mijas 63
Minas de Ríotinto 161, 184
Museo Minero 161
Mini Hollywood 26, 102, 181
Mojácar 100–1
Monasterio de La Cartuja 27, 90
Monasterio de San Jerónimo 91
money 187
Montoro 130
Moors 6–9, 22
Murillo, Bartolomé Esteban 24, 25, 149

national holidays 188
Necrópolis Romana 154, 155
Nerja 26, 65
Balcón de Europa 65
Burriana 65
Cuevas de Nerja 65
nightlife 44
Níjar 100, 179

opening hours 43, 188

Pampaneira 93
paradores 38
Parque de las Ciencias 26, 90
Parque Nacional de Doñana 158–9, 168
Parque Natural de los Alcornocales 66
Parque Natural de Cabo de Gata-Níjar 99
Parque Natural de Cazorla y Segura 124–5
Parque Natural Sierra de Grazalema 66–7, 176–8
Parque Natural del Torcal 27, 66
passports and visas 186
Peña de Arias Montano 183
pensiónes 39
pharmacies 188, 190
Picasso, Pablo 24, 52
Pitres 94
plasticultura 96, 100, 179, 181
Playa Cuesta de Maneli 26
police 189
Poqueira Gorge 92–4
Pórtugos 94
post offices 189
pottery 100, 101, 179, 181
Prado World 62
Priego de Córdoba 110–11, 120–1
Barrio de la Villa 120–1
Carnicerías Reales 121
Iglesia de la Asunción 120, 121
Iglesia de San Pedro 121
public transport 36–7
pueblos blancos 46, 66, 176–8
Puerto Banús 27, 62, 64

rail travel 36, 187
Real Escuela Andaluza del Arte Ecuestre 57

Reales Alcázares 146–7
Reserva Zoológica 102
Río Tinto 161
Romería del Rocío 20, 162
Ronda 53–5
Baños Árabes 55
Casa Juan Bosco 54
El Tajo 53
Iglesia de Santa María Mayor 54
La Mina 55
Museo del Bandolero 54
Old Town 53–4
Palacio de Mondragón 54
Plaza de Toros 54–5
Puente Nuevo 53
Vista Panoramic Jardines Ciudad de Cuenca 55
Royal Andalucían School of Equestrian Art 57

salt marshes 99
Sanlúcar de Barrameda 67
bodegas 67
Palacio de Orleáns y Bourbon 67
Sea Life Park Submarino 62
Segura de la Sierra 130
senior citizens 190
Seville 138, 142–53
airport 35
Barrio de Santa Cruz 148
bus tours 149
buses 153
Calle Sierpes 152
Capilla de San José 153
Casa de Pilatos (Pilate's House) 150–1, 153
cathedral 143–5
Giralda 143–4
horse–drawn carriages 143
Hospicio de los Venerables Sacerdotes 148
Isla de La Cartuja 152
Isla Mágica 26, 152
Jardines de Murillo 148
La Maestranza 152, 168

Museo Arqueológico 151, 153
Museo de Artes y Costumbres Populares 139, 151, 153
Museo de Bellas Artes 27, 148–50, 153
Parque de María Luisa 151, 153
Plaza de España 151, 153
Plaza Nueva 152
Plaza de San Francisco 152
Reales Alcázares 146–7
river cruises 150
Torre del Oro 152
tourist offices 142
Triana 152
Seville and Huelva (provinces) 137–68
accommodation 163–4
Aracena 138, 156–7, 182
Carmona 154–5
Costa de la Luz 138, 161–2
eating out 164–6
Écija 160
El Castillo de las Guardas Nature Park 162
El Rocío 162
entertainment 168
four–day itinerary 140–1
Itálica 160
map 139
Parque Nacional de Doñana 158–9, 168
Río Tinto 161
sherry 26, 28–9, 41, 56–7, 67, 68
shopping 42–3, 166–7, 188
see also individual areas
Sierra de Alhamilla 180
Sierra de Aracena 182–4
Sierra Cazorla 27, 111
Sierra de Grazalema 27, 66–7, 176–8
Sierra Morena 27, 138, 168
Sierra Nevada 78, 92, 93

Sierra de la Virgen 182
Sierras de Cazorla y Segura 124
skiing 95
Solynieve (Sun and Snow) 95
Sorbas 101, 181
souvenirs 42
spa 92
sport and leisure 44, 76, 108, 136, 168
stamps 189
students and young travellers 190
sun safety 190

Tabernas 181
Mini Hollywood 26, 102, 181
Reserva Zoológica 102
tapas 30–2
Taller del Telar 94
Tarifa 68
taxis 37
telephones 189
Texas Hollywood 181
time differences 187
tipping 41, 189
Tivoli World 26, 62
toilets 190
Torremolinos 63, 64
tourist information 35, 186–7
travellers' cheques 187
Trevélez 94–5

Úbeda 111, 126–7
Capilla del Salvador 126
Museo de Alfarería 126
Palacio de las Cadenas 126
San Pablo 127
Santa María de las Reales Alcázares 127
Ubrique 176

Vejer de la Frontera 68
Villaluenga del Rosario 176

water sports 44, 76, 108
Websites 186
Welles, Orson 13, 14
Western Leone 181
white towns *see pueblos blancos*
Wild West attractions 26, 102, 181
wildlife 99, 124, 158–9

Yegen 94, 95
Casa de Brenan 94
youth hostels 39

Zahara de los Atunes 68
Zahara de la Sierra 27, 66, 178
Zuheros 128
Cueva del Cerro de los Murciélagos 128
Iglesia de la Virgen de los Remedios 128
Zuheros Museum 128
Zurbarán, Francisco de 24, 59

Picture credits

The Automobile Association wishes to thank the following photographers and libraries for their assistance with the preparation of this book.
Front and back cover: (t) AA Photo Library/Peter Wilson; (ct) AA Photo Library/Peter Wilson; (cb) AA Photo Library/Peter Wilson; (b) AA Photo Library/Gettyone/Stone; Spine, AA Photo Library/Peter Wilson.
AKG, LONDON 7b, 22t, 22cl, 22cr, 22b, 25t; ANDALUCIA SLIDE LIBRARY/MICHELLE CHAPLOW 2t, 5, 17, 26b, 27b, 28b, 31t, 31b, 46, 49t, 63t, 64b, 92b, 102 (D Kinnear), 110b, 128, 182, 184; BRIDGEMAN ART LIBRARY, LONDON 116 View of the maqsura and mihrab, built during the reign of Al-Hakam II, 976 AD (photo) Mezquita (Great Mosque) Cordoba, Spain, 149 The Apotheosis of St. Thomas Aquinas, 1631 by Francisco de Zurbaran (1598-1664) Museo de Bellas Artes, Seville, Spain; BRUCE COLEMAN COLLECTION 124b, 158, 159; CORBIS UK LTD 9t (Adam Woolfitt), JAMES DAVIS TRAVEL PHOTOGRAPHY 2cb, 45, 92t; ROGER DAY 79t; MARY EVANS PICTURE LIBRARY 8c, 9c, 15t, 15b, 23, 24l; EYE UBIQUITOUS 18t, 19t, 19b, 20t, 30t, 115, 146/7, 147, 161t, 172; DES HANNIGAN 3cb, 7t, 50t, 55, 59t, 60, 66, 87, 94, 96t, 100/1, 114t, 118, 120, 120/1, 124c, 138b, 141r, 162, 169, 170, 171l, 171r, 173, 175, 176, 179, 180; HULTON GETTY 13, 24r, 25b; MUSEO DEL BANDOLERO 10tr, 10c; PICTOR INTERNATIONAL, LONDON 16, 80b, 151; PICTURES COLOUR LIBRARY 2ct, 2b, 3t, 3b, 20c, 33, 61t, 77, 81t, 84, 90, 93, 109, 125, 141l, 156, 161b, 185; POWERSTOCK/ZEFA 20b; REAL ESCUELA ANDALUZA DE ARTE ECUESTRE, JEREZ 57t photograph borrowed from The Royal School; REX FEATURES LTD 6b, 14, 18b; THE ARTARCHIVE 49cr, 88/9, 119; THE TRAVEL LIBRARY 25t, 49cl, 78, 97, 99, 101, 112t, 139; PETER WILSON 85, 112b; WORLD PICTURES LTD 10-12, 21, 28/9, 56, 79b, 80/1, 82/3t, 96b.
The remaining photographs are held in the Association's own photo library (AA PHOTO LIBRARY) and were taken by PETER WILSON with the exception of the following:
Michelle Chaplow 8t, 27t, 27c, 47b, 49b, 52, 88, 100, 110t, 111, 113t, 113b, 121, 127t, 127b, 128-130, 129, 140b, 160b, 178, 189t, 189cr; Jerry Edmanson 29, 53, 82/3b, 84/5, 86, 126, 140t, 146, 158/9; Andrew Molyneux 142r, 144/5, 145; Jens Poulsen 65b; Douglas Robertson 6t, 8b, 59c, 81c, 89, 91, 94/5, 103, 114b, 122, 123, 160t, 181; James Tims 47t, 47c, 48r, 50b, 61b, 62, 63b, 64t, 65t 189cl.

Abbreviations for terms appearing above: (t) top; (b) bottom; (l) left; (r) right; (c) centre

Author's acknowledgement

Des Hannigan wishes to thank the very helpful staff in the Tourism Offices in Alméria and Córdoba, and in the Municipal Tourism Offices in Cádiz, Jerez de la Frontera, Sanlúcar de Barrameda and Granada. Thanks once again to Paula Moreno Robledo of Carmona and Cele Cuesta of Montefrío. Thanks also to Ana Griffin, Pam and Rob Murray, Josephine Quintero, and to countless Andalucian friends and acquaintances along the way for all their help and advice.

Questionnaire

Dear Traveller

Your comments, opinions and recommendations are very important to us. So please help us to improve our travel guides by taking a few minutes to complete this simple questionnaire.

You do not need a stamp (unless posted outside the UK). If you do not want to remove this page from your guide, then photocopy it or write your answers on a plain sheet of paper.

Send to: The Editor, Spiral Guides, AA World Travel Guides, FREEPOST SCE 4598, Basingstoke RG21 4GY.

Your recommendations...

We always encourage readers' recommendations for restaurants, night-life or shopping – if your recommendation is used in the next edition of the guide, we will send you a FREE AA Spiral Guide of your choice. Please state below the establishment name, location and your reasons for recommending it.

_____

_____

_____

_____

_____

Please send me AA Spiral _____
(see list of titles inside the back cover)

About this guide...

Which title did you buy?

_____ **AA Spiral**

Where did you buy it? _____

When? m m / y y

Why did you choose an AA Spiral Guide? _____

_____

_____

_____

_____

Did this guide meet your expectations?

Exceeded ☐   Met all ☐   Met most ☐   Fell below ☐

Please give your reasons _____

_____

_____

_____

_____

continued on next page...

Were there any aspects of this guide that you particularly liked?

_____

_____

_____

_____

_____

Is there anything we could have done better?

_____

_____

_____

_____

_____

_____

About you...

Name (Mr/Mrs/Ms) _____

Address _____

_____ Postcode _____

Daytime tel nos _____

Which age group are you in?

Under 25 ☐   25–34 ☐   35–44 ☐   45–54 ☐   55–64 ☐   65+ ☐

How many trips do you make a year?

Less than one ☐   One ☐   Two ☐   Three or more ☐

Are you an AA member? Yes ☐   No ☐

About your trip...

When did you book? mm/ y y   When did you travel? mm/ y y

How long did you stay? _____

Was it for business or leisure? _____

Did you buy any other travel guides for your trip? ☐ Yes   ☐ No

If yes, which ones? _____

_____

Thank you for taking the time to complete this questionnaire. Please send it to us as soon as possible, and remember, you do not need a stamp (unless posted outside the UK).